# ASHKENAZI
# JEWS
# IN MEXICO

SUNY Series in Anthropology and Judaic Studies
Walter P. Zenner, Editor

# ASHKENAZI JEWS IN MEXICO

## Ideologies in the Structuring of a Community

ADINA CIMET

State University
of New York
Press

Published by
State University of New York Press, Albany

Production by Susan Geraghty
Marketing by Bernadette LaManna

Printed in the United States of America

For information, address State University of New York
Press, State University Plaza, Albany, N.Y., 12246

Library of Congress Cataloging-in-Publication Data

Cimet, Adina, 1951-
    Ashkenazi Jews in Mexico : ideologies in the structuring of a
community / Adina Cimet.
        p.    cm. — (SUNY series in anthropology and Judaic studies)
    Includes bibliographical references and index.
    ISBN 0-7914-3179-7 (hardcover : acid-free). — ISBN 0-7914-3180-0
(pbk. : acid-free)
    1. Jews—Mexico—Politics and government. 2. Mexico—Ethnic
relations. I. Title. II. Series.
F1392.J4C56  1997
323.1'1924072—dc20                                                95-5161
                                                                          CIP

10  9  8  7  6  5  4  3  2  1

*To my parents, Ruben and Shoshana,*
*for their unconditional support and dignified love.*

# CONTENTS

## PART 3

# PREFACE

The development of the community of Ashkenazi Jews in Mexico over the last eighty years sheds light on many social, political, and philosophical aspects of our contemporary life. Looked at internally and externally, this community is an experiment in social construction, an experiment in pluralist living arrangements, and a test of the political and philosophical coexistence of multicultural groups.

These Jews arrived in Mexico with few resources and created a network of organizations to sustain their cultural survival in a country that had its own cultural context. At the same time, the social construction of this universe defined and imposed principles of perception and judgment on its members. While on the one hand the newcomers created their social environment, on the other the context imprinted itself on them. People, both ordinary and unique (teachers, writers, painters, philosophers), and groups (Zionists, Bundists, and Communists) confronted each other in struggles in which the clarification and imposition not only of a worldview but also of a vision and control of the world were at stake. The struggles themselves (with all its participants as agents) defined the boundaries of the new social construction. Once a structure was in place, it continued to reproduce itself; its users maintained it with more or less tension.

Of course, this story cannot recount all that happened in that community, nor does it mention all the individuals who produced a worldview to sustain themselves in their goal to survive in that community. To even attempt that would be impossible; many other productive artists, writers, and others who were part of the process are not included here. Each story has, and must have, a selective angle. The criteria for inclusion as a socially meaningful agent was not so much to have an alternative worldview in that community but to have *a worldview* and *a critical mass of followers* that acted out the ideology or vision in question with direct impact on the structuring of the community.

The story of what these Jews built is in part the result of the context and their intended actions, as well as of the unexpected consequences of their own actions. While agents and groups struggled, many levels of misunderstanding contributed to what they produced. Their ideologies all included definitions of the situation and their identity, and were all used

as weapons, deployed in a struggle to control the social world being created. Six voices are presented here as part of the dialogue. They did not all
speak at the same time, but they all left enough of an echo to be heard at
one point or another. From their thoughts and actions grew a network of
organizations and resources, which became a symbolic battlefield for
competing ideologies and the material world in which all was at stake.

The choice to build the story around conflicts is strategic: it reveals
the constant *redefinition of the identity issues* of the group. Those definitions had specific consequences: they determined who would be
included or excluded from the nucleus exercising political control, and
even who could coexist in that world. The visions they held about the
world were thus the criteria for deciding who would be a stakeholder in
the new society.

To build a communal structure is to build an objective reality. These
Jews created their "truth," and it is that truth that was also at stake in
their struggles. Material and immaterial elements were intertwined. As a
result, all that this community produced is historical by definition, the
product of people's actions, in the singular and the plural. This understanding of the social process restores historicity to the project of communal life. In other words, it moves away from a false sense of eternal-
ization of the social enterprise. Therefore, when we understand Zionism
as the most important ideology for Jews today and, at the same time,
offer a critique of its effects in the community, we do not incur a contradiction. Following the logic of the analysis, it is clear that Zionism has a
fundamental function of sustaining identity for and within all Jewish
communities over the world. Yet it also created problems. We approach
these, and open up the dialogue again, addressing new, contemporary
issues for Jews.

The book is divided into three parts. Part 1, which presents a general
picture of Mexico, focuses on the problem of immigration in this century,
specifically Jewish immigration. The political context which the immigrants encountered is highlighted. Once the stage is set, the book describes
the development of Ashkenazi communal structure, from the defining of
the viable political alternatives for the minority to the actual institutionalization of the organizations that embodied them.

Part 2 describes the thoughts and actions of six key thinkers who
played specific roles as social agents. Each represents a different ideological perspective; collectively, all participated in the making of this
community.

Part 3 presents the gradual unfolding of the structuring process, after
the reader is acquainted with the agents who were the movers. The agents,
their groups, their beliefs and actions were all intertwined as in contending dialogues. These exchanges did not all take place at the same time, nor

did all the participants survive long enough to debate among themselves. But each had enough of an influence on the communal structure to warrant being included in this account.

In the process of recounting specific issues in the life of this community, interesting connections surface: the geographic transference of cultural and political visions among groups, and the sharing of international cultural and political problems among groups, all affecting the idiosyncratic interpretation of the local condition. In this process, these people found the tools to survive as an ethnic group enmeshed into a new society. But even if seen as a unit apart, as a community, their fate is, was, and will be interconnected with the actions and thought of the rest of the world. Although Mexico hosts a relatively small Jewish community, its problems as a minority and the solutions they opted for, as well as the conditions the country offers them, reflect the contemporary condition of minorities all over the world, and the political and philosophical issues we all—minorities and majorities—have to address.

The Ashkenazi Jews in Mexico are not a perfect society, nor did they create the best structure for their survival. Whatever they created they created, partly as a response to felt needs and to the pressures of the time. Examining them not only pays homage to the efforts of real people, but leaves us with the consciousness of some of the sociopolitical challenges we now face and cannot afford to ignore.

# ACKNOWLEDGMENTS

The research for this work was based on my doctoral thesis. As an outgrowth of that I am indebted to the people that guided me at the time. I would especially like to thank Prof. Sigmund Diamond, mentor, teacher, and friend. I also wish to thank Professors Herbert Gans, Arthur Goren, and Viviana Zelizer, who provided me with pertinent suggestions for the development of this book; and, I thank Prof. Saúl Sosnowski for his contribution in the latter stages of the project.

Prof. Susana R. Cimet, my mother and a sociologist in Mexico, has been my most loyal, constant, and refreshing source of support and communication. We have managed to create with much fruition a working relationship that alternates and exchanges roles from research assistant to sounding board, always with enormous respect for each other. Dr. Annette B. Ramirez de Arellano undertook the editing of my work. Not only has she been the intelligent and motivated reader any writer dreams of, but has become a friend whose experience and advice has been invaluable. And last, but not least, I thank Mike, Yaira, and Gealia for enduring my work. Within the changing demands of what a home and family life should be and are, they have helped me sustain and be who I want to be. For that, no amount of gratitude can be enough.

—A. Cimet Singer

# PART 1

# CHAPTER 1

# The Reestablishing
# of an Acquaintanceship

A society is, therefore, a structure which consists of beings who
stand inside and outside of it at the same time. . . . This is that the
individual can never stay within a unit which he does not at the
same time stay outside of, that he is not incorporated into any
order without also confronting it.

—Simmel
*On Individuality and Social Forms*

The encounter between Mexicans and Jews involved many things, including a confrontation with long-standing myths and the clashes of a new
reality. The views they had about each other and the context in which
they renewed their acquaintance played an important role. Though most
of the accounts of immigrant Jews to Mexico highlight the perplexity
they felt over the country, the geography, its flora, its folklore, the food,
and the strange sound of the language, the confusion deepened because of
the newcomers' ignorance of the recent Mexican past and their vague
knowledge of an older history of uneasy relations with Jews. Mexicans,
having been distanced from Jews for centuries, brought a mixed background to the new acquaintanceship. In addition to strong religious prejudices, Mexicans experienced great difficulty with the idea of and possible intrusion of foreigners—*all* foreigners. Both these intellectual currents
always played a part when judging Jews.

The immediate and often unexpectedly friendly encounter between
Jew and Mexican in this century required the juggling of contradictory
information; when reality did not coincide with prejudice, the Mexican
often concluded that the particular Jew had to be an "exception" to the
norm, a being very different from the picture the Mexican had intellectually internalized.[1] At times, however, this attitude toward the Jews came
perilously close to prejudice, and when the wave of anti-Semitism
enveloped the world, Mexicans did not entirely disassociate themselves
from those feelings. They remained largely detached: Jews were not physically attacked in Mexico, but neither was there any rush to help refugees
out. Even the Spanish language, a good mirror of the group that uses it,

reflected some of the feelings towards Jews. A "Judas" doll was burned in effigy during Easter Week (Semana Santa), and *Judas-like* was used as pejorative adjective. Similarly, a *judiada* was defined as an inhuman action, particularly one producing excessive and scandalous gain. The negative associations put on Jews were thus encoded in language and hence in thought.

When the Spanish came to the "New World," they brought and passed on their "Jewish experience" to America, not only by including some converts among their expeditionaries, but mostly by bringing a well-defined anti-Jewish ideology that was an intrinsic part of their thinking and acting. This ideology was reproduced in the New World, and its traces, still felt today, were part of the cultural structure that welcomed Jews in the modern immigration.

The conquest and control of this part of the world was carried out by the same institutions that had made possible the discovery of this "new" world, all created in the mother country. The desire to Christianize, for instance, used as an argument to suggest the possible "salvation of the world," was closely linked to the conquest of the new territories. The Inquisition, the institution created to search out heretics or anyone that could hamper the project, was activated in Spain in 1481, and was soon to open a branch in the new continent too. To the Spanish, then, Jews were not an unknown, and the Spanish who came to Mexico brought their ideological and institutional structures to the social world they attempted to remodel and control.

The desire to banish Jews was not new. England expelled all its Jews in 1290; France followed the pattern with massacres and expulsions in the fourteenth century; and Spain subjected its Jewish population beginning in the mid–fourteenth century to periodic massacres, mob attacks, and forced conversion. Spain ended its chapter of Jewish life with the expulsion of Jews in 1492. However, the case of Spain is different, unique, and paradigmatic, because for a period Jews, Arabs, and Spaniards cooperated in a most fruitful cultural experiment of sustained association. It is only when the Spanish attempted to reverse the balance of power and control in the search for a new social structure, when the Spanish sought to reestablish an absolute control of their territory, that these old alliances were broken. New definitions of the "other" were activated. Religion, both as a system of thought and as an institution, stepped in to offer ultimate sanction to the forced conversions and to the new political construct. This pattern of thought and action helped propel not only the desire for new territory, but also the imposition of a dominant style of control of the new territory. Because no professing Jew was allowed to pollute Spanish society, no Jew was allowed to contaminate the colonies in the New World. The Spanish Inquisition, which started as an attempt to impose a religious orthodoxy, developed as an ethnic cleansing tool, thus destroying the previous mutually enriching experience between Spaniards, Arabs, and Jews.

Little was done to allow even converted Jews into the New World in the sixteenth and seventeenth centuries. Letters and decrees, both local and European, made clear that no Jews or converted Jews could settle in the cities of New Spain. The King and Queen of Spain and Pope Paul III issued decrees to that effect. King Pedro of Portugal, for instance, enacted a Law of Extermination (1683) for the expulsion of convicted Jews and their offspring.[2] The prejudices against Jews were thus exported to the new continent, and Jews were often used as symbols of evil in the lengthy process of conversion that the colonizers imposed on the local population. Jews therefore did not go to New Spain in large numbers, and those who did did not manage to leave direct traces.[3] By the time the autos-da-fé were famous and popular in New Spain, these antiheretical executions were perpetrated against Jews by the Inquisition with such ease that ideology and prejudice were well rooted.

## An Overview of Mexican History: The Context

But Mexico and its society had an even more complicated history than this account alone would suggest. After three hundred years of being exposed to and forced to adopt Western culture, there was a sufficient cultural and demographic distance from the controlling center, Spain, so that the area was ripe for change. There was no redress possible. Some of what Spain gave to New Spain was so ingrained that no separating of cultures and people was possible. By now, Mexico sought to define itself as a new entity. Mexico was made up of a multiplicity of cultural, ethnic, and religious groups, but economic and political control were centralized by a very limited group. In addition, the French and American Revolutions provided a backdrop against which the colonized and conquered people could begin to dream. Mexico's population included a variety of Spanish subgroups: Creoles, Africans, racially mixed populations, local indigenous peoples, and other foreign groups such as the English, French, and American. Not only was it an extraordinary task for the people in Mexico to articulate and justify their desire for independence from Spain, it also required an exercise in realpolitik and imagination to coalesce the diverse multicentered forces in that vast territory. Each had its own agenda, and therefore had to be convinced and attracted to a single center to form a new political entity.

The political and economic difficulties were exacerbated by the territories' geographic and cultural situation. It was difficult to maintain control over the vast and distant north (California, Louisiana, Texas,

Florida) while also maintaining linkages to the south (Yucatán and Guatemala). The major challenge was to create a centering nucleus capable of holding all these forces in a centripetal fashion and subsume the population under a new power structure.

The nineteenth century was for Mexico a period of physical violence and intellectual upheaval. Divergent visions of how to integrate the new unit competed for attention. It was a century of war and dissension: liberals fought conservatives in their many variations. From the war of independence (1810) with its later national heroes like Hidalgo and Morelos, to the Constitution of 1824, to the Santa Anna period and the Ayutla revolution against Santa Anna, to the Constitution of 1857, to the Reform War separating church and state (Juárez, 1859), to the French invasion and the Empire of Maximilian, constant clashes were the norm.[4] The nineteenth century in Mexico was one of turmoil from which a new political entity was born and the parameters of its polity were defined.

All of these conflicts, together with the visions, the ideas, and the experiments undergirding them, were inherited by the twentieth century. As the geographical international pressures against Mexico eased, the conflicts were incorporated into an internal agenda. The issues then were transposed into the political agenda that forged the Revolution of 1910.

*Two Issues That Defined the New Nation*

There were two major issues around which the confrontations of these two centuries were fought: territory and population. In fact, each of these issues embodied a series of problems. For example, the problem of territory comprised at least three aspects: jurisdiction, control, and governance.

Territorial problems in these last two centuries have firstly been problems of jurisdiction, of which areas of land would remain under the jurisdiction of what was then Mexico. Mexico's international relations were extremely complicated. Following the war of independence which began in 1810 and the difficulties of gaining support from Spain, France, and England, Mexico faced Spain's attempts to reconquer lost territory in 1822. Then followed a war fought against France in 1838.[5] The tension over territory did not abate.

The second aspect of the territorial problem concerned how to remain in control of the bordering territories. In the north of Mexico, for instance, the American government sought to expand its economic resources by mobilizing the population of the area against the Mexican government. Thus, the colonists of Texas attempted to become independent in 1835; the final annexation of Texas to the American state occurred in 1845. Later, New Mexico and California were also annexed.

Words were exchanged over the fate of the regions of Sonora, Baja California, and Chihuahua. All of these were not just defeats and humiliations but shocks to the Mexican system; eventually the Río Grande became the demarcation line. Mexico had given up more than half its territory in exchange for an indemnization of 15 million pesos in 1848.

The third aspect of the territorial problem was more internal, and involved the type of governance an independent Mexico should adopt. Some felt it could be an empire; others thought Mexico could and should be ruled by a monarch with European support; yet others favored a republic as the best solution. At the same time, the mechanics of creating a federation had to be worked out. The political rules of the new polity had to be not only articulated but agreed upon. Decisions concerning who could "own" territory, and how much of it, were constantly debated.

The problem of population was (and probably still is) not only extremely complex, but also undergirded many essential issues of contemporary Mexico. In its original and older format the question asked was: who, among the different types of groups, was to be in charge of the new Mexico? There were many groups competing for power and control, and their confrontations demanded simultaneous intellectual elaborations. Thus Peninsulares (Spaniards from the continent), Creoles (of Spanish descent but born in New Spain), mestizos (mixed population resulting from either Spanish and indigenous marriages, and Spanish and other racial mixtures as Africans), and the indigenous population all had to find a way to coexist. Eventually, the notion that the country needed a nationalist definition took over. That would help justify and legitimate the new polity and its dominant groups. The main idea—since the war of independence—was to forge and legitimize a new civilization based on the mestizo. This was to be the new man, unsituated historically. The mestizo was the result of mixture, yet all new, carefully designed to limit the new group in power. The right to a particular culture, the right of any of the groups that lived or came to live in Mexico to their own culture in Mexico, was lost.[6]

The interaction between and among these groups slowly shaped the content of the new nationalism. For instance, the Peninsulares had been powerful people in New Spain. At the time of independence, some sided with the Mexicans during the war. They had developed a taste for independence, too, and had important positions in the army, in the government, and in the church. Some, however, remained loyal to Spain and even attempted to oppose the independence movement,[7] hoping to maintain their power with the support of Spain. Spain's opposition to the legitimacy of Mexican independence gave rise to further anti-Spanish feeling. In 1827 the first Peninsulares were expelled. Soon, expulsion became the norm. Hundreds of Peninsulares with Mexican families who lacked the resources to pay for their families' relocation had to leave the country alone. Aligned against the mestizos in power positions, the remaining Peninsulares became the new foreigners of the new state.

With Mexico engaged in wars both locally and internationally, the notion of *foreigner* became increasingly problematic; a nationalist ideology was elaborated in a parallel fashion to secure and legitimize the new political entity and its new power elite. The Juárez government of the 1850s was particularly significant in this process. Following the defeat and execution of the imposed European emperor Maximiliano and the establishment of the reconstructed Republic, liberal intellectuals took over the rebuilding of the country. The main agenda was to homogenize the country. It was understood that the country needed pacification, demilitarization, roads, railroads, foreign capital, and immigration. If, as it was then argued, the weakness of the country and its poverty were in direct relation to its being sparsely populated, the solution lay in repopulating. Some of Mexico's leaders wanted to follow the American and Argentinian models of attracting potential homesteaders, though the salaries that Mexico could offer were much less attractive than the ones in these countries. Mexico had about eight million inhabitants then, of which only two million were in the labor force.[8] That worked out to about one worker for each one hundred hectares of land. Though Spanish was the lingua franca, more than one hundred languages were actively used. One million people spoke Nahua; half a million spoke Otomi; a quarter spoke Maya; and more than 100,000 people spoke Zapoteca, Mixteco, and Tarasco. While new population was sought, the government had decided that the country's internal diversity had to be diminished regardless of its cultural-ethical price. The country's prehispanic past was felt to offer nothing but the recounting of fabulous glories of only antiquarian interest.[9] There was a need to form a new unity so that the new incoming population could be part of the new mixture.[10] That this policy would have a tremendous social, political, and philosophical effect went unnoticed.

From 1867 to 1876, raging epidemics did not allow the anticipated population growth, and neither did the desired foreign colonization take place. In 1875 a new colonization law not only authorized the government to become an active colonizing agent but also allowed the private sector to participate in such a task. Added incentives included cheap land, deferred payment on loans, Mexican citizenship, and other economic aid. But actual numbers fell short of projections: the 6,000 to 7,000 Europeans and Americans were much fewer than expected. Most of the immigrants dedicated themselves to commerce and settled in cities. They therefore did not populate the hinterland, a fact that was later used against the Jewish immigrants. The lesson was clear: a population that migrates seeks mostly urban areas, where jobs may be available and where a lesser investment is necessary to survive.

*Ingrained Ambivalence: The Strongest Characteristic*

The Mexican government's ambivalence to foreigners following the revolution was also evident in its treatment of a specific minority, the Chinese. Although there was interest in attracting immigrants, Mexico eventually adopted the types of restrictions that the United States implemented after the 1830s, when labor unions started to protest against immigration, suggesting that immigrants were the cause of the country's economic problems.[11]

In Mexico it was becoming clearer that investments were more acceptable than actual immigrants. But by 1880 there were about 150,000 Chinese who had come to the United States as part of the famous gold rush. The U.S. recession of 1871 eliminated the jobs of thousands of Chinese, and the U.S. government closed its doors, suggesting that the Chinese were "inferior and dangerous" for the country. It was also argued that cultural homogeneity was necessary; the Chinese were therefore seen as less desirable.[12]

Chinese then started to come into Mexico in the 1880s. The first Chinese-Mexican treaty was signed in 1887 in search for a balanced exchange of population and commerce.[13] In 1889 the final version of a treaty for "friendship, commerce, and navigation" was signed. Although ten years earlier the Chinese government had protested against the bad treatment to which the Chinese had been exposed, the Chinese continued to arrive and Mexico found a rationale for their presence. Again, it was hoped that the Chinese would aid the agricultural progress of the country. Yet, the same year that the treaty was signed, anti-Chinese sentiments were aired in the newspapers of Mexico. The Chinese were called "degenerates"; people who never adjusted to the countries they immigrated to since they remained loyal to their customs and language; a type of bird of prey that flies home as soon as its beak is full. The Chinese were criticized for their short height, suggesting that that characteristic in a population that would mix with Mexicans would eventually produce a "nation of midgets."

In 1896 protests against the Chinese started: it was argued that they took jobs away from the Mexicans, and that they often rejected work that other Mexicans offered them. In 1907, a Catholic newspaper saw them as reaching the limits of the acceptable: they were becoming *tortilla* workers and *tamal* experts. More and more, the attack took on racial undertones. Descriptions of how the Chinese ate, and their habits, were published.

Absurd rumors took hold of the imagination of the local population: it was said that *chorizo*—a sausage—was being made by the Chinese of children's meat, and that the Chinese were not hygienic, and were therefore a menace to the Mexican population. Pressure against mixed marriages heightened.[14]

In the 1800s other groups of people arrived: Italians, Japanese, and Mormons. None assimilated, not even the Italians, who were judged to be the most "assimilable" type.[15] But none faired so terribly as the Chinese, who in 1911 faced a terrible massacre in the northern part of the country, in Torreón, where about three hundred people were killed. Some sectors, in an attempt to justify it, claimed the massacre was brought on by the "wealth and greed" of the Chinese people. These events, so much like pogroms, were too well known to the foreigners to be ignored. The victims were always blamed; there was very little hope for justice, reason, and civility.

## Nationalism and Political Control

Once a body politic had been formed and its rules stabilized, the different groups, through contention, sought to define how the country would develop, modernize, and achieve social justice. Mexico went through a major social revolution; 1910 marked the beginning of a period of convulsion and struggle during which a variety of commanding army chiefs—*caudillos*—attempted to gain control and redefine the goals of the country. Fights and alliances as well as enmities characterized the next seven years. The country pacified and controlled some of its violence during this civil war only under the presidency of Plutarco Elías Calles (1920–1924).

In the thirties, the rules and the system that President Calles had initiated started to take root. They established an electoral process that would offer a longer life expectancy and routinized transitions that increasingly legitimized rules and rulers.[16] More and more, it became an attempt to move away from the Hobbesian state of war of all against all. The issues that had been hitherto fought in military struggles became too costly for the country to benefit anyone any further.[17] As groups were being disarmed and depoliticized, they also reconfigured the political life of the country.

Physically, whatever had been achieved during the pre-Revolutionary calm was soon destroyed. Roads and railroads—crucial for war and for peace—had been extensively damaged. The mining, metallurgy, and oil industries needed foreign currency to restart production. In the early part of the century, economic tensions grew. Salaries did not follow past growth; strikes broke out all over the country. About 88 percent of the country was rural, and the agricultural sector had to support half of Mexico's 14 or 15 million inhabitants. This majority did not have the power to participate in the economy. The market was possibly used by 3 million people only.

About a million people died during the Revolution over issues of leadership and presidential succession. The expansion plans of the United States also remained a source of tension. In 1914, in the midst of the power struggles following the murder and coup d'état staged against President Francisco I. Madero by Victoriano Huerta, the northern states of Mexico requested help and military supplies from the United States. President Woodrow Wilson sent troops to Veracruz. The reaction in Mexico was fierce: many interpreted it as an attempt on the part of the United States to secure the oil fields of Tampico (near Veracruz) and to get a permanent foothold in the national territory. Mexican nationalistic sensibilities were and remained raw. Only in 1932 did the United States recognize the then-president of the country, thereby officially acknowledging the sovereignty of Mexico.

As soon as there was some peace, the issue of repopulating the country resurfaced as the most efficient and immediate solution to the country's internal problems. But the inherited dislike and distrust of foreigners and of Jews specifically had not disappeared. The nationalism that had taken root in Mexico during the years after the war of independence now also incorporated elements of nineteenth-century positivism, which was an ideology very much in fashion in European circles. In its social version, it suggested that the betterment of a society required the "whitening" of the races by establishing a racially hierarchical structure to direct society. In its Mexican version, the social hierarchy implied that those at the top were also in control of the economy and polity. This was to come about as the Europeans mixed with the local indigenous population, producing a culture and a group, the mestizo, that incorporated the "whiteness" of Western European culture biologically, culturally, and religiously. Though it appeared that this brand of positivism invoked universal principles (i.e., the mixture of "all" the races), in practice its xenophobic and anti-Semitic content was never fully hidden. It linked the betterment of society to a predefined homogenization of the population, usually in support of "white, western, Catholic" culture.

Yet the idea of an immigrant population, when discussed in abstract terms, seems to have been attractive. Despite the specific nationalistic feelings, everyone agreed that the immigrants were an economic asset. Immigration as an idea was never totally rejected; but the ambivalence over it always lurked.

### On Immigration: Policy and Politics

Taking as its source an immigration law that had been enacted in 1823, after the independence movement started, immigration and colonization were often topics on the political agendas of the groups fighting for control of the country. However, Mexico never achieved what the United States achieved in the area of immigration.[18] When the government once again stressed the issue of immigration in 1856, Mexico was still immersed in a civil war that never allowed the country to offer the economic attractions required for populations to come.

The immigration laws changed often, refining the language about immigration categories following what other countries were doing at the time. During the first years of the century and until 1923, the country based its policy of immigration on the 1908 law that examined only the health condition of those foreigners coming into the country. This followed the selection criteria that were used in the United States. Limitations were set against people with epilepsy, communicable diseases, mental diseases, and physical defects, as well as beggars, prostitutes, and, in a category of their own, anarchists. But slowly, new restrictions were added. By 1917, not only physical and mental undesirables were excluded but "economic and political undesirables" too. As more laws were enacted, reports that the laws were not regularly enforced increased and the bribes paid to circumvent the laws became more frequent.

While the United States was closing its doors to immigration in 1924, Mexico sought to attract the immigrants that were being rerouted from the north. Though the United States had developed a mystique of success,[19] the country of "streets paved with gold," the reality of political life was at odds with the prevailing image. During World War I, many attempted to avoid the draft, Jews among them. Some managed to enter Mexico even when documentation was missing. The Mexican inspectors were lax on the requirements and may have felt some sympathy for what they may have perceived as the immigrants' "anti-Yankee" stand.[20]

In 1923, President Obregón refined the immigration law, establishing male and female age requirements, as well as favoring only young adults; restrictions were also placed on illiterates, users of toxic substances, and anybody who did not have sufficient economic resources to subsist for at least two months. The law was amended again in an attempt to attract the postwar influx from the United States. The Jews who settled "temporarily" in Mexico were offered a special "privilege" to wait for visas to enter the United States; but, because the number of years required to wait changed between 1921 and 1928 from one to five, many were forced to settle in Mexico after all. Once they had developed basic skills, established themselves in some line of work, and learned the language, the move again to the United States was less attractive; it would involve a difficult and exhausting effort, for an undetermined benefit. As if against all odds, Jews were arriving in the country. Little by little, and totally unplanned, Mexico was hosting immigrants, among them Jews.

In the aftermath of World War I, immigration to Mexico occurred in larger numbers, and the laws on immigration became more complicated. Reforms adopted in 1926 defined categories such as *colonizer, tourist, emigrant, immigrant,* and so on. By July of 1927, the economic crisis led to the imposition of additional restrictions by specific area or country: Armenians, Arabs, Lebanese, Palestinians, and Turks, among others, were all deemed unacceptable. In 1929 the increase of the undesired categories of people included the Polish, Russians, and Chinese. For a few months, albeit temporarily, immigration was prohibited completely. Though later it was phrased as only limiting the entry of "Syrians, Lebanese, Armenians, Palestinians, Arabs, Turks, and Chinese," the law amounted to a closed-door policy.

Nationalist labels often masked the fact that the restrictions were aimed at Jews from certain countries; only in 1933–34 did the regulations openly limit Jewish immigration. This, of course, was at the height of the need for Jews to immigrate, as Nazi persecution rose. The law thus decreed:

> This Ministry deems it convenient to attack the problem created by Jewish immigration, which more than any other, because of its psychological and moral characteristics, and because of the type of activities to which it dedicates and the procedures it follows in pressing business of commercial nature that invariably is its choice, comes to be undesirable; and consequently will not be allowed to immigrate to the country, neither as investors in terms of the Agreement of the last 16th of February, nor as traveling agents, directors, managers, representatives of businesses established in the Republic, workers of responsibility, rentists, students, the individuals of Semitic race; adding . . . if it will be discovered that he is of Jewish origin, regardless of the nationality he belongs to, his entry will have to be prohibited and the Ministry shall be advised immediately by telegraph.[21]

In 1938, the international effort to place Nazi-persecuted Jews as refugees did not make Mexico into an immigrant haven. However, the rules were bent for other groups: in 1937, five hundred Spanish orphans of the Spanish Civil War were taken in; in 1939, Spanish republicans were also allowed in as refugees. With respect to the Jews, like some other countries, Mexico intended to be helpful, but the terms of its help were so vague that the numbers of immigrants considered acceptable were absolutely minimal. Nevertheless, the application of the many new and changing Mexican rules on immigration were never enforced so rigorously as to inhibit all immigration.

But the Mexican government still sought to solve its chronic internal economic problems by using immigrant population. Agriculture and industrialization were both areas of the economy which required attention in Mexico. Mostly they required large amounts of capital. Agriculture required infrastructure: irrigation, dams, and the transport of water. To industrialize, there was need for money to generate the technology necessary or even to import it.[22] This also required the development of infrastructure—roads and railroads. To attract immigrants, the government offered facilities: limited free land, low prices for land, time to pay off land, and exemption from military service and taxes. But the government's propaganda was neither accurate nor widespread. Any propaganda on immigration that reached the Jews became a bureaucratic problem because they had no particular international body to represent them. Most attempts were made by either American Jewish organizations that helped Jews internationally, such as the B'nai B'rith, HIAS (the Hebrew Immigrant Aid Society), the Joint Distribution Committee (commonly known as "Joint"), or colonization associations that were often organized and supported by a wealthy Jew who financed most of the enterprise.

Mexico had not clearly defined its immigration policy; when it came to Jews, the ambivalences were further exacerbated. In addition, there were diverse opinions within the country as to the specific desirability of Jews. The latent and intangible prejudices of the Catholic Church against Jews, at least in the abstract, exerted an influence. The image of Jews crucifying Jesus and the connection between contemporary Jews and the crucifixion were actively maintained. In addition, Jews were hardly physically known in Mexico for a few centuries, as the Inquisition had eliminated the few who had managed to settle centuries back. Because of their small number, Jews were not encountered as a group. Yet the negative images of Jews held by the population at large were not counteracted. The Church fostered anti-Semitic thinking for practical reasons: the Catholic Church owned half of all the real estate of the country; it was thus not interested in sharing territory with immigrants who would get it "free" from the government.[23] However, all anti-Semitic actions were not attributable to the Catholic Church.[24] Church and state had been separate since the latter part of the nineteenth century. There was too much ambivalence and anti-Jewish feeling on the part of the government to blame those actions solely on the Church.

*Attempts to Redress the Antiforeigner Mood*

The ambivalence to foreigners that was imbedded in the actions and reactions of the Mexican government had many facets. In 1920, before the country had achieved peace, President Carranza faced the problem of most of the leadership positions in the country being held by self-made military men. The value and aim of a civilian government seemed utopian, as a civilian within the existing power structure was totally alien. Carranza, however, decided to introduce his ambassador to the United States, Licenciado Bonilla, as a civil candidate to the presidency. Bonilla was relatively unfamiliar in the Mexican scene. Speculation arose concerning his national background, whether his family name was really Mexican, who his parents were, and whether he was Catholic. The fact that he was married to a Protestant Englishwoman was regarded as a liability, and raised questions about the education and religious beliefs of his daughters. The lack of sympathy for Bonilla was fanned by an entire campaign to discredit and eventually disqualify him as candidate.[25] In this story all the political elements of the period conflate: civilism versus militarism; nationalism versus openness to foreigners; Catholic versus other religions.

In 1922, President Obregón made the first public invitation to Jews, but by 31 October 1922 he was urging that the Mexican Constitution grant privileges to any race. The new invitation and its clarification seem to have eliminated the possibility for colonization, and weakened any immigration. The B'nai B'rith had potential projects for colonization in Mexico, and had contacted President Obregón without being in contact with local Jews. A group of sixty Jews in Mexico wrote an open letter to the Jewish press in America, suggesting a halt to the ideas of immigration.[26] The local economy was too precarious and unwelcoming, they argued. Similarly, Anita Brenner, an early settler and writer, recalled that when Yiddish was first heard in the streets of Mexico, a wave of alarm went through the Jews who had settled there. Their good fortune would be spoiled if competition increased and Jews started to be recognized. This reaction, encountered again and again in many communities, reveals, at the very least, the perpetual insecurity of Jews.

Whether the original invitation from President Obregón was aimed at countering these feelings of the local Jews, and the later modifications to the invitation were a response to internal pressure, is not known. We can conclude, though, that conflicting pressures and rationales existed in both sectors.

*Projecting an Image and a Reality*

The Mexican business representative in Berlin and later deputy Alberto García Granados told the Mexican government in 1879 that since Jews in Rumania seemed very unhappy, it would be wise to induce them to go to Mexico if they would bring their "considerable capital." The Alliance Israelite of Paris[27] began planning the migration of between 12 000 to 15 000 Russian Jews to Mexico. Because the Mexican government wanted farmers, the plan was to settle them in San Luis Potosí. But the plan quickly fell apart as the potential immigrants were found not to be farmers.[28]

In 1881, the newspapers *El Monitor Republicano* and *El Siglo XXI* reprinted a French article concerning a proposal for the establishment of Russian Jewry in Mexico. Incentives to the would-be immigrants included free grants, transportation, tools, machines, animals, and exemption from military service. The same month, the English *Jewish Chronicle* also suggested possible emigration for Russian Jews to Mexico. A year later, a German Jew living in Mexico, Guillermo Müeller, offered to buy land in the state of Veracruz for the resettlement of one hundred Jewish families.[29] Similar proposals arose periodically, and as late as 1957 diverse groups were still attempting to settle Jews in Mexico.[30] The local Jews never made great efforts to attract, support, or expand the government's invitations after these were issued and published; little on this topic was publicized in Mexico.[31] As a result, there was never a formal organized plan, neither from the hosts nor from the Jewish immigrants.

In the period immediately preceding the more formal settlement of Sephardic Jews in Mexico in 1912, there were other major projects to relocate Jews; all ended unsuccessfully.[32] There was an attempt, for instance, initiated by Baron Maurice de Hirsch (1831–1896) in 1881. While focusing on Argentina as a possible solution for some of the masses of impoverished Jews, he also briefly considered Mexico. Prominent Jews in France and New York cooperated with him in his effort; most significant among these were Jacob Schiff (1847–1920), the New York banker, and Ernest Cassel (1852–1921), financier and railroad magnate involved in the construction of railroads in Mexico. The discussions continued until 1892, but again nothing materialized. Baron de Hirsch was never fully convinced of Mexico as the right place for Jews, and he eventually abandoned the plan.

The attempts that the Alliance Israelite had initiated in 1882 in response to a Mexican overture did not lead to anything either. In 1887 another project was sponsored by Lionel Samuel, a member of a London Jewish family living in Mexico; this also failed. This was the period when the President Díaz expressed interest in Jewish immigration, declaring that Jews could "teach [Mexicans] to think preventively." Their example could be, he said, beneficial to the country. The Catholic press declared itself against the project.[33]

A project launched by the Territorialists, a group formed by the British Zionist writer Israel Zangwill (1864–1926), also failed. They propagandized sporadic attempts for colonization in Mexico, which they printed in their journal *Freeland* in Mexico. Even as late as 1945, *Freeland, Periodical of the Freeland League for Jewish Territorial Colonization in Mexico*,[34] suggested a novel theory of immigration. This posited the view that immigration did not displace the local population economically, because the process did not decrease wage levels or employment. Instead, they saw immigration as a potential job-creating experience, as the case of the United States proved. The Territorialists produced a list of immigrant groups such as the Italians and the Irish, and attempted to show that cotton manufacturing, whaling industry, iron-clad steamship, and the building of bridges, railroads, and dams were all activities whose development was due to the immigrants' ingenuity and resources.

But in creating colonies with potential massive immigration of Jews, Mexico often wanted "capital and sufficient remuneration" that made the projects prohibitive and unfeasible. The problem of the daily sustenance of the newcomers was left unresolved. How would they earn a living? The country needed the building of an infrastructure and population, and resources to do it all. It also wanted to develop the country's agriculture. Jews could certainly not finance the first part of the project, not even part of it, and they tended to be more of an urban population. In Mexico, the only type of urban immigration that was welcomed was that of technically skilled people who moved temporarily to the cities to provide specific services. As a result, all the Jews who entered the country in the 1920s made it mostly on their own, with no official structural support.

In 1910, before the Revolution, Mexico had about sixty colonies: sixteen official ones and forty-four private ones. Eight of the official ones and ten of the private ones were formed with Mexicans; of these, five were comprised of repatriated Mexicans. Of the other official ones, six were settled by Italians, one by nationalized Guatemalans, and one by American Indians. Of the private efforts, twenty were North American, two German, and two Cuban. Each of the following groups also had a colony: French, Belgian, Spanish, Boer, Japanese, Russian, and Puerto Rican. It is very hard to come by the exact numbers of people that were housed in these colonies. We can assume, in general terms, that the total population fluctuated between 6,700 to 8,500 persons.

The Mexican official position was ambivalent to all foreigners but in particular to Jews, who were in constant search for a territory and a safe haven, especially during politically and economically discriminatory periods in Eastern and Western Europe. When invitations were issued, they were inevitably accompanied by statements that ample privileges could not be offered to the new population; financial support and capital were almost always requested from the world Jewish organizations. Thus, although the Mexican government toyed for a long time with the idea of attracting an immigrant population to help develop and colonize the vast country, and Jews, for the most part, were eager to participate, a formal match was never consummated. Jews never seemed to fit the exact type of immigrant the Mexican government envisioned.

*A World That Dismisses Pluralism*

The fact that Mexico was in search for ways to achieve new defined goals for itself was in and of itself not new. For a long time, diverse groups in Mexican society had put forward their own blueprints of what they thought Mexican society should become. The modern history of the country can be read as the confrontation among groups with varied ideas on this matter.

The last two centuries have been for Mexico a period of not only rebuilding the physical and political boundaries of its nation but also of building its internal psychohistorical identity. After being a colonial enclave of Spain, Mexico struggled to create a new cultural definition of itself sufficiently distinct from the Spanish one to further its claim to independence and sovereignty. Although independence meant primarily separation from the Spanish, the process itself suggested that many "others," individuals as well as cultures, could be perceived as potential or actual threats. The distaste for the "other," the stereotypical Jew, helped to create scapegoats to explain the country's internal economic problems. After all, blaming foreigners for most social evils has a long history.

The concepts of *mestizaje* (crossbreeding of racial groups) and *crisol de las razas* (crucible of races) were the two central concepts embodying the idea and the experience of Mexico's cultural melting. But more than anything, *mestizaje* and *crisol de las razas*, as used in the later part of the last century and the current one, became parts of an ideology that defined the cultural entity of the new Mexico. The concepts helped identify who was in charge and in control of the new body politic, who were the legitimate owners of modern Mexico. Mexico was for the mestizos and for no one else. At the same time, the ideology evoked the homogenizing forces that were at work for those who wanted to join the new Mexican experiment. The fear of the "other" led to the fear of diversity; diversity was seen as an inherent threat to central authority and to the authentic. This lack of pluralism had consequences that have spilled over the political style of the country into areas that are very far removed from cultural areas: as soon as any group was defined as "other" in Mexico, it was excluded from full participation in the political space of the country.

This ideology also overlooked a historical, ethical, political, and cultural fact: the indigenous population of Mexico. This population had not turned mestizo. Thus, the ideology expressed a desire for a homogeneity, but did not describe a reality. Moreover, the homogenizing ideology promoted and imposed a violence onto one of the most deserving sectors of the population: the indigenous groups. This population had incorporated vast elements of Western culture and the Catholic religion, and, to some degree, the most structural characteristic of the Western society that controlled them: the language. But many indigenous groups, perhaps as many as a hundred, diverse in size and spread out over the country, had remained, despite this history, distinctive cultural and linguistic subgroups. Mexico reflected the liberalism of the Enlightenment, offering a similar response to its cultural wars of identity. As in the Enlightenment, most ideals of man and society were stated in abstract, universal terms. On the one hand, this meant a unification of the conceptualizations of the human condition. On the other, it meant an effacement of immediate historical specificities. Thus, the ideology and the nationalism it produced was a composite of cosmopolitan, rational design that negated its own pluralism and its diversity.

Mexico's political culture did not encourage respect for pluralism. It developed an abstract definition of Mexicanness, expecting the social groups to fit into it. If the internal diversity of cultures was not accepted, how could Mexico tolerate diversity from the outside? It is interesting to analyze the thinking of the influential Mexican philosopher, politician, and writer José Vasconcelos as an example of the problems intrinsic to such an ideology. Although by no means the only thinker on the issue,[35] as a politician in the early part of the 1920s Vasconcelos became an active proponent of the "Mestizo ideology." In his interpretation, mestizaje produced a new race. In this "new race," Hispanism would prevail. While he advocated the fusion of all races out of which a "cosmic race" would emerge, the fusion would not affect all races equally. He was especially proud of his Hispanic background and ancestry and thought that this Hispanism represented a higher cultural stage and should therefore predominate. During his years in public life, the ideological racial hierarchy that he promoted was either veiled to most or acceptable to some. It was only in the 1930s, when his political standing had weakened and he felt his personal power threatened, that his original distaste for other cultures took the form of a very clear anticommunism, anti-Americanism, and, finally, a vitriolic anti-Semitism.[36]

The condition and problems of the indigenous population of Mexico have been effaced from the political agenda of the country. The indigenous population was not sufficiently integrated linguistically, economically, geographically, or politically to be able to fill the economic gap that mestizo society wanted. Their general culture and existence were not fully accepted, their economic and political status were misunderstood, and the mestizo culture saw them as an undifferentiated group in terms of the dominant, conquering Western culture. *Indians*, in itself a historically inaccurate term that directed attention to the colonized status of these groups, were deemed a lazy, backward, useless group, all old stereotypes taken from the conquering culture. There was no recognition of their painful past, no recognition of their culture, no respect for their identity, and no historical awareness of the sociopolitical and economic limitations that were imposed on them. Indeed it was only in 1994 that the Mexican Constitution recognized the fact of the indigenous population as a minority in its midst.

The number of languages the different groups maintained were—and mostly are—unknown to the Mestizo population at large. Maya, Tarahumara, Aymara, Guarani, Tzoltzil, and Tzeltzal are all one undifferentiated mass. If communication was difficult,[37] cohesion was then almost nonexistent. And, although language need not be a requisite for cohesion and nationalism (as the case of Switzerland shows), the diversity of languages in Mexico coincided with socioeconomic and political divisions. Seventy percent of the total population over ten years of age was illiterate at the beginning of the twentieth century.[38] Understood in a different way, this multicultural context could have served to develop views about multiple ethnic-cultural social arrangements. But Mexico was unable to address this issue.

Immigration was therefore a detour to avoid a direct confrontation of how to incorporate the indigenous population into the body politic. The Mexican government justified the need for immigration by stressing the country's unexploited national richness, the lack of population, the local limitations to exploit the natural resources, and the greater value of the foreign worker. If the policy of immigration of the nineteenth century was aimed at correcting the global deficit of population and the unequal distribution of the population of the country, the government acted at best ambivalently in its attempt to solve these problems. Since 1856, Article 27 of the Constitution had specified that only Mexican citizens could own land. The same was true for companies. Special care was given to place foreign colonies at specific distances from the border, to avoid the potential changing of boundaries within the territory. The government could officially offer special rights to foreigners as long as they renounced the protection of other governments. There was no desire to incorporate foreign entities into the country, only an intellectual desire that somehow seemed to make muddled numerical sense.

How then, is one to describe Mexico's position? At best, one can say that the political position on immigration remained always ambivalent. However, what seemed a problem of the past (immigration) and a policy of the past (the interrelationship with foreigners) became a basic characteristic of the state. The issue still colors the state's internal relationship with the minorities and calls into question the democratic character of Mexican society.

*Jewish Testimony of the Early Mexico*

Testimonial information from immigrant Jews who arrived in Mexico in the late teens, twenties, and thirties,[39] ranges from individual life histories to a view of the economy and politics as lived and felt in the streets, and from a view of lifestyles to the clash of cultures of the peoples of the world. What emerges is a picture of a world that no longer exists, but a picture that contains the seeds of much of what developed later into the more mature and elaborate political culture of this system.

The immigrants give us a Mexico which in its strangeness appeared to them as a land of extraordinary, magical beauty, a land in which nature, food, culture, and people present the landscape of a very different world. The colors, the light, the sun, the heat; the flora, the leaves, the trees; the smells, the shapes, the textures; the roads, the dust, the air, the sounds; the dress, the shawls, the hats, the sandals; the houses, the food, the songs, the drinking, the extreme feelings: everything is noticed because it is different. A picture of old Mexico can thus be reconstructed, coming alive through the voices of the immigrants.[40] In viewing this strangeness, and their aim to be part of it, they reveal much of themselves. Their fears and their anguish suffuse their recollections of the beginning. But, more than any other feeling, we find hope in their voices: hope that a future exists, hope that survival is possible, hope that coexistence is something within reach, hope that they will bond, and hope that the world's vast problems, when reduced to their life-span and immediate context, will permit life.

After their first assessment of their new environment, the immigrants began to make sense of themselves and their life in the new world in more reflexive terms. Then their self-definition became a priority. Their concerns—who are we, who can we be here, and how are we to become that—reflect the political make-up of the country. Many of the new writers identified very strongly with the indigenous population. For, if they felt themselves to be in exile, they sensed and identified all the more with the parts of the society that were also exiled.[41] When Salomon Kahan, a journalist, begins his 1945 book *Yidish-Meksikanish* (Jewish-Mexican) with a short essay on the drama of the "two Mexicos," he is chronicling not only Mexico's problems but also his general problem of belongingness in Mexican society. The issue of belongingness is his central motif, and he describes it as a raw nerve of this society. He studies the country: the indigenous groups and the mestizo. While he identifies with the tragic fate of the first, he also attempts to understand the difficulties of the second.

The main issue for Jews in Mexico was whether they would be able to belong. But to belong is not a one-way street. One must *want* to belong, but one must also be *allowed* to belong. The complexity of this dynamic was not clear to the immigrants at the beginning, but neither was it totally hidden. The government had not adopted an explicit and definitive immigration policy; instead the flexibility of rules and rulers allowed Jews to arrive and settle, giving them some space in which to expand. In addition to the economic problems that Jews, like most immigrants, faced (lack of resources, lack of language skills, etc.), what they had to contend with was the creation of a political space.

Anita Brenner, an early observer of this community, concluded that, except to cultured Mexicans and foreigners, a Jew was either a "Judas toy" or an "evil spirit," but not a person.[42] Being limited in number, Jews could escape prejudice. They remained mostly unnoticed. However, they could also cope with discomfort by concealing their identity. Prejudice served them well, as Brenner suggests, and being a "monster" had its compensations. No one could identify them as Jews; horrid Jews were nowhere to be seen. For a time, they were considered to be of any other nationality and for as long as possible they remained hidden as such. Being called Arab, Russian, Turk, or Pole—it all served a purpose.

The Mexico that received these Jews is variously described through different lenses, from the disheartening feelings of dashed illusions to the romantic hopefulness of the dreamer. A foreign transient observer, Leon J. Pepperberg, a geologist and engineer, thus wrote to the *American Israelite* in 1922: "A colony in this desert territory is like exile. I ask myself if European Jewry could adapt easily to these agricultural conditions." He explained that railroads and roads were rudimentary; there was a lack of irrigation and water. "I am not a Zionist," he wrote, "but I would prefer to invest this money in Palestine rather than Mexico . . . the land of the forefathers . . . there is no future for the agricultural colonies of Jews in Mexico."[43] Though this thinking prevailed, attempts to help individual Jews continued. In 1923 Rabbi Martin Zielonka from El Paso, Texas, a special liaison of the B'nai B'rith, studied the possibility of Jewish colonization in Mexico. He found wages to be too low for immigrants to subsist, and the market too limited to be an incentive; Jews would therefore not be able to support themselves. As a result, neither the urban centers nor the agricultural projects received a seal of approval. Zielonka suggested that, even if attempted, massive colonization could be prohibitively expensive. Finally, the American Jewish Congress also vetoed the colonization projects. Opinions like these, harsh and disappointing, projected a disenchantment that had a strong impact on the American Jewish organizations and philanthropists who were considering Mexico a possible location for the colonizing experiments.[44]

Descriptions of Mexico differ according to their sources. For most adults, Mexico was foreign and difficult: exotic in its food, different in its climate, strange in its language and customs, enigmatic in its people and culture. Jews who came as young adults had to face questions of survival in the midst of such a perplexing environment. J. Belkind described the country as a "Switzerland of America, with magic scenery." The magic would enrapture him and make it possible for him to forget temporarily that he was an immigrant, as well as the almost inhumane conditions of the trip and the approaching hardships. Awakened to reality, though, he concluded that this country must really be the "bottom of paradise!" The dream evaporated all too soon, when "the economic questions of the new life [arose]."[45]

Situations were hard for immigrants, and some paid a price they never imagined. It was not just the losing of a needle which kept a family without food, nor the ordeal of getting by with bread alone, that marked their experiences. Some found themselves in desperate situations that finally broke them. Brenner reports that Jacob Muze, a Jew from Bukovina, hung himself, supposedly because he owed six hundred pesos to a German roommate which he could not see his way to repay. Further, the only Jewish cemetery did not give him burial, due to the "excessive rates demanded."[46]

At the same time, we have from Anita Brenner one of the most poetic and deeply loving descriptions of the Mexico of that time. Her life in Mexico was very different. Born there, she grew to love the country. She observed all and learned to live as a secular Jew. She went to Texas as a young adult to study at a university, where she was faced with anti-Semitism and the reality of "No Jewesses allowed." Yet she became attached to that country, too. Perhaps for Jews there was no conception of a more welcoming environment anywhere. After all, history had never allowed them such an option. She expressed her deep love of Mexico: "once the dust of [Mexico] has settled on your heart," she wrote, " you have no rest in any other land." She loved the country, the people, and the culture. Her testimony, however, is also a telling description of the tensions Jews faced and Jewishness presented.

While Brenner was expressing her heartfelt attachment to Mexico, she noted that Jews could live there well because of the wonderful qualities she found in the Mexican people: "There is an emotional and intellectual rapport with Mexican and Jew, . . . because in Mexico a Jew is not primarily a Jew but rather a tailor or a musician or a wit or a handsome blonde." As social concepts, she found that others saw two Jews in Mexico—the "bogie" and the "legend."[47] The first is the devil with horns and a tail; the second, the prophet, the wandering Jew. The devil and the hero—two sides of the same concept. For her, the existence of these concepts did not interfere in daily exchanges or with coexistence. However, she ignored the part of her own observations which testified to the unacknowledged status of Jews, and did not ponder whether the acceptability of those "tailors or musicians" was not contingent upon their not being perceived as Jews. Brenner thus speaks for the immigrant who has not been joined by large numbers of others of her group. She can, to some extent, choose to merge with the larger population and not feel the need to think in collective terms. The group is not numerically significant enough for these concepts about Jews to be evoked.

But, what happens when Jews are noticed, when they form a group and when they are seen as a group by the others? What happens to those who want to remain a cultural religious group as they have to face and contend with the image of the "bogie" or the "prophet"? Brenner herself was never indifferent or marginal to the Jewish community, and felt proud of its development. But her early testimony un-self-consciously shows that a Jew-qua-Jew would have trouble accommodating in Mexico. For her, a Jew-qua-person—if such an abstraction exists—could easily merge with the population at large: if one was "not primarily a Jew," then life in Mexico could be beautiful. She truly loved the country and was neither puzzled nor repelled by the latent hostility to Jews she inadvertently portrayed: "One may grow symmetrically," she wrote. "One may find, relish, shape one's own appreciations unhurriedly, unstopped. Perhaps that is why Mexico to me is indivisibly bound up with a beautiful picture of Jews."[48]

Different Jewish immigrants experienced different Mexicos. Most started peddling goods or doing other unskilled work. Each one experienced the new country and his or her new life in different ways. And each one adopted different ways of being. These immigrants had a unique challenge and opportunity: coming from diverse countries, they had to regroup themselves into a cohesive whole. They had to find sufficient commonalties to share and to want to recreate to be able to come together. At the same time, they had the opportunity to recreate themselves: their dream of becoming was now possible. All those potential writers, poets, musicians, doctors, engineers, scientists, and artists had an opportunity for self-creation. There was the need to recreate and to create anew some recognition of the old status-set that each had or wanted to have. The exercise of describing oneself and the old social environment to others, to build up one's persona so that others could "recognize" and return the desired evaluation, all for the purpose of establishing social recognition, was a first requirement. They were engaged in establishing a group, with all the status valuations and exchanges a social group has.

Furthermore, however debilitating their first experiences, the immigrants managed to overcome formlessness and use the possibilities and abilities they had to build their own social milieu. Out of nothingness came a communal network that was willed but not predestined. That became the framework of their lives.

*The Old Identity: A New Problem*

Because the Jews were building a new communal substructure in Mexico during a period when the country itself was restructuring its political, cultural, and economic life, they were able to concentrate on themselves: to a large extent, they were left undisturbed. The majority of Jews had a predefined identity which included all the ambivalences that accompanied secularization. It included a desire, both conscious and unconscious, to adapt as soon as possible to any new country that let them be. In Mexico, they wanted to learn the new language while they continued to use their own familiar languages, Yiddish and Hebrew; they wanted to work and earn a living while they sought to create a school for their children. They wanted to understand the new country and find expression for their own inner world. The houses of prayer, the school, the cemetery, and all early assistance and cultural groups seemed both experiments in fulfilling Jewish needs and experiments to test the extent to which Jewish life would be tolerated in the new country. If broad political discussions were conducted concerning whether the mass immigration of Jews should be accepted or rejected, no such discussions took place within the "Jewish street." Those who were in the country—a couple of thousand perhaps[49]—focused on their immediate options. Jews were left quite to themselves to address only their internal struggles. The benevolent disregard in which Jews were left masked the complex and contradictory nature of the interrelationship between the majority and the minority. Jews concentrated on redefining their "new" identity internally. The lack of dialogue between majority and minority on the issue has kept the problem dormant—not solved, but just volatile enough for it to become constantly a problem.

The new experience involved a renewed effort to try to take in cultural and sociophilosophical elements of the new social surrounding. The poet Jacobo Glantz and the journalist and musical critic Salomon Kahan tried to answer the question "Who are we here?" Their concern, however, was the exception to the rule; it was not the majority's conscious aim to find a satisfactory response.[50] The notion of assuming a double identity or becoming "hyphenated Jews" became an issue in Mexico only much later.[51]

Not all in the community struggled consciously with problems of identity.[52] Most retained a kind of historic memory of uncertainty with respect to the treatment they got from the "others." The desire to integrate became a desire to adapt, to merge. In this second version of Jewish desires, what developed was an uncertainty that Jews faced in their wanting to be in "another" social world: uncertainty of their old world and uncertainty of the new world. Secularized Jews who incorporated much of their surrounding societies implicitly criticized and abandoned cultural and religious elements of their own before they even knew whether they would be able to accommodate into the diverse new societies. Some tried to exchange elements from one culture to another, while others juggled both cultural loads. The result was an enormous uncertainty of their inner beings. Few focused on these issues themselves. They let themselves drift into a variety of positions that some expressed and attempted to implement structurally. As a result, the uncertainties they felt and lived by were embedded in the communal structure they built.

Whether issues of identity were met directly or addressed obliquely, the acceptance of the Jews in the new land was not immediate. The land was observed, lived in, and empathized with, but it takes a long time to feel—and to be allowed to feel—that one belongs. After all, belongingness is a reciprocal process. But who cared about the minority-Jewish problem in Mexico? The process of consolidating the Mexican political system allowed Jews in the second decade to develop their own substructure with minor interference from the government. Only occasionally were there newspaper articles and reports indicating that not everyone was indifferent to or ignorant of the existence of Jews in Mexico. Underlying thoughts and feelings about Jews surfaced sporadically, evoking in Jews their old and not-forgotten fears. On some occasions, a causal connection between Mexico's economic and political problems and Jews was implied by some individuals in ways that added to the despair of the Jewish community. But, all in all, the establishment of Jews into Mexican life occurred with relative ease.

The intellectual encounter between Mexico and Jews is best described as tentative. The encounter combined ambivalence on the part of the Mexican government and an undefined, unqualified unease on the part of Jews. Despite the small number of Jews in Mexico, the enterprise of creating new interdependencies was neither unplanned nor unwilled. These interdependencies had a voluntary and deliberate quality. The immigrants had a level of self-awareness that oriented these actions and choices towards a communal existence. Theirs was a collective enterprise. The desire and ambition to build a "world" included a spread of intensity and commitment unequaled in their short new history.

# CHAPTER 2

# The Development
# of the Communal Structure

Nothingness craves thingness and hunger is desire expressed in the
first verb: *Fiat* (Let there be).

—Jacob Boehme

To study this community we need to reconstruct the structural development of the community, yet we do not want to ask only the conventional
questions (i.e. the demographic growth of the group, its economic
changes, etc.). While these questions are basic, they are not the only ones.
In addition, the available data allows only a general reconstruction of
overall trends. At the same time, there are other issues that are crucial in
the understanding of this community: Jews who arrived in Mexico were
not transplanted from any *one* location. These were Jews from different
locations; few knew each other. Ideas, ideologies, languages, rituals, and
folklore were not shared. It is therefore important to trace the process by
which these Jews became a group. The communal expansion and the network of organizations became then the subtext of a more interesting
question: How did these people become a group and create a structure for
themselves? This question in turn gives rise to others: How was the main
ethnic definition of Jewishness elaborated so that all could partake in its
meaning? How were the parameters of acceptable group behavior
defined? How did these become accepted? How were different patterns of
thought and action institutionalized? And how were these patterns
enforced?

The process of communal structuring described in this section, then,
is not a chronological account of the organized development of the community. Although the evolution of the communal network will emerge
from the description, its focus is on the historicity of the agents, and the
ideas, views, and resources they confronted, deployed, and acquired as
they created a new social world. We then explore the possibilities and constraints of their activities.

Schools, synagogues, cultural organizations, leaders, writers, painters,
teachers, and ideologues—all created, established, and reproduced,
through their acting and thinking, the limits of the structure. The action of

one specific agent was not the cause of the structuring process. It was from the confrontations among groups, and the limits they imposed on themselves, that the structure was created: a vision of the world and its control was always at stake. For that, all were willing to fight to win. This is, then, the description of the gradual emergence of the principles of differentiation which eventually provided a definite structure for the community.

## The Accommodation

The encounter between the Jewish and Mexican cultures was at first cautious and uneasy. The ambivalence displayed by both groups was based on different causes. Mexicans, as hosts, were exploring the benefits to be gained from an immigrant population. Their requirements included a population that could merge with and assimilate to the country and its culture.[1] But none of the earlier immigrant groups had merged in that fashion, and Jews, of course, were no exception. The taking on of a new identity, as the Mexicans expected, was almost impossible for any group, and not always desired by the minority.

The Mexicans were reluctant to extend national identity to others. This was an attitude fed by diverse sources, first among these the desire for Spanish and Christian hegemony. The centuries of Spanish dominance were thus layered with more modern ideologies, which in turn reflected the attempts of the world powers to control the country. No tendency towards tolerance ever was articulated; no push for pluralism was seen in Mexico or in most of Latin America.[2] The immigrants themselves seemed to have disappointed the government in their inability to "perform" according to expectations: the government's views of the immigrants were self-fulfilling.

All too often the Catholic Church, or factions strongly identified with the Church, linked up and supported antigovernment movements with anti-Semitic ideas and activities, following the pattern of scapegoating Jews. The anti-Jewish press—e.g., *Omega* and *El Tribunal*—emphasized such themes as the "Communistic and Jewish character of the government," "Sovietism and Communism as of Jewish origin," "Jews avoiding taxes," "Jews as exploiters," etc.[3] In these incidents or periods, nationalistic and xenophobic ideas were expressed and minor riots were often staged. Anti-Semitism was seldom attacked, with the result that Jews were not attracted—as a mass—to the country. But Mexico allowed some Jews to settle there, and most of these Jews had decided to build a Jewish life for themselves.[4]

An important step was sporadically to clarify to others and to themselves their social role, given the conditions that existed. It was mostly the already established Jews[5] who attempted to justify their being in the country by pointing out their achievements in the economic and cultural fields in which they participated: "Jews as joining the expanding middle class"; "developers of industry and of new industry," "helpers in opening sources of work," "creating new markets," "increasing levels of consumption for the population," "expanding development of the provinces," etc.[6] The idea of an immigrant population as an asset and contributor to a country was an idea that was often put forward by Jews themselves. Using a different approach to the same subject, Dr. Abraham King, the most active territorialist in Mexico, suggested in *Freeland*:

> Before, there was fear of the immigrant and of foreign capital. No more. In the U.S. they are fighting against the Walter McCarran immigration act. The fact is that the representatives of the A.F.L. and the C.I.O—the largest unions in the U.S.—have asked for the increase of immigration, and this will surely have a response with the unions and government of Mexico."[7]

In the United States, more than anywhere else, and among Jews more than any other group, an ideology of "immigrant gifts to America" proclaimed successfully that pluralism was a national need.[8]

In Mexico, pluralism was not rationalized to that degree, and Jews were certainly less daring in identifying it as a "need" for the country. There was no underlying ideology in Mexico that Jews could apply and elaborate as in the United States. Therefore, Jews in America could become "exaggerated Americans," as Feingold has called them,[9] even though he suggests that Jews possess a cultural identity not rooted in territorial space. This could not have happened in Mexico as easily, and it did not. Rather, the opposite image had taken root in Mexico: the idea of homogenization seemed to have been elaborated by the "mestizo" population as a way to link politically to the indigenous population and legitimize their own power. It was not meant for foreigners who desired to maintain their distinctiveness.

A more tentative attempt by Jews to formulate a rationale for their being accepted in this new society was found in Mexico. The desire to feel accepted, wanted, and thereby secure in the host society in the midst of insecurity and ambivalence was, of course, present. In the Mexican case, the whole Jewish community often felt at the mercy of the likes or dislikes of the majority rather than an integral part of the political culture of the country. Mexico was not an immigrant country. From a multiplicity of groups, the government sought to forge a unity.[10] Mestizo culture dominated, and to accommodate the "others" was not part of the mestizos' historical consciousness. In fact, the whole idea of foreignness was disturbing to anyone who tried to claim roots in this new country. Jews could not apply, then, the experience of the United States to their case. They only used their social and economic productivity as a theme to justify their being a positive entity in the country.

## THE BUILDING OF A STRUCTURE

*First Stage: Regrouping, Redefining, and Networking*

Despite the lack of international organizational Jewish support, Jews traveled to Mexico. The despair of Jews in their countries of origin, be it for economic, political, or intellectual reasons, led them to search for other options, no matter how temporary or limited. The lack of means to initiate a venture in Mexico on Mexican terms did not make the place too congenial an environment. Finding their way through the narrow doors of Mexico in the early 1900s, individual Jews began arriving. German and Alsatian Jews, the very first immigrants of the century, kept their Jewish alliances submerged, and they were very few in number. The Syrian Jews, who had been there since the early part of the century,[11] identified among themselves by their city of origin—Aleppo or Damascus—and somehow guarded their Jewish identity by the religious activities they wanted to maintain.[12] They offered help to the Ashkenazim, and the building of a structure got started. After that, their history becomes our story.

The first traditional role of the rabbi—or *chacham*—was filled by Shlomo Lobatón, one of the few knowledgeable Sephardic Jews in Mexico at the time. Versed in Hebrew and Jewish sources, he performed circumcisions, taught, and directed prayers. When the reality of death shook this incipient community, Rabbi Lobatón helped establish the first Jewish cemetery in 1912. The Ashkenazi immigrants of the late 1920s were helped by the pioneering Sephardic Jews, whom they joined until differences (and the means to fight for them) separated them again as subcommunities.

A transitional frame of mind was apparent in the Jews' relation to the country; however, their thinking also contained a hidden desire for affirmation. When the first secular Jewish school was formed (1920s) and its curriculum debated, one topic of discussion was whether or not to include the English language as a subject matter. The argument for inclusion suggested that, in the transitional years, one could at least learn a language that would be useful later in future geographical stops. The argument itself is revelatory, as was the decision of the Jews. English was not further officially encouraged. The American Jews who came to Mexico between 1917 and 1920 to escape the war draft were not at first eager to establish themselves; but the expected duration of their stay was slowly lengthened.[13]

At least two factors helped change the feeling of temporariness the Jews in Mexico had about their own relation to the country: first, the United States closed its door to immigration; second, the rudimentary organizations created by other Jews in Mexico satisfied the immediate needs of the newcomers: shelter and jobs, a network of support, and some structure for religious life. The welcome that this cultural and linguistic network offered to the Jewish immigrants eventually changed their perspective. The network generated and allowed new activities, and with them a new approach. Slowly, "long-termness" began to be seen as a viable option, one of the few left to European Jews.

This change of perspective did not create a feeling of total comfort. Many different elements inhibited that feeling. Whether because of the historic Jewish political fear of diaspora, the immediate insecurity of the Mexican experience, or the ambivalence that Mexican society and government reflected back to the community, a general sense of insecurity and an obsessive need for legitimization tended to prevail. Communal newspapers occasionally wrote about how "welcome and positive an element" Jews were for this society. In an effort to justify and support those statements, the favorable opinions of non-Jews were often cited. Thus, the views of the chronicler of old Mexico, Bernal Díaz del Castillo, or of the muralist and painter Diego Rivera,[14] were often quoted to exemplify the reactions that diverse intellectuals had about Jews. The implicit hope was that others, less favorable to Jews, would come to share similar thoughts. However, these efforts were not sufficient to prevent the sporadic anti-Semitic attacks that occurred in diverse states of the Republic[15] where some of the Mexican press often incited and supported them.[16]

An invitation made to Jews by President Calles in 1924, for instance, produced a strong reaction in Mexico on the part of a group called "Cristeros."[17] The Cristeros aimed to attack the anticlericalism of Calles, his general policies, and what they felt was his pro-Jewish position. The Cristiada, the Cristero movement, became then a reaction to two forces that were hostile to Catholicism: antireligious freemasonry and the labor movement within the state, with its Iberian anarchist roots. The government attempted the incorporation of diverse groups into its structure, and the growth of Christian syndicalism in the country seemed to them a threat.

Jews found themselves in the middle of these tensions. The escalation of those reactions had reached a notorious climax by the end of the 1920s and early 1930s. The world economic depression and the expulsion of Mexican workers from the United States contributed to the uneasy feelings of the general Mexican public, who accepted the scapegoat suggested by the anti-Jewish Cristeros with relative ease. This anti-Semitism was later taken up by another group, the Camisas Doradas, who got support from the already established Nazi government in Germany. Calles's successor, Pascual Ortiz Rubio, yielded to the pressure of the local larger economic consortiums and called for the elimination of street-salesmen and pushcarts from the Lagunilla Market in the center of Mexico City. The peddlers were mostly Jews. It had been suggested that these merchants were having a negative effect on the sales of the large, well-established stores owned by "real Mexicans." The poet and storekeeper Jacobo Glantz was physically attacked[18] in 1929, and the treatment of these and other events in the media was used by some to further justify the desire to "expel all Jews" from the national territory.[19] Calls by Nicolás Rodríguez, the leader of the Camisas Doradas, for the formation of a Jewish ghetto;[20] an attempt on the life of Jacobo Landau (1935), then-president of the Yidisher Handls-Kamer (Jewish Chamber of Commerce); and the public request in 1937 to check the status papers of all foreigners were all reason for Jewish unease in Mexico. All were seen as frightening incidents by Jews, and were considered of sufficient concern for the Jewish community to take steps against them. But none of the events was enough to indict Mexico as a host country and a viable home for Jews, particularly in the 1930s when few other options were available to Jews. The Jewish community hardly ignored the incidents. It formed the Central Committee (Tsentral Komitet), an umbrella organization of all subcommunities, whose first objectives were to deal with anti-Semitic activities, to offer legal protection to Jews, and to respond to all defamatory activities.

The celebratory memoirs of the first twenty years of Jewish communal life in Mexico show the subdued and unpleasant awareness that not all was "perfect," no matter how much the documents express feelings of success, amalgamation, and comfort. There was an understanding that the local acceptance of Jews was not based on love, and that their being tolerated was not unconditional. The fact that many Jews still identified themselves at the time as Polish or Russian rather than as Jews, that the celebration of twenty years of communal life could "not be performed in the open," that the Jewish bank was never called by and identified with a Jewish name but was rather known as the Banco Mercantil, all point to the undefined and undetermined space that Jews occupied in Mexico.[21] Thus, after two decades of work, dedication, adaptation, and the search for some integration, Jews were still struggling with the unclear balance between their needed insulation and their burdensome isolation: one was a chosen, self-protective measure; the other, an imposed condition.

For those Jews who had an assimilationist approach but opted to take advantage of the help their brethren had provided and so stayed "within" the community, as well as for those who sought to build a Jewish life to sustain their cultural identity, the choice led to spatial segregation. This insulation offered basic economic and linguistic comfort, while on the other hand allowing Jews to live as a religious, national, and/or ethnically distinct group. Some level of insulation was required for the affirmation of one's identity. A neighborhood in the center of town— the oldest part of the city—became the first Jewish neighborhood. Downtown streets such as Tacuba, Palma, Donceles, Jesús María, Bolivar, Mina, 5 de Mayo, etc., became the Jewish quarter in the second decade, the 1920s, and the 1930s. The networks of help, services, and communications, as well as religious needs, all implied a certain level of insulation.

Insulation, however, also represented an active state of being "on guard" with respect to the wider society. In the urban space in which Jews found themselves, it became difficult to handle the rationalization of a modernizing society, its controls, competing and conflicting commitments, and the simultaneous desire for relationships based on intimacy, subjectivity, and protection. Jews had to provide these for themselves, and they achieved them with insulation. Isolation, however, was never desired or attempted; that meant disconnectedness, separation, and detachment, none of which were desired goals.[22] Formally, no isolation was imposed by the general society. Nevertheless, in critical moments, when the role, status, and space of Jews in Mexico were publicly questioned by the hosts, the Jews experienced feelings of being cut off, set apart, and distanced.

During these formative years, the American B'nai B'rith was the only major organization that provided Jews in Mexico with resources such as money or representatives. During the crucial early years, this help was extremely important. But the help had strings attached: with it came suggestions, directions, and even conditions. If B'nai B'rith was to be a joint builder of the community, they sought to voice an opinion and exert some control over what was being built. However, local Jews had plenty of opinions to choose from, and some were very different from those suggested by B'nai B'rith. The B'nai B'rith was functioning under the premises and with the aims it had in the United States: secularization, integration, and homogenization with the local population. They not only assumed that the locals would want the same as their American brethren, but that the host society was equally willing and able to receive them. Although the Jews in Mexico needed help, differences surfaced and Jews in Mexico broke off the dependency. There were at least two areas where suppressed differences eventually forced the parties into adversarial positions: one concerned the aims of education when provided by the community; the other, how to offer economic help.

The first confrontation revolved around the idea of who the immigrants should become. The American immigrants aspired to "shed their foreign character" and aim for something similar to the American Dream while not disturbing the already established Jews; B'nai B'rith wanted Jews in Mexico to do the same. Jewish education was thus seen as a tool to facilitate acculturation. It was not an education specifically aimed to sustain cultural, ethnic, national, and religious differences. Because the latter view prevailed in Mexico, the relationship in that area was severed.

A second confrontation occurred over the issue of initial economic help. The wealthier American-linked Jews aimed to offer economic support to individuals according to their specific problems, keeping all its decision-making discretionary. The socialist-oriented Jews, most of them recent immigrants themselves, disliked and opposed this idea of philanthropy and aimed to reorganize the Hilfs (help) organizations as "credit centers," with greater access to decision-making on the part of the beneficiaries. Again, the latter view prevailed, fueled by the more socialist-oriented immigrants. While the Hilfs Fareyn did not always get its given credits back, the style and principle behind it gave respect and autonomy to the "creditors."[23]

This conflict created in the community not only a sense of autonomy, but also a sense of control and direction. It helped raise an awareness of the value and meaning of the actions taken. After that, ideological conflicts produced a network of organizations and institutions, which was surprising given the resources and time needed to create the network, all of which were never in large supply.

Religious needs for prayer had been fulfilled in private houses and, later, in large rented rooms used only on the high holidays.[24] The Sepharadic Jews, maybe one hundred families in all, had already had a synagogue ("Monte Sinai") since 1906. In later years, Ashkenazim and Sephardim had disagreements, especially over prayer rituals and traditions. Resembling the *landsmanschaftn* of the United States, the Ashkenazim broke away from this first organized religious group to form their own prayer centers.

Eventually, another issue further separated the Jews internally. The then-joint cemetery committee requested a father to pay what for him was an excessive amount for the burial of his child. The money was not available and the child was not buried in the Jewish cemetery. In the ensuing uproar, a new plot of land was purchased by the Nidkhei Israel group, who took control of the new cemetery for Ashkenazi Jews. Divisions and breaking away occurred with greater frequency: groups divided, split, and began anew. The community did not decline with these apparent changes; rather, it entered an unparalleled period of effervescence.

The channels for Jews in Mexico to express themselves were not strictly limited to the internal political field. The outpouring of literary material was enormous. A hunger to express themselves dominated sensitive minds engaged in ceaseless searching. The number and variety of journals, magazines, and newsletters was amazing. These were mostly temporary efforts; eventually, the publications became fewer and more stable.

Usually, an organization sponsored a new newsletter aiming to attract a specific audience. A still smaller group was involved directly in writing.[25] Three or four people constituted a group; often linked in small teams to produce a journal, they functioned as audiences to each other, as peer groups, as a forum to exchange ideas and generate new ones. When a paper failed, for either lack of economic resources or internal disputes among the writers, a new alliance emerged. Soon there was renewed enthusiasm for the production of another publication. The fact that so many other seemingly more vital areas (e.g., jobs, loans, education, health care) were also being addressed raises the question of how resources remained to be allocated for this exercise. The energy needed to carve out time and money for the cultural production was extraordinary, but the job was done.

Where did this hunger for writing come from? It has been suggested that a written tradition provides a basis and a focus for stability.[26] If that is so, a desperate sense of stability and assurance was sought by these immigrants. This hunger for writing may also represent the indefatigable aim for affirmation. This does not mean that ingrained notions of transiency disappeared. However, the desire and need for affirmation and stability prevailed, and their cultural production soon became a forum for the discussion of local and international problems.

Despite the desire to affirm, the keeping of records and the method of historical self-recording were neglected to an astonishing degree. Was this due to a fear of potentially exposing their communal profile? Was it a self-denying respect for their own enterprise?[27] Or a combination of both? Or was it a way to postpone addressing their very existence in Mexico and waiting to see the host's reaction when the raising of the question would require an answer? Maybe, as was suggested by some early observers, the involvement of the pioneers in building impeded their having the necessary perspective to record their actions. In the words of Meyer Berger,[28] the first formal director of the Yidishe Shule: "our pioneers didn't record the first protocols, they didn't guard the reports . . . they didn't keep a diary. They were involved in the 'Maase bereshis' (creation process) of the community." It may very well be that the years of creation required that all the pioneers' energy be put into the production of something before attempting to record the process. For all the written legacy, Jews did not seem to think in terms of being "rooted" and feeling "permanent"; it thus appears that much was purposely left unsaid.

Emblematic of this craving was Itzkhok Berliner's attempt to publish a book in Yiddish using Latin characters; there was no Yiddish type available in Mexico in 1922, so he resorted to what was at hand. His peddling and selling of Madonna pictures to the indigenous population was a survival tactic, a matter of livelihood. But ever present behind it was the attempt to alter this anomic condition. Life was not just a matter of food and shelter; it could have meaning, but meaning had to be created. The self-preservation of the immigrant contained a desire for affirmation. "Hunger" seems to be a fundamental human drive, linked to hope.[29] The hunger to build, to be able to carve out a Jewish intellectual life in a totally non-Jewish environment, was then and still seems today an impressive effort. Newspapers, journals, gazettes sprang up like mushrooms, however fragile and short-lived they were. Even a Jewish theater functioned for some time in 1925.[30] Much before Jewish peddling was superseded,[31] the intellectual work of some immigrants amidst still extremely precarious economic conditions was beginning to flourish.

Towards the second decade, the Young Men's Hebrew Association—the Y—was formed; its name reflected the fact that the majority of the immigrants were men and American-oriented. Its activities were primarily social, but also cultural and economic. The Y was started by Jews who left the United States during World War I. In 1920 all were identified as "American" by the later-arriving European Jews. The Americans spoke English among themselves, and were soon "wealthier" than the East Europeans were at arrival. The Americans had no strong religious affiliations or other specific ideology except a general sympathy for Zionism as the supporters of another Jewish settlement. This sympathy was the central and most visible integrating force in their Jewish identity. Their newspaper was printed in English and later added some Spanish. They attempted later again to add some Yiddish, printed in Latin letters (since there was still no type available to them), to serve and attract the newcomers. By that time the Y had close to one hundred members.

A small group of socialists who could not adapt to the format and content of the Y formed the Y. L. Peretz Fareyn. Shortly thereafter, further leftist forces joined to expand into what became the Kultur Gezelshaft. This organization was formed by Bundists, socialists, communists, and some Zionists, all of whom felt that they could reach a meaningful existence by retaining the variety of their positions and detaching themselves still further from the Y. Yosef Yehuda Zacharias, Halperin, Kutcher, Salomon Kahan, Jacobo Glantz, and Itzjok Berliner were the activists, some of whom maintained until later years important positions as organizers of Jewish political life in Mexico. In 1927, when the first Yiddish lettering set was given as a gift to Jews in Mexico by the American *Forvertz*, the first independent Yiddish newspaper appeared: *Meksikaner Yidish Lebn.*

The late 1920s and early 1930s derived their basic force and energy primarily, although not exclusively, from Jews with ideologies on the left, even though it was not a homogeneous and unified left. Communists, who would not merge with the Bundists, felt strong enough to separate and create another private organization: Radikaler Arbeter Tzenter. Although they expected that about four hundred Jewish workers could join them, the actual number of members was much smaller.[32] Left-Zionists often worked and cooperated with them, as well as with other institutions serving the community: for example, the Jewish school and all welfare organizations. Some infighting over the leadership of organizations was beginning to occur. However, the fierce debates did not flourish until the 1940s, when organizations fought not only about the organizational structure, but also about the alliances of the public to legitimize their positions, to obtain a larger area of control in the communal life.

By the end of the 1920s the Y bulletin had become *Undzer Vort*, printed in Yiddish.[33] Interestingly, the later wave of immigrants, although theoretically still interested in going to America, was against using English as the language of the paper. It is probable they had to learn that language, too, and were not immediately interested. They were searching, first of all, for a life with meaning: "We brought with our habits, concepts, a thirst for spiritual life. Who will satisfy all this?"[34] The general changes in the Y, and the transformation of the bulletin into the *Undzer Vort* newspaper, reflected the change of audience, membership, and direction of this organization. By the end of the 1920s, the writers had a well-defined, interested, and responsive audience that bestowed recognition on their activity and on them. The original peer-group activity expanded its operations by incorporating a broader public into the debates and discussions, all of which had important consequences.

The bulletin of the Y in its *Undzer Vort* incarnation gave much attention and support to the settlements in Palestine. Because the paper was financed by the original Y members, and because these issues were of utmost importance to the paper, one of the oldest of Jewish Ashkenazi institutions in Mexico (and later the community at large) came to be identified with Zionism. The initial interest and intellectual support for the Zionist political movement did not immediately develop further. The first attempt at organizing a Zionist movement occurred in 1922 and was unsuccessful. A second attempt in 1925 succeeded in establishing a more permanent contact with the central organizations of the movement, but did not command a massively strong or large response. However, from the content and style of this early press and the linkage to the idea of the Y as the organization of the Ashkenazim, a perception arose that the majority of the community was Zionist. While the general interest that Palestine elicited cannot be denied, a more active Zionism had not yet taken root. Nevertheless, the view of the community as Zionist did prevail, even though these years saw rather an active left.

The excitement emanating from world events—especially the social-ist experiments—was felt in Mexico. Those whose thinking included left-ist paradigms felt themselves at the center of the changes. At the same time, the differences between their more specific visions and dreams col-lided. Some socialists joined in the Peretz Fareyn, while communists and left-Zionists joined in the Kultur Gezelshaft. However few in number these immigrants were, their meanings and the languages with which they approached their worlds propelled them to build wider contexts. The network was expanding.

Towards the end of the second decade, Jewish participation in the economy of Mexico was entering a new stage. Many Jews still needed economic help and credit to be able to work, though the development of small industry was already beginning and Jews seemed to be building a part of it. Ironically, this process got an unexpected impulse through the government's anti-Jewish policy of 1931, when the Jewish street mer-chants of the city market "Lagunilla" were expelled, and they needed to find alternative work locations and alternative types of work.

Within the community, however, the economic change was slow to be assimilated intellectually and ideologically. The Radikaler Arbeter Tzenter was formed after the Kultur Gezelshaft was closed because of ide-ological disagreements among its members. The Radikaler Arbeter Tzen-ter was, as the name reveals, an attempt to highlight the radical political leanings of the working force. However, no Jewish "workers" in the classical Marxist definition of the concept really existed in Mexico, cer-tainly not in great numbers. Jewish workers were peddlers, owners of small stalls, workshop owners, tailors, etc. In a climate of poverty and economic hardship, most developed economically by working on their own. The Tzenter in 1928 did not in general attract this working group either.[35] Another attempt to organize the Jewish workforce was the Tai-lors' Union, formed in 1931. But again, this effort did not succeed.

### Second Stage: Organizational Expansion

The structuring process of this community soon entered a new stage. Diverse ideological postures had been brought, rephrased, and rebuilt within the possibilities and restrictions of both the host society and the minorities' internal resources. From the community's beginnings until the end of the 1940s, the variety of Jewish organizations in Mexico and the speed with which they proliferated illustrate the intensity with which the immigrants examined social issues. At the same time, the European Jewish ideologies that fed these groups were transplanted to America, and the issues in the new territory were still to a large degree "Euro-pean." The divisions were the same; their quarrels were also similar.

These ideologies also transposed a deeper structure, an ambivalence in the Jewish identity of the thinkers. Emancipated Jews had started out with an unelaborated premise that was presented as an interest in the "modernization process" of Jews (assimilation). This was mixed with Jewish concerns (particularism) as well as with general social concerns (universalism), forming an identity in the form of what J. Murray Cuddihy calls a "cubist collage."[36] Beyond the specific content of each Jewish ideology, all of these ideologies were secularized enough so that their assimilatory attempts combined with the Jewish elements they retained to produce this collage.[37] Caught between contradictory positions, the Jews felt both a need to retain private and subjective definitions of themselves while being part of a different larger society. In other words, Jews took universal problems into their ideologies and visions, and addressed and elaborated them into particular paradigms, as the frameworks for their ideologies—Bundism, Zionism, and communism—show. Some engaged in the reverse: particular problems were woven into universal paradigms.[38] Each ideology attempted to solve the conflict between particularism and universalism.

The American case seemed to offer room for "solutions," and Jews worked on them. The Mexican case left little room for solutions. Jews retained and suppressed the conflict, but the problem of inserting a subculture into another culture did not disappear. The host society tolerated the newcomers; however, it did so better at some periods than at others. Yet tolerance is not necessarily acceptance. When Jews were called "a menace" (1931) and the press played upon this prejudice, the society and the subculture found themselves at odds. Their acceptance into that society was being questioned. From within the subculture, this deep-seated ambivalence carried over into the project of the building of the community. Jewish continuity was, of course, a given, but not how much of it. During the initial period, adaptation required some attention, too. In this second stage, the choices made in the first period begin to manifest themselves. The initial adaptation soon raised the problematic issue of continuity.

Learning the new language was perhaps the first formal step in adapting; this was followed by a constant search for any new opportunities the new society offered. Some level of adaptation seemed indisputably necessary to be able to cohabit in the new society. However, when this entailed a desire to shed some of one's cultural differences to achieve a quicker and more secure integration, then the behavior labeled "adaptation" really became "integration," "distancing," "homogenization." Here Jews once again got caught in the historical conflict between adapting enough to be accepted, or at least tolerated, while avoiding assimilating to the point of losing their identity. Some found themselves in that conflict more deeply than others.

Formal schooling was supposed to reproduce certain cultural messages (e.g., language, general culture, national feeling), but offered weak political connections for the children. At the same time, the home—the all-pervasive socializing agent—was weak in supporting the school message: the ethnic language was used less and less often, and feelings of continuity were unsystematically and selectively mixed with efforts to adapt and integrate, which were never presented as contradictory.[39] If the formal status given to the ethnic language within the various organizations gave intellectual recognition to the issue of continuity, the daily behavior of the vast majority of the community did not show equal commitment to continuity in the private sphere of life. Private support for the public posture was minimal.

Other inconsistencies surfaced. During the same period, when it was clear that leftist ideology of any shade would not take root among these Jews who were moving away from that way of thinking, the Gesbir—a communist-backed group—had the largest command over the small audience. In 1934, Gesbir—the Gezelshaft for Birobidzhan—reopened and took over the hegemony of the left. This Jewish communist group had long attempted to focus attention on the issue of colonization in Birobidjan as a solution to the question of Jewish nationality. By this time, the prestige of socialist ideas and their embodiment in the Russian government were generally and loosely accepted, even if they did not result in greater activism among the masses. The 1930s and a large part of the 1940s were years when a general acceptability and sympathy to Russian affairs flourished. This pattern, which was evident in intellectual circles in England, the United States, and other countries, also prevailed among the Jewish left in Mexico. The only exception to this were the Bundists.

Other inconsistencies were manifested at the individual level, too. The authors Jacobo Glantz and Salomon Kahan provide two examples. Both early immigrants, they arrived in 1925 and 1921 respectively. The fact that links them here is related to their active and open request to the community to "adapt further," "deeper" into Mexican culture. What exactly this meant was not made clear. But it appears that this adaptation was to be attained through a one-sided conscious submersion into all things Mexican. Glantz and Kahan felt that the immigrant should soak up Mexico's history—its past and its social problems—while also setting aside those aspects of the past that only heightened an awareness of one's differences. The message was contradictory because neither Glantz nor Kahan ever suggested openly that they wanted to leave their Jewishness behind or that others should do that; nor did they ask for parallel reciprocity from Mexicans. They only wanted, they said, to create an awareness of a different present.

Glantz wrote an epic poem on Columbus as a personal attempt to follow his own prescription. The reenacting of the voyage to the new continent, the new society, was his way of entering that social world, a rational exercise mediated through historicity. But his message was veiled and confused. While his readers were adapting as a matter of course, creating a Jewish framework to survive as Jews, he was (while writing in Yiddish, editing Jewish newspapers, and working in help organizations) advocating for a metamorphosis into the new culture which required abandoning parts of one's own to take on the new. However, he did not feel the contradiction; thus, he did not feel the need to articulate it further.

Salomon Kahan joined Glantz in this plea. Yet, in the late 1940s, both writers opposed both their own positions and the results their own ideas had helped to bring about. Neither, however, was conscious of the contradictory character of the "new" message when juxtaposed to the first one. They later advocated for a "return" to one's culture. They could both "enter" a foreign culture and then "return" to their roots at least in theory, because they were part of a generation that "left" and could "go back" to their place of origin. But to the newer generations whose lives had begun in the foreign culture, the return was impossible. There was no cultural base to return to. Many did not understand what there was to return to, or even want to. Kahan had first made explicit the need for hyphenated identity. "Jews-in-Mexico," as opposed to "Mexican-Jews," he said, were part of a conceptual island whose main characteristic allowed for religious continuity only and inhibited a commitment to the new country.[40] In his book *Judeo-Mexicano* he advocated an intense mode of life in the new country in which all facets—social, political, economic, and cultural—should be absorbed, producing what he hoped to be a new identity. Mexican-Jews would be then something new, something that they had not yet become. The host society's expectations would presumably make this outcome possible.

Two decades later Glantz, in his book *Kezais Erd* (*A Morsel of Land*), and Kahan, in his journalistic work on the Yiddish language, called for a return to one's roots.[41] Glantz expressed it in his poetry: "If earth will join to a mother be it only, where the wide expanding stems root not to tear apart"; and, in the same poem: "For whatever it becomes, it is to hold oneself onto the root."[42]

Kahan reversed his original plea by focusing on the language: "Spanish is not your language. You cannot consider Spanish the instrument to express the hidden corners, the deepest depths of the Jewish national historic experience."[43] When the structure of the social, religious, and cultural life of Jews in Mexico was crystallizing in the late 1940s and its political contours were being defined, Glantz's and Kahan's calls for return seem inexplicable. They make sense as a personal reaction to their earlier calls for integration, but were unclear to the general public. The authors did not seem aware of their convoluted thought processes, which suggests of a lack of self-reflection on their part. Their calls spoke of a reality they had helped to create, in whose "solution" others could not follow.

Given the general ideological context of the community, their thinking was always "anachronistic": in the early years, when all immigrants were adapting themselves to the host society as a matter of course, Glantz's and Kahan's call for "further adaptation" must have seemed unclear. In the 1950s when they, among others, were calling for a "return" while the institutionalization of the community was well under way, their calls again seemed out of context. Glantz and Kahan had at first articulated an ideological tenet that was inherently antithetical to the continuity objectives of other Jews in the community, though necessary for their adaptation. In the 1950s their reversal was perhaps also the result of a sensitive perception of the institutionalization process. Fresh as it was, they pointed to the initial signs of the abandonment of the new social structures. In the increasing euphoria, the message they sent could be misunderstood. Few knew how to cope with this ambiguity. The only link these thinkers did not acknowledge or understand was the extent to which they themselves had actively paved the way for the cultural distancing that had occurred. They had not understood the rationale for continuity earlier. Now it was otherwise, but it was late.

Here were to be found the first signs of the unexpected consequences of an earlier ideology. A series of political, social, and linguistic inconsistencies were beginning to emerge. The echo of these original conflicts, however faint, suggests the inescapable conflict for secularized Jews between continuity and integration. The cultural distancing between generations was first widely exposed here. Here was the unsolved dilemma for the Jew in Mexico as well as for the modern diaspora everywhere. The subcultural society Jews had built in Mexico was to become not so much a social reality in which the group found itself, but a private reality in which each individual participated to the degree appropriate to his own ideology, with the added incongruities between host and minority. Over time, the distance between generations widened: the thinking of one generation would not be understood by the following one. What was passed on were only the answers—the structure as form—and not the queries and the logic of thought which had given rise to the structure. The meaning of the issues was obscured. The mechanisms that ensured integration eclipsed the mechanisms that attempted cultural reproduction. The inability to connect across generations seems, then, largely a self-inflicted condition.

In the 1930s, some social and religious organizations were already well settled. Nidkhei Israel (1922–23), the synagogue-congregation which became the most important one of its kind, had subdivided its activities into credit, schooling (Talmud Tora), and, later, support for the Yidishe Shule, Gmilas Khesed fund, and, most important, the cemetery. When it came to religion and tradition, the Ashkenazim had a variety of experiences that could not easily be subsumed under one style in one religious organization; they were diversified from within. But most characteristically, religion itself was never the central dimension through which these Jews defined their activities. Polish Jews decided to center around the Agudas Akhim Congregation, and had their own agenda. They continued for a time to be strongly connected with Polish Jewry, to the point of sending a representative in 1934 to the World Conference on Polish Jewry in London. They maintained their own rabbi, and never fully joined Nidkhei Israel, with which they never were able to compete in scope and breadth. They also did not attempt to counter the activities of Nidkhei Israel, which had a constituency made up mostly of Jews from Russia. In keeping with this diversity, the Jewish religious authorities in Mexico were never subordinate to a central figure. Even though Harav Yosef Dovid Rafalin, a Lithuanian who was the Kehillah rabbi for over forty years after Nidkhei Israel imported him from Cuba, was main rabbi, other rabbis had positions of their own and areas of relatively independent authority and prestige. (Today, the number of rabbis has risen, possibly in response to the increased activities of the Sephardic Jews in the religious sector.)

In this second stage, each group, though, functioned as an experiment in organizational alternatives in terms of style, content, and scope, and each helped to train and establish a hierarchy of local Jewish "politicians." The political vibrancy and effervescence of the community led to organizational change, but with small variation among the incumbents. This group of people established a context in which they could see their values and the symbols mirroring them. In a way, as argumentative and combative as they appeared, they were often very flexible, and searched for connections among themselves in spite of their ideological differences. Few in number, they needed each other and mostly chose to relate to each other. They never ignored their differences, but often chose to highlight what they had in common. When the differences became more salient, however, the organizations broke into factions, or were transformed. Conflict divided and delayed efforts by reducing budgetary and human resources, but political effervescence and a sense of possibility were at their highest.

To some, this fitful making and remaking of organizations, publications, and groups must have appeared to reflect the gropings of an insecure, uncommitted society. Some people actually voiced their opinion at the time that the changes in the community were puerile and revelatory in their immaturity.[44] Yet the almost unlimited internal resources that the process required, and the almost insurmountable hurdles that the early immigrants overcame in order to organize and express their thoughts, are vital testimony to the creative and adaptive resources used for cultural survival. This pattern of behavior persisted long after the original need to cluster together had passed.

*Experiments in Politics: The Preparation
for the Institutionalization Stage*

The 1940s was a disturbing decade for Jews in Mexico, in unforeseeable ways. The horrifying experience of the Jews in Europe was tempered by the improvement of the Mexican economy: annihilation and destruction for Jews in one part of the world coincided with some prosperity in another. Increasingly, the response of the organized community in Mexico was for representatives of diverse positions to coalesce and cooperate. Was this a case of uniting in the face of a common threat? Or was it a moment the leaders used to further their own political aims? Zionists, for example, wrote and published in the Jewish communist press. At that time, none of the newspapers published was basically Zionist, although some were very sympathetic to the Zionist cause. Those that were thoroughly Zionist were short-lived. As a group, the Zionists were not interested in financing their own paper. Economic resources from the Zionists were usually channeled to and for Palestine. Different types of Zionists worked together for a time within the Jewish communist framework.[45] All joined in an effort to fight fascism. That became the slogan and unifying force for many intellectuals who were either independent or allied, but sympathetic to the communist platform. The Bundists, however, remained independent, with their own forum. Their political differences with the communists never eased and were at times acute. Furthermore, the Bundists differed dramatically in their interpretation of the immediate reality of the war and what the outcome could be or should be for Jews.

Bundists differed from Zionists and communists, then, and sustained their position. The differences were substantial. Bundists were fighting to rescue and retain the vanishing European Jewish world, while communists and Zionists were dreaming of new worlds. While the actual dreams of these latter groups differed, they could—by the mere act of hoping— momentarily come together. For them, the war was seen through the lens of the dream and the hope. For Bundists, however, the war implied the shattering reality of social death, and no dream could mitigate their pain. Their writing is full of despair. If anything could be built, it had to be from within that vanishing world, and not away from it. They were perhaps not fully aware of how destroyed that immediate reality was.

There was despair in their inability to act, and there was despair and frustration with the other Jewish political dreamers who did not seem to mourn.

For the masses it may have been more comforting to hear the uplifting rhetoric of dreams than to be consumed by the growing consciousness of Jewish destruction. The Mexican government—which was in theory open to immigration and could have taken a politically active role advocating for refugees—remained at the margins of the issue.[46] The leaders and the country remained fairly silent. In the Evian-Les-Bains conference on refugees (1938), most of Latin America rejected the immigration possibility. Chile, Ecuador, Uruguay, Venezuela, Peru, Argentina, Brazil, Nicaragua, Honduras, Panama, and Mexico all voted against taking in Jews. The only exception was the Dominican Republic, which took in a small number of immigrants. The old feeling of "Judea Capta" was, in 1938, as a witness expressed it, already pointing to the unescapable destiny of Jews.[47] If any group conveyed this message in Mexico, it was the Bundists.

The dreams at this time, however much they hurt the Bundists, were instrumental for the group. They provided concerned Jews a forum for action and participation. By collaborating with the communist journal *Fraivelt,* the Zionists kept their issues at the fore. Avner Aliphas—the left-Zionist teacher, journalist, and school builder—is a good case in point. Aliphas joined the Jewish press of the left not only to fight Nazism-Fascism, but also to express his socialist leanings. *Fraivelt* was a forum where different ideologies could converse, as long as socialist hopes were built into the premises of all other beliefs. Aliphas could then clearly state his linkage with the communist group while he attempted to gain active support from the Soviet Union for Jewish purposes. Because he expected that after the war the "world would be redivided,"[48] he tried to make the Soviet Union conscious of Zionist Jews. In 1944 Aliphas saw the Soviet Union as participating in deciding, together with a few others, the geopolitical division of certain parts of the world. He clearly felt and hoped that World Zionism should be present at the time of these political partitions. In speaking to the communist leadership and to World Zionism, he hoped that both entities would find their common elements and assist each other.

The divisions of the communal groups were as important and decisive as the alliances in the intellectual and political life of the community of the period. During World War II, the balance tipped towards alliances, and most cooperated with each other in some form or other. But even that time was not devoid of polemic. As much as the 1940s echoed a desire for unification, the multiplicity of voices and opinions was highly productive for the expression of thought. The alternatives for this decade were either unification or division. Thus the general attempts at a unified political interpretation should not obscure the bitter divisions that gave rise, for instance, to four new schools with diverse ideologies. This school system became a kind of "second front" where the dialogue between and among ideologies remained active. Although the issues were narrowed, the fight transferred the issue of internal hegemonic control to an acceptable arena, given the context of the past world war.

*External Influences: The Holocaust and the State of Israel*

The years of World War II and after are crucial for the understanding of changes in the structure of the Jewish community in Mexico. Bundist concerns over the tragedy of the Holocaust did not subside, even though they were unable to stir up the protests that some of them wanted.[49] Each of the ideological parties within the community was acting on its own issues. But there was a sense of expectation that the war would come to an end and that new ways of thinking and acting were going to be needed.

Prestige and authority dramatically changed the structure of the community after the war. The Holocaust and the creation of the new Jewish state in Israel were the two events that influenced the resulting changes. Not only did the Holocaust eradicate the actual and potential audience of the Bund, it also curbed, dampened, and crushed the ability of Bundists to think and act on their ideology. If the world had failed, part of their universalistic ideological thinking had crashed, not only because of it, but with it. Who could persist in defending the ideas of gregarious life in this world? Was the war going to be rationalized as a period of political aberration? Or was the Holocaust linked to the cultures of prejudice and anti-Semitism? The blow of the events was of such magnitude in both quantity and quality that the Bund and other groups could not begin to address the issues. Those who remained committed to the ideology were like religious zealots holding on to their idea of hope against all hope.

Israel, its creation and physical reality once achieved, meant everything to Jews: hopes, dreams, intertwining past and future. In the midst of the debasement and confusion to which the post-Holocaust period further condemned Jews, the new Jewish state became the most relevant and uplifting factor for Jews politically. It was a tonic of strength and hope. More than anything, it was what it was: an overwhelming new reality that directly affected Jews everywhere, giving many the opportunity to live and helping the vast majority of Jews to channel their Jewish solidarity and concern.

Both the Holocaust and the creation of Israel altered Jewish thinking: the former, for its disturbing and shocking effect; the latter, for the elation and exaltation it provoked. The closeness of the two events diffused and confused the ideological dialogue. The problem of physical survival over-shadowed most issues of content, especially the philosophical issues of Jewish practical living. The agenda of practical, political, and socio-economic concerns of Jews also changed for most. For Zionists, the founding of the nation-state led to a process of consolidation of power. All groups who had debated and fought for the interpretation of their reality had to take into account the larger reality of international politics. Local conflicts for power now had broader implications. In the years after the war, the prestige and control of the communists weakened. Bundism lost strength, credibility, and its own ground. Zionism in Mex-ico gained much of what had been lost by the others. What took place then was a political reaccommodation rather than the forging of ideo-logical consensus. Zionism's political and ideological local ascent was thus the result, in part, of international political events.

This climate facilitated the formation of the largest and most encom-passing organization of the community: the Kehillah. Its tone would be ipso facto Zionist, and that would bring in again ideological issues that were somehow extraneous to Jews in Mexico but part of the political scene in Israel. For the groups involved, the international context was analogous to accompaniment in music. Local issues coincided with inter-national ones. A last fight was to take place. All ideological groups and organizations involved in the pre-Kehillah period reinforced locally what was occurring on the international stage. This was the backdrop to the last and most acrimonious battles of the ideologies of the old world.[50]

*Towards the Third Stage: Definition of Viable Political Alternatives*

Although international variables played a definitive role in determining the overall Kehillah ideology,[51] the Kehillah structure, ideology, and char-acter cannot be understood if the local confrontations are not addressed. In all the political confrontations preceding the creation of the Kehillah, different groups attempted to impose political limitations and behavior parameters to ensure a set of basic core principles for Jewish survival. This process of definition took place within the power exchanges of the groups that fought for centrality and control. Each tried to define and protect their own views so that, once successful, the political agenda would reflect their ideology. The aim after conquering was, of course, control. In the power fights between groups, all political tools were used: cooptation, cooperation, pressure, and/or expulsion.

Without explicit elaboration, each fight and the success of any pre-vailing group sent the message of what kind of political behavior was going to be acceptable and what was not. These all formed part of the local political consciousness on which the Kehillah later built its rules. This control resulted in the blaming and questioning of other groups, as well as the indirect enhancing of the Zionists for representing authentic Jewish values.

Three examples will illustrate how viable political alternatives were defined internally. The first two share the fact that the source of control was well defined—the school—and had the power to impose its rules at least within the parameters of its constituency. The examples differ, though, in terms of the actual political groups involved: one was a Zionist-Bundist confrontation, the other a Zionist-communist one. In both cases, Zionist concerns were presented as more nationalistic, authentic, and central. The third example is more complex because control was not imposed from a single source. It presents itself as a conflict of voices, in various degrees of elaboration. It is the most complicated conflict of the three, as it touches on the issue of the concerns for survival and representation of Jewish people. All three examples show how the dominant political alternatives affected the day-to-day lives of the people, and how the "winners" always claimed to define the core nonnegotiable principles for the group. These parameters became slowly established and entrenched in the communal life.

The first example revolves around an early power exchange in the Yidishe Shule, a first major confrontation between teachers and students. In 1931 the school had close to a decade of work behind it, with an established curriculum that had also been the result of contentions over time.[52] A Yugunt Klub was formed for the older students with the help of some of the teachers. Active in it were Meyer Berger, the long-time director of the school, and Yosef Tchornitzky, a Zionist teacher who later moved to Israel. The club sought to offer the student body a forum for the promotion of their (adolescent) cultural development. Berger and Tchornitzky defined themselves as Zionists with differences. Although the teachers kept a close watch over the activities of the club, some autonomy was given to the students to direct their activities parallel to their interests. The students decided to invite Salomon Kahan as guest-speaker. Kahan was a well-known personality by then, respected, among other things, for his knowledge of music and his varied contacts with non-Jewish circles. He had not yet developed his later documented love and respect for Israel,[53] but was well known for his socialist and anti-Zionist views. The two teachers, however, perceived him as a Bundist and a negative influence on the students. In the confrontation that ensued, the unequal relationship between teachers and students tilted the results. The teachers abruptly canceled the meeting, and a year later (1932) discontinued the club. They had the power to do so, and decided to impose control rather than let Kahan or the likes of him "influence their youth."[54] The episode was a display of control and power, not only of statuses, but of ideas and ideology. This censorship was a stepping stone towards the final definition of acceptable views among competing political positions.

Another interesting case, illustrating the same delimitation of the accepted alternatives, revolved around a student, the daughter of a well-known communist Jew, Shmuel Maguidin.[55] Maguidin was a Russian Jew from Belorussia who participated in the Red Army in 1919. He arrived in Mexico in 1928, and was soon in contact with locally known communists such as Julio Antonio Mella. Maguidin was active in Gesbir, the communist Jewish organization seeking to establish a Jewish home-land in Birobidjan. His daughter, then in high school and soon to graduate, was also interested in political issues. During recess one school day, she was seen and heard by a teacher reading a pamphlet on issues between the Soviet Union and Israel to other students. The group seemed interested. The zealous teacher broke up the group and confiscated the material the student was reading. In addition, because the content of the material was not approved by the school's authorities, the girl was expelled from classes. After protests by her parents and herself, she was given a nominal punishment: she was suspended from school on a weekend, when no classes take place, but she was "expelled." The effects of this episode spilled over into the graduation ceremony of her high school, when she proudly protested the treatment she had received from the school. Control of acceptable thinking was being implemented and expanded outside of the formal political arena; again, the different political groups were fighting for control and publicizing their messages.

In the competition for Jewish followers between the Zionists and the communists, a majority clearly favored the Zionists. The communal institutions had been supporting Eretz Israel, which was seen as the true, unquestionable Jewish national cause. Advocacy or espousal of the Soviet position was rejected as counter to communal interests. The stakes were clear: communist positions were beginning to be successfully defined as anti-Zionist and anti-Jewish. The choice was clear: Jewish communists had to choose between their "Jewishness" or their belief in "world communism." Sympathizers of both groups and onlookers were taught a lesson.

The process of selecting viable political alternatives is also an example of the changing dependencies of political groups. The Maguidin case is a particular example of how the limiting of political choices directly affected the daily lives of people. The diminishing tolerance towards certain positions took on a special meaning when specific thoughts and those holding them were censored. It shows, further, that thought in general and political thought in particular is not expressed in a vacuum, and that control and censorship exist even when institutions do not have specific authority to enforce them.

The last example of community-imposed controls on thinking is the case of poet-painter Yonia Fain, who lived in Mexico in the late 1940s and early 1950s. He experienced control and censorship imposed not by a specific institution but by the narrowed intellectual space available for expression once political options had been defined. That control created a situation against which he could not fight.

Fain survived World War II thanks to luck and to some painting jobs. He escaped through Shanghai, as some others did. Arriving in San Francisco, he was contacted by former colleagues from the Bund to go to Mexico and teach in the Yidishe Shule. Because the fame of the Mexican mural painters had not escaped him—he was familiar with Orozco, Rivera, Tamayo, and Siqueiros—and painting was his passion, the hope of meeting them made him embrace the opportunity. His impact was felt immediately in the education field.[56] Young, knowledgeable, handsome, and a magnificent reader, his Yiddish poetry took on a special meaning for his students; he also wrote, participated in conferences, and was fully active in the cultural life of the community. He began painting again, stimulated by the immediate connection he developed with the local muralists and painters, including Diego Rivera. With the support of a network of acclaimed painters, he exhibited his work in Bellas Artes a few months after his arrival.

The exhibition was received positively. The communal press publicized and expressed pride in it. Art critic Anita Brenner judged the work highly. Salomon Kahan called him "the painter of pain and wrath." Fain was not the painter of beauty and niceness, he said; he was the painter of the tragic. Kahan quoted the poem of Morris Rosenfeld, "Nit zukh mikh dort vu mirtn blien," to describe the fact that Fain would not be found where "myrtles flower"; the world of beauty was not the one about which he was destined to speak.[57] Persons of other communities felt they could identify with and appropriate the pain and suffering Fain experienced in his own life and expressed in his work. Mexicans felt he could understand their tragic past, and expected him "to paint as a Mexican." Spanish refugees also found their tragic fate in his paintings.[58]

The Jewish community, Fain felt, reacted with more detachment; with praise, but little understanding. It is not clear whether this was a result of their inability to allow visual expression of the still open wounds of the Holocaust; whether it was a desire to escape from this pain; whether it was the difficulty of dealing with the display of private grief and its appropriation by others; or whether there was then no way to judge the events of World War II. Fain felt lost. Though he aimed for a universalistic level of expression, he nevertheless needed Jewish support. His poetic endeavors had met with success, but he did not view poetry as his main means of expression. While Fain had not yet fully articulated the relationship between his particularism and the universal concepts he wanted to convey, he was uneasy about the reaction of the Jewish community to his art. He aimed to offer testimony, but he was not sure if he was reaching an audience.

When Avraham Golomb, writer-pedagogue and the director of the Yidishe Shule under whom Fain worked, criticized Fain, suggesting that he was not a "Jewish painter," the artist hastily concluded that he would be denied the support and recognition he craved. Golomb may have recognized and rejected Fain's thinking about the Jewish condition and his attempt at universalizing this message. Golomb was, however, an important symbol of authority for the community and for Fain. Fain could have attempted a rebuttal, but he did not. To the Nazi world, Fain was a Jew; for Jews, he was not acting sufficiently as a Jew. Golomb was attacking the "collage identity" of a secularized Jew. Fain was beaten, as was the movement he belonged to, the Bund. The defense of "authentic Jewish principles" was at stake. Eventually, Golomb's and Fain's animosities developed into an open confrontation, although not over these issues.

Fain's unsettled position coincided with what he saw as Nidkhei Israel's disrespectful treatment when he was commissioned to paint a mural in the Jewish cemetery. Fain saw this as a commission to paint a chapel; it evoked in him associations with the great masters' chapel. When the work was done, there was some dispute over his payment. Diego Rivera was called in to make a judgment and the congregation promptly settled. But Fain was ready to leave; he felt he lacked space in which to work and Jewish space in which to live. His duty as a witness to suffering and as a voice of the generations lost to Nazism had no way of being expressed. He felt alone, and left for the United States to pursue his work without compromising his feelings and thoughts. The community did little to keep Fain. He was let go, and with him a world of unaddressed issues.

The issues underlying the delimitation of political alternatives acceptable to the community were linked to conflicting ideas concerning self-definition, identity, and ideology.[59] Thus, for instance, to label Jewish communists as either for or against "Jewish national interests" at a specific point in time, or to determine the artistic expression of a Jew as either Jewish (particularistic) or universal, and then assess its impact on local Jewish interests, was to engage in pigeonholing based on abstract general premises. These more abstract visions were linked to the *continuity-integration* dichotomy. These views became basic postulates and played an enormously complex role in the building of ideological responses towards specific contextual problems.[60] *Continuity* and *integration* represented two philosophical visions of survival for Jews. The dichotomy, however, represents two poles of a continuum. But in reality, all ideologies were hybrid versions.

Continuity and integration are both responses to a common Jewish past, and all local ideological positions reveal a position taken on these options. Continuity and integration represent different survival patterns and coexist as visions within the ideologies—mixed, ambiguously defined, and on occasion cryptic. Following the Enlightenment, Jews used new modes to organize the views of their collective past. In addition, different groups competed to reconstruct a "past" to define Jewish group memory, recovering and claiming only specific portions of the past as vital and relevant, and systematically denying that status to other elements recovered by other groups.[61]

For example, the Bund's interest in local Jewish life was never questioned. It was taken for granted that their concerns were for local continuity. If any group should have been "strong" in the community, it should have been them; however, the Zionists emerged as the hegemonic group. Bundists shed certain elements that they considered obsolete: religion, rituals, etc. There was a period in Mexico when they were critical of the school and offered little support to the institution engaged in cultural reproduction. They would not allow their youth to become quixotic "Menakhem Mendlakh"[62] as they judged their parents had been. The school, they claimed, should not foster and "feed on the past, but link [the youth] to the reality of today and tomorrow."[63] While officially committed to local Jewish life, they attacked the existing cultural institutions and offered no alternative.

Zionists, on the other hand, tended to ignore diaspora history in their attempt to build an artistically preconceived image of what Jewish identity should be.[64] Tanakhism—the biblical viewpoint—was to them the only valid link to Jewish culture. The diaspora episode—its values, culture, and issues—seemed to them ill-fitted to the building of a new identity. While interested in a specific solution, Zionists were very strong in the local power structure. Each group, then, had psychological, historical, and sociological ideas that became part of their political and pragmatic aspirations. In political practice, they often banished all sources and facets of thought they chose not to use. Yet each tried to impose its vision as if it encompassed the totality of what was valid.

The process of delimitation of acceptable political alternatives in the community was placed within the concrete political exchange for power and control, but it reflected and refracted the unstated ideological premise still left untouched within the political agenda of each group. The ambiguity over continuity contained in all these secular ideologies suggests a mindset that affected the extent to which continuity in all its variations was incorporated as a communal goal. The eclectic tolerance among the groups appeared as a democratic tendency which led to initial coalitions in the preinstitutionalized period. Following the crystallization of the

Kehillah in the 1950s, tolerance became more constrained. The structuring process had produced a vast network of organizations, with general rules of politically acceptable behavior. Once these were defined, the stage was set for competition over the final central power structure.

## EXPANSION AND CULMINATION OF THE STRUCTURING EFFORTS: THE KEHILLAH

*Third Stage: Institutionalization of Political Life; Harmony and Consensus*

The third stage of communal development stemmed from the cohesion of the community. The Ashkenazim were not inherently a group, but had to *become* a group. They all were immigrant Jews who had little in common with each other outside of the fact that they defined themselves, and were defined by others, in ethnic terms. The broad delimitation of the acceptable political alternatives, and the specific behavior that was sanctioned, took on a special meaning: the idea and reality of the group and its protection became essential. One of the sources for these feelings was the shared experience of the first immigrants. The roof of the now-demolished Hotel America where many immigrants were housed was the scene of the beginning of communal life. The public reading of newspapers and the sharing of economic and cultural resources constituted the first experiences of the "brotherhood of Jews." Who could imagine then that the building of a new communal Jewish life would take on such deep meaning in the context of the destruction of European Jewry a few years later.

The early ideas as to how the community should be organized were varied,[65] and were already dominating the imagery of many. What should the group do? Whom should it help? One point seems to have become central to the thinking of these immigrants: they wanted to reconstruct what they felt was the "club-life" character of the old country: a feeling of unity, fraternity, and association. It seems plausible that the idea was further championed by the leaders at the time, who had attained a status quo they were eager to maintain. The "club-ideal" became a paramount objective: club-life, unity, harmony, peace.

Jews in Mexico—especially the established ones—felt that joining the Young Men's Hebrew Association should be experienced as "taking a brother into the family." With the new organizational umbrella that these Jews were offered in the Y, they did not expect to legitimatize any one particular political position; they were rather hoping to form a "community that should stand outside of any political influence—a community for the comfort and usefulness of each." Economic survival, mutual help, and the avoidance of the disturbances that come from political differences were the goals: Jews helping fellow Jews because they shared a common fate, because they needed each other. The immediate here-and-now was their focus of attention. All political consciousness seemed to them to polarize and threaten an idealized desire for peace.[66] The desire to achieve peace, both with the host society (the "other") and internally, undergirded the unwritten law that Jews should avoid political disputes. This thinking, linked to the instinct that, being few in number, they had to stick together to survive, suggested that the quality of communal life would be enhanced if it was conducted as a club. This metaphor of the "club" also became the answer to the issue of continuity. The logic was: to survive, we must unite; to unite, we must coalesce; to coalesce, we have to think and behave harmoniously; to sustain harmony, we must think apolitically, because this allows for self-help and survival.

Questions on how to be linked to world Jewry, how to deal with the social and political problems of the other communities—Palestine, Europe, and eventually their own—were not foreseen as unavoidable political problems. These were not remote theoretical problems. Jews had internal differences at the most elementary level—over prayer styles and internal policies on economic help, among others—that they intellectually glossed over with this argument. While they were connected to other Jewish communities in many ways, they avoided the intellectual elaboration necessary to decide how to link themselves with them. Although there were already then many well-defined positions on how and to whom Jews should relate, they were eager to avoid "problems." Despite the social pressure the early leaders were ready to use to achieve the idea of the club, Jews in Mexico generally were only superficially amenable to living in a unified fashion, sharing certain premises, and maintaining an organization that called itself a "club." Nothing and nobody convinced them to homogenize and limit their thinking by avoiding political issues. Few wanted to pursue what to the more socialist-minded Jews seemed an empty ideal of peace.

Soon enough, the established status quo was broken. From within the ranks of already established Jews in Mexico and with the help of newcomers, the ideal of the club was destroyed by the unavoidable differences among the people.[67] Individual opinions were fiercely sustained. A bitter competition for the control of the definition of the situation emerged, and each group defined the terms through which their activity could be seen as meaningful. Socialists were separate from the wealthier bourgeois Jews; Bundists distinguished themselves further from other socialists by retreating into their own organizations. Communists and Zionists began defining their separate lines of action. Nine years after the creation of the Y, the existence and hegemony of the club-style philosophy as embodied by this organization were so threatened that its originators fought desperately to retain and reinforce the existing structure. When the leaders called for the need to uphold "our choice," they were making a last futile attempt to exert control over the community as a unit. Yet this decade of less political diversity helped solidify regular life for the Jews, allowing the flourishing of greater political diversity in the next decade. "Harmony" in the club had been a way of taking care of Jews, all Jews, in their early settling years; now, it was less useful.

Despite the immediate need for unity, the seeds of pluralism and confrontation were planted at the beginning. Immigrants, particularly those who brought with them an elaborate code of political loyalties and nuances, could not detach themselves from their immediate past and their political interpretations. Many felt that their new freedom gave them a chance to express their thinking, and they were not about to give this up. Others saw this new moment as an opportunity to gain status in a newly forming hierarchy. Once the structure began expanding, almost none were willing to accept the idea of club as a unit with uniformity. *Drai Vegn* (Three Ways), an early book, was symbolic of a joint enterprise of three writers who openly held on to their individuality and separateness even through their common project.

Yet the club-ideal, with its view of a harmonious community, became part of the legacy of the pioneer organizers of the community. The Kehillah, the umbrella organization of Ashkenazi Jewry and the quasi-absolute representative of Jews in Mexico, solidified and managed the internal political rules of the Ashkenazi community. By enforcing a centralization of political power, an apparent harmony surfaced. Harmony was again presented as an acceptable and desired mode of political behavior. However, the renewed value was labeled "consensus." Shimshon Feldman—the Rosh Hakohel (head of the community)—established the style and tone of his political rule. Persuasion and discussion were used to achieve consensus for most decisions. Rarely was majority vote used for decision-making. But the consensual process[68] is an ideal that is empirically unreal. Society needs some ratio of harmony and disharmony, of association and disassociation, in order to gain a shape. It therefore seems that if the structure and its leaders have an interest in maintaining the image of harmony, it is as a legitimizing tool. With the Kehillah, conflict did not disappear but was rather controlled. By coopting and allowing different ideological positions and personalities to exist visibly and powerfully in the Kehillah structure, it built channels for dissension into the structure. When differences surfaced, they were addressed through various subcommittees. Thus, conflict existed and was a stabilizing factor. The structure had its own safeguards.[69] "Harmony" and "antipolitics" became "consensus" and "cooptation." The image of consensual decision-making and the pressure to sustain it were instrumental in the centralization of power. While "consensus" and "cooptation" are not unique to this political structure, what is distinctive in this milieu and links it further to the older ideal of the club is the intense veneration in which these two tools are held.

## The Quest for a Kehillah

The Kehillah has been a particular form of European Jewish internal political organization. It has served a variety of purposes, and it has protected Jewish political self-definition over the centuries.[70] Democratic trends have always been in conflict with any other form of behavior in this structure; this testifies, according to Elazar, to its republican character.[71]

In addition to religious and judicial obligations, social welfare was probably always a major concern of the Kehillot, to which we can add the education of the poor, since the well-to-do either paid for private instruction or took care of educating their children in some other way. Kehillot were very often transplanted into the diverse countries Jews moved into. In the modern period of the nation-state, the Kehillah became a voluntary entity, since the Jewish community members were admitted as individual citizens to the different bodies politic. That meant that, as a group, they had to gather in a voluntary association and limit themselves primarily to religious services.

The nineteenth century witnessed a decline in Kehillot. Many of their functions had been fragmented among different associations.[72] The pressure to conform or to remain apart was there, and integration versus continuity was an issue. But as separation from the host society had diminished with emancipation, the need for some Jews for so central and total an organization had also diminished. These feelings of acceptance and integration, however, ended for European Jewry with World War II.[73]

Whether the Kehillah was voluntary or compulsory varied by country and time.[74] In Latin America during the nineteenth and twentieth centuries, the Kehillot based their organizations upon ethnicity, including religious and cultural elements, rather than on religious affiliation only, as some German and French Jews had done. In general, Jews tended to be nationalistic and succeeded in transplanting all or most of the ideologies that existed in their European world.[75]

The quest for a Kehillah-type organization in Mexico arose early, in part as a desire to shape the voluntary and political framework to which these Jews were exposed: "It would be a national representational body of the Jewish collectivity"; "it could enlist and press to fulfill the obligation of belongingness by collecting an internal tax"; "all have to bring their bricks and help build the Kehillah here."[76] Some Jews requested a Kehillah as a conscious attempt to establish a link to their old political institution.

Others saw it simply as a better way to coordinate internal affairs and organize and control the potential chaos of multiple organizations.[77]

By the outbreak of World War II, when the quest for a Kehillah was articulated as an unquestionable need, the idea had begun to take root. Avraham Golomb suggested that the community be reconstructed under a special unit to fortify group identity and provide guidance for ethnic survival. Golomb wanted to create a "people consciousness," a "folk totality"; a Kehillah, he thought, would promote and embody these ideas.[78] Others insisted that the justification for a Kehillah came from the need to better protect the community; the Kehillah would perhaps counteract the inertia of the established organizations. It thus represented a way of planning for the future, to reduce the sense of being merely transient. Whatever the reasons, none devised or clearly conceived how it would function.

In 1945, Golomb counted between fifty-seven to sixty-five organizations,[79] reason enough to consolidate. To think in terms of numbers of organizations only shows a very subdivided community. Looking at the community by blocks of thinkers, however, highlights the cohesive nature of the relationships among groups and their interaction. It also provides a better way to understand the interdependence of most of these organizations and the process by which they submitted to the centralized power and authority of a Kehillah once it came to exist.

The appearance of the Kehillah in the late 1950s was neither the result of a specific crisis nor the culmination of one particular organization.[80] Three factors converged and facilitated its formalization. First, the first thirty years had trained enough leaders to create a cadre of politicians interested in consolidation, centralization, and control of power. Secondly, some leaders were able to become "professional politicians" by having the financial security that allowed them to leave their jobs and still have a livelihood. Increasing affluence allowed some leaders to engage in politics on a full-time basis and to manage a small but growing bureaucracy of paid workers. Finally, there was an increased awareness in the community in Mexico of the need for a formalized channel to represent Jews in Mexico vis-à-vis Israel.

Attempts at such centrality had begun earlier. There were three precursor organizations in 1938–39: Nidkhei Israel, Tiferet Israel, and Hilfs Fareyn. The three organizations each attempted to unite the community,[81] together with the Central Committee and even the Zionist Federation. Though as a political group, the Zionists were badly organized and weak, and so could not unite the community either, as an ideology they were well represented everywhere. This would turn out to be a crucial difference.

Despite a consensus that a new organization was needed, the Central Committee (Tsentral Komitet) formed in 1938 to defend the community against the outside, tried to fit the bill. It had taken strength by 1942, when it dealt with the government and attempted to help the few Jewish refugees who were interned in the Santa Rosa camp, as well as to address the anti-Semitism that seemed to surround them.[82] Since 1937, Jews in Mexico (with the help of American Jews) had been working with the government to set up settlements for refugees: Baja California, Tabasco, and Guanajuato had been selected as possible areas for that. The Baja California project was seen in Mexico as an attempt on the part of Jews to take over land and thus failed almost immediately. The project in Coscapá, Tabasco, was also scuttled; the government argued that its duty was to protect the local workers, and placed their interests over those of the refugees. The project was canceled by the president's office and the land given to Spanish refugees.

The final attempts on behalf of Jewish refugees to be housed in Santa Rosa, Guanajuato, and San Gregorio, Coahuila, met similar fates. The Quanza boat with eighty-three refugees was returned to Europe, while the attempt to at least allow one hundred Jewish children to immigrate also came to nothing.[83] Though always claiming that they understood the humanitarian needs of the European Jews, the Mexican government never acted on their behalf and the Central Committee was never fully successful in changing the government's position.

The Central Committee also attempted to coordinate all sub-communities, and to function as their representative towards the government and other entities.[84] However, the internal power struggles between Zionists and Bundists stymied the results.[85] The organization was further weakened by the rapid turnover of representatives, which inhibited the formation of leaders within.[86] While organizations of the community joined the World Culture Congress (Alveltlekhn Yidish Kultur Kongres), the Central Committee refused to join, triggering a protest from the Bund, which withdrew its representatives. The Bundists also protested the imposition of the "politics of the majority," which in their view was a stand against tolerance.[87] Thus, the idea that a "new" organization would be the best way to centralize the structure did not fade. However, the Central Committee did not give up, claiming to fit that category.

A second attempt by the Central Committee to establish its hegemony concerned the collection of funds. There had been a practice of separate campaigns to collect funds for different causes. But collections of money were becoming increasingly complicated, and failed to raise the projected amounts. In 1946 Nidkhei Israel stepped in and attempted to organize and lead the fund drive. The independent effort in 1947, when most groups worked for themselves, was labeled a crisis because of the unimpressive results; it was hoped that a joint program would succeed in

1948.[88] In the meantime, Nidkhei Israel was turning out to be the most successful of the organizations; in comparison, the Hilfs Fareyn was raising little money.[89] General Zionists seemed to have the upper hand, because they were active in the Nidkhei Israel, and even attained control of the organization. Some cynically suggested that the Zionists were becoming religious in order to obtain control. This alliance, which proved to be very successful in the future, highlighted the Central Committee's weakened role in centralizing and conciliating the different factions. As a result, the Central Committee was unable to supersede the efforts of the Nidkhei Israel.

As fights between factions in the Central Committee continued,[90] there were growing pressures to distance the Central Committee from any party line: the Central Committee was supposed to avoid partisan conflicts.[91] However, even after a joint fundraising effort was made, the campaign of 1948 did not further the Central Committee's intentions. It was an ineffectual attempt, and central direction remained unachieved. The Central Committee attempted to control, but the debate on how the funds should be allocated, always a difficult issue, did not allow them to take over. Should funds be mostly for Israel, or also for rebuilding Jewish life elsewhere: that is, diaspora needs or Zionist needs?[92] There was some talk of giving the Central Committee oversight for the cultural affairs of the community in addition to its other roles, but by then the Central Committee was becoming weaker. How could the Central Committee do cultural work—the question was raised—when it had no experience with cultural activities?[93] Further, it was argued, how could cultural work be centralized when it had been the activity of diverse parties all along?

The Central Committee failed in attaining legitimization for a broad spectrum of activities. The outcome was that the Central Committee was left with a much narrower and specific objective: attending to local "public affairs" issues rather than to Jewish internal life, establishing and maintaining cordial channels of communication with politicians and intellectuals, and working on antidefamation.

The Central Committee later devolved into a branch organization of the Kehillah, and it remained so, although it has become more distant from the Kehillah since the 1980s. In time, it obtained more autonomy. At the same time, the Nidkhei Israel was able to remain economically sound and Zionist, two characteristics that would be essential and advantageous in the creation of the Kehillah. The congregation downplayed its religious functions while highlighting its economic efficiency. Both issues helped it in the successful negotiation of its role in the new Kehillah. While it entered the Kehillah as a passive, accommodating, orthodox body, it was successful in gaining visibility and coexisting with the community, which remained secular.

The first forty years of community life may have been less efficient and coherent, but they were full of Jewish cultural and intellectual activity, and also full of variety. The years between 1920 and 1950 were the foundation years, when the cultural organizations solidified. These decades were also training and experimental decades in which leaders had a forum to practice, and began testing their relative power. Organizations were formed and dismantled, and the alliances and interdependencies of the members gave rise to conflict and cooperation. A wealth of ideas, approaches, and questions had been tested. Jewish life in Mexico was being defined and redefined in the context of the host society and world affairs.

## The Dominant Ideology

Whatever the groups involved, all the political developments and contentions of the community bolstered the idea that the institutional life of the community had to favor ethnic continuity, fend off any threat to Jewish survival, and promote Jewish solidarity and autonomy. Zionism emerged as the ideology that best furthered these objectives.

Zionist organizations proliferated slowly.[94] More than any of the other political platforms, Zionism had groups on the left and right, and some reproduced these nuances at the youth level as well. After a failed attempt to organize in 1922, the first Zionist organization, Kadima, was established in 1925. This group was not subdivided according to shades of ideology. The aim was to form a united front to raise funds for the pioneer settlers in Palestine. In fact, the first representative from Keren Hayesod (the Palestine Foundation Fund) who arrived from London in 1926[95]—a Sephardic Jew, Ariel Ben Tzion—reorganized the existing weak structure, suggesting the need for new leadership to reach out to the more affluent groups. Younger activists who headed the group were dismissed in favor of older and economically more powerful ones. This change established and reinforced a pattern whereby philanthropic work and the raising of funds were the basic practical aims for Zionists in Mexico. The recruitment and education of youth for an ideological dialogue was relegated to a secondary level.[96]

A mindset specific to most Jews (and Mexican Jews were no exception) gave Zionism a unique grounding. Palestine was understood to be "a settlement," but it was also the location of the very old Jewish dream and part of the root of the whole culture. Nobody in Mexico opposed helping Jews attain and retain Palestine. Initially, the dream of Zionism did not strongly disturb other political aspirations; thus "the Zionist dream" found a general level of acceptability among Jews.[97] This does not mean that Zionist thought did not have opponents, some virulently

intense and articulate. However, in the diaspora, "Palestine" was not a
threatening idea. Many Jews made a distinction between a Jewish Palestinian settlement and the more specific implications of Zionist ideology. It
became possible to be an "economic Zionist" without being a "physical
Zionist." Thus a commitment to go to Palestine—Eretz Israel—was not
an absolute requirement to self-identification as a Zionist. Further, the
majority of Jews in Mexico could define themselves as Zionists if some
sympathy existed for the idea of a Jewish state in Israel, without their
being forced to think or rethink local alliances, diaspora identity, and
local Jewish continuity.[98]

The Zionist leaders in Mexico who were engaged in fundraising gave
immediate attention to Zionist international politics. However intricate
the different nuances of Zionism, the group in Mexico followed the general international Zionist pattern of interpretation, whereby local issues
were subservient to Palestinian issues. In other words, built into the ideology was a lesser interest in the local problems and politics of the Jewish
community.[99] At the same time, the interpretation of local Jewish issues
was always presented with alarm. "Alarmism"—as it was called—was a
mechanism Zionism used in viewing local problems, whose solutions
were invariably found in the ideals of Zionism. Zionist ideology posited
that all the "local" problems of Jews stemmed from their being in a geographical location that did not offer them their own polity. Eretz Israel
was always portrayed as the single viable solution to this condition.

Despite this, individual activists also took an interest in the internal
fights. But the majority of early Palestine sympathizers used the reorga-
nization of the community's power structure at the time of the creation of
the State of Israel, so that their linkage to Zionism and their positions in
the higher echelons of the community was not a coincidence. Internally,
Zionists in Mexico had their polemics. The most active group of all was
perhaps the Poalei Tzion (Workers of Tzion),[100] which since 1923 had
been using the newsletter *Undzer Vort* to air its thoughts.

Still, real control and power remained in the hands of the "General
Zionists," who were, in Mexico, a nonrigorously defined group. Their
sympathy for Israel was open and manifest, but they managed to incorporate without feelings of contradiction a strong commitment to the local
community, and with the other elements that had occupied the work of
the community: traditions, selective use of orthodoxy (mostly when a
ritual would need to be performed), and use and support of the Yiddish
language. This was all done in an eclectic way, a tactic that later proved to
be the best policy for the cooptation and cooperation of other parties.

General Zionists in Mexico were aided by the ideology of their sub-
party.[101] This subgroup followed—as others did—the Herzlian ideal of
working to create a national home for the Jews with the support of the

other communities: the famous "conquering of the communities." However, what distinguished them from other Zionists was their affirmation of the continuity of diaspora Jewry, at least until Israel became the national center of the majority. They saw the majority of the Jewish people as "middle class," with the same traditions, the same desire for security and freedom, the same destiny, and the same responsibility. General Zionists claimed they were the only group that set particularistic politics aside and concentrated on the economic need for the reconstruction of Israel. In fact, their distancing from the left-Zionists emerged from the generalists lack of interest in destroying private capital and the middle class. Their separation from the right came from their recognition and relationship with the worker's organization, Histadrut. In general, the General Zionists realized that the Jewish bourgeoisie was too assimilated, while the left was searching for a synthesis with Marxism that was forced, ideologically remote from a large number of Jews, and did not allow for ethnic minorities: no European socialist leader gave support to the Jewish worker, "not Passfield, Bevin or Ilya Ehrenburg."[102] Had not Marx, too, accused the Czech movement of independence? they claimed. They felt detached from Marxism, and this thinking pushed them to the center of the spectrum.

This type of Zionism evolved into something like the American "Palestinianism,"[103] restructuring and limiting the former ideology to "aiding Jews to build a Jewish homeland in Palestine." However, in the case of Mexico, it also included the peculiarities described above. It became a flexible inclusive group rooted strongly in the local power structure. Its power was enhanced with the advent of the new state in Israel, and when its prestige rose it overpowered all other political alternatives. In the Mexican case, the consolidation of General Zionist power was the result of these parallel processes: the local political confrontations, aided by the interdependence of world Jewry.

But General Zionism had another element that helped it gain acceptance in the community: its socioeconomic outlook for the middle class was not at all threatening to the local majority and recognized and accepted their diaspora condition. Here was a way out of the internal contradictions other Zionisms posed for these Jews. This does not mean that all other voices in the communal spectrum were silenced. By the 1950s the other positions were structurally weakened, but persistent and charismatic personalities of these positions managed to integrate themselves into the structure while sustaining their own voices. Because of its ideological flexibility, the Kehillah became an eclectic construct of tremendous stability. The consequence of all this, however, was that the community and the Kehillah forfeited the necessary debate over many issues about continuity, adaptation, and identity that were vital to its own life. In other words, diverse definitions coexisted with a consequent loss of intellectual dialogue, and innovation and ethnic self-reflection were curtailed.

## The Kehillah As Institutionalization of the Communal Structure

After the first year of work (1958–59), the Kehillah presented a report of its activity to the community. All major organizations were present, and the list is evidence of the Kehillah's new "umbrella" position: it included the Central Committee, the Zionist Federation, the Yidishe Shule, the Histadrut Tzionit Bemeksiko, the Poalei Tzion and Tzeirei Tzion Party, the Herut Party, the General Zionist Party, the Mapam Party, the Mizrachi and Hapoel Hamizrachi Party, the Froyen Fareyn (Women's Organization), the O.S.E. Health Organization, the Hilfs Fareyn, the Agudas Israel Congregation, the Yiddisher Handls Kamer (Chamber of Commerce), the Froyen Pionern (Women's Organization), the Kultur un Hilf, the Bund, the Keren Kayemet, the Keren Hayesod, the Kultur Tzenter, the Gezelshaft far Kultur un Oifboi, the Sport Center (C.D.I.), and the Tiferet Israel and the Adas Israel Congregations. The Kehillah functioned with fifty-four board members (of which only one was a woman) and eleven volunteers that represented all the local organizations subsidized by the Kehillah. The Kehillah required payment for membership on individual basis or as head of families, and reported 1,331 member-families that first year, with a suggested 3,500 as the general number of families for all subcommunities.

The Kehillah formed subdivisions which eventually collapsed into a smaller number and a simpler division of labor. Originally the subdivisions included Education, Religion (the transformed Nidkhei Israel congregation), Budget and Finance, Culture, Help (Hilf), Social Activities (old-age home "Eishel," Medical Center, O.S.E., etc.), Interorganizational Relations, the Central Committee (representing all subsectors of the community), Help for Secular Jewish Organizations, Construction and Kehillah Patrimony, and Propaganda-Clarification. Centrality was followed by shrinkage: soon, departments merged under the authority of a few more central and charismatic leaders. As the old ideologies lost relevance and were remade, if at all, by a core of activists, the same thing happened to this "wider" Kehillah: it soon had fewer activities and leaders.

The formalized new alliances between groups, with the Kehillah as their embodiment, defined and determined the viability of certain groups, people, and beliefs, while others had to break away.[104] In the confrontation of styles of thought and languages, the newly created structure with its ideology proved itself strongest. There had always been "winners and losers," but most of the outcomes reflected the new power structure and its hegemonic ideology. The Nidkhei Israel Kehillah was orthodox in the way it performed rituals, although it never enforced strict observance and adherence to Jewish law on private individuals. As a congregation, it had also been involved in other functions (welfare organization, education, raising funds, etc.); it therefore had experience and exposure in different fields that it used when becoming the Kehillah. Until now, no other organization has remained as attached to its original philanthropic objectives as the Kehillah. Although other organizations manage large sums of money—e.g., Sport-Center C.D.I., Bet-El congregation—they do it mostly for the furtherance of their own institution. The Kehillah, however, subsidizes a variety of local organizations, including the schools, the old-age home, cultural activities, and Israeli-linked youth movements.

The underlying tone of the Kehillah was Zionist; it incorporated all local ideologies that actively or tacitly accepted and supported the existence of Israel. However, the cultural and ideological elements relating to the Jews in Mexico were also incorporated. These gave the Kehillah its distinctive character. In the 1930s and 1940s, for instance, the desire to link to the national intelligentsia and its political forum was a paramount objective of the communist, Bundist, and Zionist agendas. This effort represented not only a process of public self-justification and self-reassurance, but also an attempt to secure acceptance and control. For example, the philosopher Eli De Gortari and the leader of the C.T.M. (Confederación de Trabajadores Mexicanos) Lombardo Toledano were sought after by all these groups. However, the success of any group—specifically the Zionists—was not linked to a victory in the internal Mexican political milieu. The continuous attempts to find support in non-Jewish circles remained a legitimizing practice in internal debate. Even in the 1980s, the top Kehillah leader, Shimshon Feldman, highlighted his connections with local politicians as a way to establish the centrality of his organization, its ability to deal with any anti-Jewish sentiments, and the security that came from these relationships.

The Kehillah has always claimed to be an organizational response to the problem of Jewish continuity, which it sees as paramount. In the search for a balance between continuity and integration, these two visions were often treated as two equal components. While adaptation was more a natural response to issues of surviving in a new society than an ideological imperative, "integration," its derivative, was imbued with ideological meaning. When Jews called for adaptation, their aim was really immersion in the new culture of the host society. Jews in Mexico did not probe into the complexity of continuity, despite the fact that adaptation and integration were of crucial importance in each generation and were always somehow linked. The conflict between continuity and integration was left unarticulated. The later attempt at consolidation and centralization was disguised as pluralism and failed to overtly address ideological choices.

Political exchanges shrank in leadership and constituency. The result was that the Kehillah incorporated not so much a party, but the personality of a party. The team became an elite, becoming almost impenetrable, with the protection that absolute "consensus" and "cooptation" offered. The assertion that "all" or "most" positions could participate in the Kehillah was misleading, for "few" or "none" of the outside positions could participate. Positions that are not aligned with the center have neither survived in the Kehillah nor outside it. Whoever was not in or with the Kehillah, or could not apostatize, could not survive politically in the community. A shedding of positions occurred. When the Kehillah took full form, it withdrew its support of all the then-defined "extreme" political positions in the community. The political "game" as they knew it was over. Because the Kehillah's ideology did not include a built-in mechanism for change, any outside challenge was portrayed as an attack on the main institution.

The creation of a Jewish state immediately conferred authority, prestige, credibility, and power to the Zionist representation in each community in the diaspora.[105] The need for formal Jewish representation in the diaspora was now an operational necessity. As a result, the Zionist organizations and leaders were strategically placed to take central positions.[106] This important historical juncture was felt in the Jewish community in Mexico, too. While General Zionists had been active in different positions in the community, their political future as the center group was not assured. Although they had representatives in many organizations, their concerns for the local community were only elaborated insofar as they connected and subordinated to the Israeli state. Diaspora life had no clear perspective and was an empty issue. For the Zionists to have prevailed in the community in Mexico was largely the unexpected result of world politics.

The process of internal solidification of loyalties, concerns, and issues forced a redirection of the identity issue. The new Israelis had to define themselves vis-à-vis Jewish identity in the diaspora. In the struggle to define the new Israeli identity, choices were made that had mixed effects on Jews of the diaspora. Alternative views of diaspora Judaism were attacked to enhance the viewpoint of the new formal Israeli-Jew. Bitter struggles ensued over the relationship between Zionism and the diaspora communities. The gains and hopes embodied in the creation of the new state also unleashed new ideas to which diaspora Jews had to accommodate while sustaining old definitions of Judaism. The linguistic fight between Yiddish and Hebrew is perhaps the saddest and most agonizing example of this confrontation. The decisions around it in Eretz Israel were perhaps the most confused, chaotic, and mistaken decisions Israel enforced and exported to the diaspora. Those communal arrangements that did not align themselves with Israel after 1948 were left on the periphery of world Jewry.

In the new climate, the Kehillah was very resilient. Not only was the Kehillah not an ideologically active body, where substantive issues could be implemented according to a relatively well defined party line, but it became a consensual body, technically efficient to deal with communal needs. The democratic image dwindled, not to disappear altogether but to resurface sporadically. Voting—the anchor of a democracy—seldom occurred, with little change in the outcome. No channels for the expression of a political platform were left active, so any conflict that arose was solved within the established parameters of the institution, among the in-groups that had a fairly stable division of labor and power. The Kehillah was not only the culmination of a process of structuring and consolidation, but also the historical symbol and monitor of the political game, ending any political exchange outside the institution. Politics was confined to the Kehillah; thus, it initiated and increasingly enforced a pattern that inhibited ideological production outside itself.

The espousal of a common denominator by the Kehillah left no room for differences to emerge, be heard, and be politically challenged. The vested interests within the structure, with their access to control and power, made the organization progressively more remote and inaccessible to the ordinary member. To the public the message was that politics as an activity was solely the Kehillah's domain. This message furthered the Kehillah's apolitical image and eclipsed the political nature of its actions. But, if the issues were left unchallenged, their consequences became visible unexpectedly and unforeseeably. What developed was a Kehillah that was first unwilling and then unable to socialize the community into politics in its effort to control and maintain its power; it was also unwilling and then unable to train people for its organization. The younger generations remained for the most part unengaged, and learned to define themselves in relation primarily to the noncommunal values of others.

The Kehillah became increasingly bureaucratized; as the political rules of the game became slowly institutionalized, fewer confrontations occurred. Close attention was given to the fact that all problems or disagreements had to be dealt with within the Kehillah structure. Extreme caution was exercised to avoid fissures among the groups already within the Kehillah, and negotiations were launched to preclude competitive structures from emerging. Even partial structures such as separate cemeteries, other congregations, and professional groups were squelched.[107]

Once Shimshon Feldman emerged as Rosh Hakohel, he became the most powerful figure in the Kehillah. When cooptation was used and a rival personality was incorporated, areas of relative autonomy developed. This was the case with Tuvia Maizel and the culture department.

Maizel became the "czar" of all cultural activities in the community. His judgment and decisions were undisputed. His Bundist ideology would find an outlet in this field, even though the Kehillah was not a Bundist institution, nor did the Bund have a significant vote. Maizel, however, had earned his authority and power with a charismatic personality and long years of work, and it was deemed proper to have him "in" rather than "out." The areas of work which were entrusted to him were never threatening to the central power.

Differences in the ideologies of most parties were smoothed over. Some criticized the fact that too many parties existed in name only, with few real differences among them.[108] To others, the new alliances were incomprehensible in the light of past differences. The larger visions had eroded to a great degree. World War II and the Holocaust had left Jewish ideological discourse relatively speechless. Outside of Zionism and Orthodoxy (that in Mexico played a minor role), all other visions seemed powerless and aimless. None had the strength to devise mechanisms to safeguard existing and emerging principles.

Jewish leadership in Mexico never took on the challenges that national Jewish leadership took on in the United States.[109] Both communities struggled to (a) help establish new immigrants, (b) work for local communal unity and survival, (c) defend the Jewish public image, (d) provide relief for other Jewish communities overseas, and (e) come to terms with the success of the multiple dimensions of Zionism. But unlike the United States, the Mexican "culture creators" were never "culture brokers."[110] In the United States, for instance, Jewish leaders managed to define Jewish issues as American issues. Kraut suggests that Jews in America were not soliciting special favors when they pleaded their cause. America had to live up to its ideals as a pluralist democracy: "Even defending the rights of non-American Jews abroad became an issue because of the putative American responsibility to foster American ideals across the world." This never happened in Mexico. The Jews there attempted systematically to link up with the non-Jewish politicized world to legitimize their being in Mexico. But this symbolic legitimation only allowed Jews to remain as a distinct group in Mexico. It was not as if "visions of Judaism were taken to the marketplace."[111] Jewish leaders in Mexico, as consensual and accommodationist as they were internally, were not consciously building a synthesis between Jew and non-Jew, as in the United States.[112] Jews in Mexico searched for space, adapted to the new country, aimed at some merging into the country, but did not openly search for a "hyphenated identity."[113]

Eventually, the Kehillah's unofficial main objective became the maintenance of stability.[114] The combination of the newly centralized power and the infused value of cohesion became the basic idiom of the Kehillah's legitimacy. Cohesion, homogeneity, and unity became not only tools for specific activities or a way of problem solving by the new administration, but rather the indispensable objectives of Kehillah life. The ideology held by leaders and administration became a self-fulfilling mechanism to strengthen loyalty to themselves. The solidarity of the people involved was not contingent on the particular ideologies they subscribed to, but rather was the result of this systematically rewarded behavior. The renewed idiom of harmony assumed a role in maintaining the new status quo. Once the club ideal became a consensus mechanism, harmony became used as a cooptation method, and the already delimited and political alternatives were well established, the Kehillah appropriated enough power to establish a structure that was not to be easily displaced or altered.

## The Political Heritage

New established social controls in a society maintain and reproduce solidarities, and can become what Gouldner calls "system and privilege-maintaining falsifications of reality."[115] The new, growing bureaucracy was systematically repressing ideological thought and inhibiting ideological creativity. The institution diverted attention from the ends being sought to the means used to seek them. This focus away from goals allowed the bureaucracy to work "better." This system of thought conditioned the intellectual passivity of the people and led eventually to passivity of action, too. The enormous consequences of this were not foreseen. This shift in focus diminished the interest of people in ideological innovation.[116] The short-term benefits of not being ideologically challenged turned years later into an unbridgeable chasm between generations. The structure became alien, and its content cryptic to the outsiders.

The Kehillah elite presented their goals as given, unchangeable, and beyond debate. The structure maintains conformity and discourages ideological skills, sensitivities, and openness. Any critique of goals, it is suggested, must be defended ideologically. But because the organization has habitually fostered and rewarded technical or other skills rather than ideological ones, it has become impoverished in ideological content. By including too many political views, bureaucratizing the umbrella organization, and homogenizing Zionist success, the structure discouraged all ideological dissension in thought and action and stymied the development of the necessary skills for innovative thought and discourse.[117] Protests against this state of affairs have been voiced by those who feel the lack of a mass following. The lack of ideological creativity and diversity has not gone unnoticed.[118] But a problem was defined with no clear diagnosis of what had to be done to address it. When the claim was launched by peripheral activitists, it was simply ignored; when the claim came from the leaders, the apathetic "others" were blamed.

Youth was and is more powerless than others in the community. More distant from their culture, less knowledgeable of Jewish sources, more detached from the social structure and its functions, and lacking economic resources, they were unconsciously freed by the elders of social loyalties that would help them define themselves in relation to their history and structure. Gulfs of experience and perception and cultural knowledge divide one generation from another. Lacking economic means to impress their views, members of the younger generation were not perceived as potential participants within the formal community structure, and they became less meaningful a force.[119]

The "end of ideology" that was diagnosed and often applauded by some in contemporary society was, in the case of this community, a matter of intellectual incapacity fostered consciously and unconsciously by the elites. The lack of ideological manifestation during this period can be traced to the combined effect of inhibiting factors—structural, cultural, behavioral—which have made innovation extremely difficult. The apathy of youth and outsiders represents a crisis of an imposed action and thought pattern that organized experience for that generation.[120] The institutionalized structure did nothing to foster critical thought in adults or youth. There was an "ideological deafness"[121] that Jewish politicians had embraced, and a corresponding "ideological muteness" that all others acquired.

The Kehillah structure—for all its relative bureaucratic and fiscal efficiency, its economic support, its centralizing and coordinating the representation of the community vis-à-vis the host society, and its extending the existence and life of Jews in Mexico with a long-termness that was inconceivable to the early immigrants—has inhibited the mechanisms and relationships required to enhance Jewish ideological thinking.[122]

From the individual's standpoint, the problem of adjustment had been dealt with. Jews of the first and second generations were integrated, although they always carried the inner conflict that this adjustment presented. Jews in Mexico remained "marginal men,"[123] living in two worlds—as they do in most diasporas—as cosmopolitans and strangers, and only partially transmitted to the next generation the elements necessary to sustain their "strangeness" affirmatively, so that the second and third generations have become partial strangers to their own strangeness. The community survives considerable political apathy, and its structure today shows complexity and diversification, centralization and homogenization, as well as much political silence. Notwithstanding all this, the Kehillah remains the central institution of the community. The Kehillah imposed the view that detachment and distance were to be socially and politically rewarded. The process, however, went beyond social intention.

# PART 2

# CHAPTER 3

# Profiles of Thought:
# The People Behind the Ideologies

... the recuperation of men's expressive acts; ... gathering
together and conservation of what was most worthwhile in what
they saw and did; it is the domain par excellence of Being ...
—Merleau-Ponty

We are ... incomplete or unfinished animals, who complete or
finish ourselves through culture.
—Clifford Geertz

A close examination of the actors involved in the structuring process
must be seen within a context that imposed specific constraints and limitations. The ideologies of these actors were "imported" ideologies that
were developed in another time and place. They were then modified and
colored by the actors' experiences in the new context in which they found
themselves. Yet, as with plants, ideologies or visions often root with
extraordinary strength, going beyond the original context; at other times,
they may remain loose or temporary. It is interesting to see what part of
the cultural baggage travels with its proponents. After all, what traveled
with these immigrants was not just their meager material possessions but
their very rich cultural baggage, which translated into many patterns of
thought and action.

This section shifts the angle of attention from a macro perspective to
a more micro one: the selected actors and their thinking. This reflects
the famous and widely quoted statement by Marx that "men make their
own history but they do not make it just as they please; they do not make
it under the circumstances chosen by themselves, but under circumstances
directly found, given and transmitted from the past."[1] The actors are
simultaneously purposeful movers and doers, and entities affected by
society and its history. Because systems of thought are not self-contained
realities, always reified or reduced to affect only the thinking and feeling
of a privileged few, focusing and recognizing systems of thought and
who used them is crucial. It may explain how and why certain ideas were
promoted, how and where they became accepted or discarded, and what
consequences they had.

Viewed from the individual's perspective, it is difficult to imagine that an immigrant wanting to adapt and integrate into a new country would and could immediately arrive in a locality and deliberately seek to pursue that goal. Jacobo Glantz (1902?–1979), who came to represent the integrationist approach, did not start like that. "Alien are for me your mountains with perpetual snow," he wrote; and "I will with your happiness never be happy, your pain I will never cry."[2] He was at the time a more typical lost immigrant, an alien. Others mourned the loss of their old country, of those that were left behind; it was not so easy to look at reality anew and initiate a process of understanding. But Glantz, as most others, subsequently changed and changed again.[3] This section will examine the asymmetry between leaders and followers as well as the asymmetry of the changes and the effects these had on the group, while the changing structure continued to manifest its constraints and possibilities to the community.

We focus here on a double process: thought as it both reflected and refracted the social context. The actors enforced their thoughts on both society and history, constrained by past and present. To approach the actors as agents, we need to look into their ideologies, their systems of thought. In portraying the intellectual profiles of some of the Jewish activists in Mexico, we do not attempt to offer biographical descriptions; rather, we are identifying and distinguishing some of the intellectual voices that affected change. For this we need to understand the changes and continuities of an individual's choices. While tracing the ideologies of the actors, we must examine the substantive issues they developed in their agendas. At the same time, their languages and issues must be seen against the backdrop of the social structures that affected them and which they in turn affected.

Thus this exercise of linking past and present, contextually and substantively, attempts to suggest why things became what they became. Further, it may uncover certain consequences of thought and action that may become problematic for the group at a later stage. Weber always insisted that ideas must be carried by powerful social groups in order to have powerful social effects, and that the thought system must become institutionalized for a social vision to be translated into a material one. The thinkers selected were all surrounded by a following at one point or another. These groups helped them develop parts of their thinking. The actors may have moved in and out of groups, but they usually managed to rally others behind them and then leave a social mark.

The reconstruction of the thinking of an actor may evoke many ideas that may be known from other older traditions; it may also evoke a mixture of cultural references that may be idiosyncratic. Not all that is said by an actor is acted upon. Some ideas may become so accepted that they become part of tradition or "common sense." Some ideas are perceived as problems and are deferred, never "resolved," or "forgotten." Some fall into oblivion, and some issues resurface suddenly, and may gain currency in a new situation. Ideology may play a role in the effort to recapture and politicize some issue and exclude it from the realm of common sense. Actors then speak to each other as well as to the past. In these dialogues what is said is always less than what is spoken about; and for us, the challenge is to understand the meaning and consequences of the implicit.

The protagonists described here are neither the "greatest" thinkers nor are they necessarily intellectually extraordinary. They are, however, emblematic figures which allow us to comprehend what an ideology offered as well as what it overlooked or excluded. The dilemmas that affected the protagonists and that continue to affect the community today are intimately linked to the issue of belonging. At stake is the answer and emphasis that each gave to the complex problem of being both Jewish and Mexican.

### Continuity and Adaptation-Integration: Two Visions

Whether conscious of it or not, all of the actors were children of a period. Because no group, however effective in transmitting its values, culture, and thought, can expect to achieve the perfect socialization of its younger generation, the changing context raises the question of identity for each generation. Their experiment in building a communal structure gave these Jews the opportunity to deal anew with the issues of continuity and adaptation-integration. In doing so, they had to understand their identity, conceptualize these dual forces, and materialize their thinking into social structures. These are not free-floating ideas, but rather specific attempts to achieve social control.

If a project is grounded in historical and subjective considerations, it will embody the actors' interpretation of the meaning of everyday life. But new interpretations cannot be presented in ordinary language; they need to be expressed in their "own new language." The Ashkenazi immigrants used Yiddish as the "new language," one that helped them remake themselves as a group. After all, this language was their personal depository of cultural difference.[4] Language was the tool of their first project: to regroup as a minority. Yiddish contained all the necessary ideological elements to mold the people into a group. Over time, however, further refinements occurred, and groups subdivided, requiring them to develop additional nuances—"languages"—somewhat different from the original one. Within the language, new discourses had to address the new perceptions. Avraham Golomb, ideologue and philosopher, provides the most graphic example of that process. Not only was he aware of constructing a "new" language, but his audiences felt his discourse on continuity (in Yiddish) as if presented precisely in a "different language." The immigrants were not an undifferentiated group; neither were their intellectual/political projects. In their dialogues we find some of their guiding tools for their social construction.

## THE FIRST IDEOLOGICAL CONFLICT:
## JOURNALIST AND CRITIC SALOMON KAHAN
## AND POET JACOBO GLANTZ

The communal structure that developed was not the result of one mind's activity; this was not a period with one charismatic leader. Indeed, everyone felt the opportunity to rebuild his or herself and status. All had ideas concerning what to do for the community. The early immigrants eventually began to address, publicly and with broad implications, the issue of accommodation into the host society. Those who fancied themselves writers started to write. Most of this particular group were sympathetic to socialist ideas, and most attempted to combine their relocation with social renovation. They were also reacting to the original attempts of the already settled "American Jews." By creating the Y (Young Men's Hebrew Association), the American Jews were addressing their social needs. However, the European Jews, who were later immigrants and less economically established and perhaps more socially sensitive, felt that the Y was not addressing their concerns. These more socialist-oriented Jews sought to promote the vision that they could belong to this new society. Because all of their work was done within the community, in Yiddish, the new arrivals did not raise the question of making open and further commitments to continuity, nor did they define the kind of continuity they were aiming at. These thinkers faced the problems of most immigrants. The solutions they offered, however, were their own. They were certainly not the only possible solutions, nor were they permanent ones. But the effect on their social behavior was decidedly long-lasting.

As the new settlers began to address issues of their identity in the new sociopolitical space they were offered, they inadvertently furthered the social process of integration. This implicit acceptance of integration reflected some of the desires of the majority of the immigrants. Yet assimilation was not included as a goal. While integration seemed the most urgent agenda, nobody was forcefully attempting assimilation. The focus on continuity did not have an immediate urgency. To integrate seemed to be the watchword; yet, it was all done as they defined their Jewishness. Soon, the issue of group definition became salient enough for some to devote time and thought to it; the future of the group seemed to be at stake. Unknown to them was the fact that the tools to forge this future required, foremost, a reinterpretation of the past.

Poet Jacobo Glantz was dissatisfied with the use of the Jewish past as the centralizing thought for these immigrants. Past should be past,[5] he claimed when he analyzed the Yiddish writer Itzjok Berliner's (1899–1957) work. "Where and to whom?" "Wandering?" said Glantz, quoting from one of Berliner's poems. For most, past experience and definitions were invoked and the mere living within a new majority did not absolve them, as minority, from the need to redefine their own self and the other. Jews, again and again, evoked the unresolved sociocultural condition of their particular situation. The question of how to live as Jews included for some the question of whether they should stay in the new society. This thinking annoyed the integrationists, for whom the new oportunity allowed them to construct (so they dreamed) a new identity, Mexicanized and unproblematic. As they saw it, "suffering" from the influences of the old home was something to be overcome.[6]

Salomon Kahan[7] (1896–1965) shared the same concerns. He arrived in Mexico from Bialostok, Poland, in 1921, sympathetic towards socialist ideas and having rejected religion and tradition very early. His Jewish education was self-taught. In Mexico he received a formal education in music, and taught for thirty years in the Escuela Normal de Maestros (Teacher's College); he also taught for a time in the communal school, the Yidishe Shule. With an unusual talent for languages, and after having worked as a bus conductor while he learned Spanish, he very soon established intellectual contacts with the intellectual elite of the country. Among his friends were Antonio Caso, the philosopher and one of the most important intellectuals of the country in that period,[8] as well as other prominent politicians and intellectuals from the Cámara de Diputados (House of Representatives), where he worked as translator. He cultivated many friendships in those circles.[9] He published in the Mexican newspapers *Excélsior, Universal,* and *Tiempo,* and occasionally in the *New York Times* and in a Berlin newspaper. He shared with others of the Jewish community a special interest in Russian workers and the fate of the Russian Revolution. He wrote often on the problems of Russian workers' organizations, their practices and ideology. He therefore was known as much for his socialist inclinations as for his musical analysis.

Many of this generation in Mexico were sympathetic to socialist ideas. Jews in Europe had their own socialist movement—the Bund (General Jewish Workers' Union)—which was established in 1897, but had been in formation since the 1870s. It started as an attempt to spread socialist ideas among Jewish people in their own language, and matured as a movement between 1870s and 1890s, when Jews began to feel that their enemy was not just their capitalist employers but also their gentile coworkers, who were often anti-Semites; their separatist movement started then to take form. Further, when it was felt that the Marxist position on the emancipation of humanity required the emancipation from Judaism and other religions, Bundists felt a need to separate and address and fight their own battle, under their own definitions. The consciousness of the Bund, then, was more a reaction to the outside than the result of internal convictions. Later, pressure from Zionist and Territorialist[10] circles moved the Bund and its ideology to broadly accept Jewish culture and think it worth preserving: they supported the right to have a national, educational, and linguistic context for a "legal minority."

For anybody calling himself or herself a socialist in Mexico, a gamut of options was available; these ranged from a left close to communism to the defense of Jews as a national-linguistic minority. Many so-called socialists—secularized Jews—felt a connection to socialist ideals without having fully worked out the content of their identity. For this type of Jew, the Mexico of the 1930s offered a kind of haven: it appeared to them as the embodiment of the socialist ideal. President Lázaro Cárdenas[11] was "the president of a Socialist government" (1934–1940) in a changing world. The Jewishness of these socialists was untroubled, and the differences between Mexico and their old social world seemed enormous; in Poland, they said, Jews had to carry identification papers; in Mexico, one could just about walk anywhere, anytime, undisturbed.[12] Kahan and Glantz shared an interest in integrating Jews into all that was Mexican. Kahan, in fact, suggested[13] for the first time to create a new social hybrid in Mexico. He wanted Jews in Mexico to redefine themselves as Mexican-Jews, assuming that being in Mexico was tantamount to acceptance into that society. According to him, it was up to the Jews to become that which Mexico allowed them to be.

Both authors developed their vision of an ideology of integration in the years when Jews were consciously taking active steps to adapt to their host society. Kahan and Glantz articulated the desires, logic, and hopes of those in the community. This initial position was not controversial, largely because it did not elaborate on its meanings and consequences. It also did not pose the questions in political or philosophical terms. The argument was emotional and psychological, and produced no counterargument. Its affinity with what immigrants were doing while adapting was undisputed. It highlighted the feelings of gratitude of the immigrants and tacitly coexisted with other ideologies of continuity.[14]

Kahan collaborated with the new Jewish publications in Mexico. He became editor of *Undzer Lebn* (Our Life) (1927–1928), a monthly of the Radicaler Arbeter Tzenter (Radical Workers Center), he collaborated with the newspaper *Der Veg* (The Way) (1932) from its start, as did Glantz. (It is Glantz perhaps, however, who can be seen as the most active and versatile of the organizers of most early Jewish publishing efforts in Mexico.)

Some of the socialists, Kahan among them, soon realized that the socialist ideology that united some was not reinforced by the economic reality in Mexico. Instead, their "ideological positions" were separating them from their milieu. The work that these Jews performed did not link them to the working class of the country. In fact, their peddling and small businesses, and their incipient industrial work, as well as the antiforeign regulations of some unions, all banned them from the organized working world, and made it virtually impossible for Jews to link the ideological socialism they brought with them to the reality they were now facing.

Although Kahan wrote for many Yiddish Mexican newspapers (*Baitrog, Di Tzait*, and *Der Veg*),[15] his antireligious position led him not to support other organizations. For a time, he felt no urgent need for a Yiddish school. He rejected what he called the "spiritual isolation" of the Jewish community from the rest of Mexico. He did not want to see an extrapolation of the values brought from Europe. He called for the rejection of a purely physical-geographical relation to Mexico which produced only the social category of "Jews in Mexico." What he advocated and thought possible was the need to transform organically the relationship of Jews with Mexico, so that a new hyphenated type should be produced: the Mexican-Jew. It is obvious that he as well as Glantz were interpreting—not mirroring—the reality they faced. In this exercise, they sought to transform their own interpretation into reality. In Mexico they felt a new freedom that activated their desire to participate in the host society.[16] Although the host society did not offer exactly what they sought, they wanted to be part of the historical process and become active actors in Mexico.[17] Glantz and Kahan wanted to join a new "history" and participate as "authentic actors" in its new chapter.

Jacobo Glantz was born in Odessa, Russia, in 1902, and arrived in Mexico in 1925. He worked tirelessly to root himself in Mexico and felt he succeeded. With what seems to have been unlimited energy, he joined or initiated almost every early journalistic effort of the community, from newsletters to small journals, whether their printing life was one or two issues, or one or two years. He published in *Der Veg* for fifty years. He aimed to create a role for himself, transforming himself from a highly russified Jew to one who, wanting a central communal position, appealed to Jews of different backgrounds by using the common language Yiddish.

To support himself and his family, he worked as a dentist for a few years and then had a variety of small stores at different times. Later he had a restaurant that often changed location, which offered him the possibility and the dream of a salon à la nineteenth-century Europe as well as space for an art gallery. He met artists, writers, and painters, local as well as foreign, and cultivated their friendships and acquaintanceship.[18] He became a painter, too, and met with Diego Rivera, with whom he could converse in Russian, a language Glantz loved. The two thus shared conversations on the two topics of politics and painting.[19]

Glantz always wrote. In Russia he had started to write in the vernacular, but with the many changes in his life—the separation from his family, the move to Mexico—he turned to Yiddish to communicate and write in Mexico. This was the early language Ashkenazi Jews shared; if he was to have an audience it had to be addressed in that common tongue. In his epic poem "Cristobal Colon"[20] and in his writing on the Spanish Civil War, he worked on an agenda for the Jews of Mexico: an elaboration of what he perceived to be a Jewish need to enter and be part of Latin American culture. His daily life also attempted to merge Jewishness and Mexicanness: the people he associated with and the topics he wrote on reflect his concerns with this duality. His Jewishness—although always present—was rather latent in his thinking, the subtext; he clearly undertook to provide an apology for his more general and, in his mind, more universal interests.

At first, his objective was clearly stated in a poem. After months of feeling displaced, alien, and depressed, he exploded in his own newly found way:

> I will not solder links
> of a broken chain
> I am tired of singing
> what time must forget . . .[21]

Many were feeling confused yet very clear about the difficulties that rooting into another culture presented: "I lost my village and I want to find it here, at least in my imagination. . . . I have in me the aroma of my uprooted life and I transport it to the land I now live on."[22] Glantz's personal struggle led him to focus on the future, jettisoning a past that not only claimed his memory but was also forcing him to maintain a link he wanted, ambivalently, to break. He suggested that his personal solution could be a general possibility for Jews in Mexico. He was thus legitimizing the very opposite of what was actively being pursued by many Jews: to forge a memory, to strengthen an awareness of the links to Jewish history and weaken any forces that eroded those links.[23] In Glantz's thought, continuity and integration were in confrontation, but integration was to have the upper hand; it became, for a time, his agenda.

When his colleague Itzjok Berliner published *Shtot fun Palatzn* (City of Palaces), Glantz's criticism of the book revealed this same thinking. Glantz also claimed for himself the mantle of the "correct" ideology.

Indeed, Glantz saw no need to recover any part of his past social world. He felt that others doing that needed to modify their views on this issue.[24] Interestingly, others saw in Berliner's book exactly what Glantz was looking for and did not find. Others criticized Berliner as "too Mexican,"[25] and saw him as betraying his roots by concentrating on alien problems. Berliner wrote in *Shtot fun Palatzn* about hunger and misery in Mexico City. He described the contrasts in the Mexico of the 1920s between palace and shack, showed compassion for the people in poverty, and conveyed a sense of protest. He was critical of the modes of thought which Mexico inherited, particularly the hypocritical elements of Inquisition thought: the priest who can pray for the soul of a sinner and then simultaneously dishonor him in the daily practice of the auto-da-fé. Berliner perhaps felt uneasy about the culture of the country, and at another point wrote, "The desire is to wander."[26] But Glantz had no patience with Berliner's feelings, and criticized his colleague for not being rooted, misunderstanding his unease with the prototypical Jewish propensity for wandering. It never occurred to Glantz, however, that rooting is not only a matter of geography,[27] that Berliner either needed more time to feel rooted, or did not want to take root in the same way Glantz did. In the statement "the desire is to wander," we do not find a man with an inability to settle; wandering seems rather an act chosen by a man who wants to remain detached from what he cannot accept, and perhaps still searches to take root in a different way or grow into something else.

When Yosef Glikovsky, one of the writers collaborating in *Drai Vegn*, wrote about the generally difficult sociopolitical condition of Jews everywhere, Glantz showed no patience with that either. When Glikovsky suggested that "there are in the world black suns," Glantz carped: where was he looking? Surely, Glikovsky could not be seeing "black suns" in the beautiful blue skies and bright sun of Mexico. Glantz suggested then that the "black suns" must be reminiscent of a past that was a bleak unnecessary memory. Literature that is not rooted in present reality, he suggested, as if past were not reality, is not literature.[28]

Anything that seemed to be a link to the past was for many the best way to retain a culture. But what may have been an intellectual springboard for some and an intellectual relief for others was a limitation for Glantz. This evocation of the past was for Glantz an obstacle to the idealized possibility of integration to the new society. That objective was for him a first step towards a new authenticity, and he thought it should be so for all other Jews, too.

During this early period, the issue of integration competed with that of continuity. But, because continuity was pursued by the community and taken for granted as a general goal by organizations and publications and through the use of the communal language, no one saw the arguments of the integration supporters as a threat. Nor were they aware that each ideology implied a different way to organize social action. Who could reject becoming immersed in Mexican culture, empathizing with its condition? However, each position suggested different emphases on the solidarities to be pursued.

The inherent tension in these two positions was eclipsed by more immediate concerns. The lack of response by immigrants—who, after all, were adapting day by day—left the integration position underdeveloped. As a position, it was not socially rejected, probably because it addressed and responded to the partial desires of most immigrants. The position, though silent, remained active. When pitted against each other, both ideological positions failed to sustain their politically differentiated character and were rather quickly adopted—albeit partially—as part of the commonsense culture of the community. In a way, they depoliticized each other, but the problems they addressed did not disappear; they were only covered up and postponed. For the most part, this early unfinished dialogue continued, although it was inaudible to most.[29]

When the issues resurfaced twenty years later, at the time of the establishment of the state of Israel, new problems of belonging tapped the consciousness of the community. It was then that the old issue of belongingness—continuity versus integration—resulted in a full-blown confrontation. Although the argument was framed as if it were entirely part of an old *past*, it really defined the *future*, as emblematic of power issues relating to the structure of the community. However, the outcome of the confrontation had been sealed earlier by the shared ambivalences about belongingness that all secular Jewish ideologies implied. In addition, the intellectual development of the continuity position had always been weakened by the contradictory actions of daily life. Those who called for integration as well as those who did not adapted to some extent.

When people in the late 1940s and 1950s—Kahan especially—accused the youth of "passivity," "lack of ideology," and "lack of interest," presumably within their Jewish life, it all seemed inexplicable. No link was ever established with the pioneers' own original objectives, not even when the pioneers reflected on the structure they built. The "youth" saw their elders' achievements as part of the structure which forced them to deal with a different set of problems. Both generations could not be looking at the same challenges.

In their personal lives, Glantz and Kahan shifted from communism and socialism towards a strong sympathy for Zionism. Kahan translated books for the World Jewish Congress in 1948, and Glantz started collaborating with the paper *La Voz Sionista* in 1950.[30] When the first Jewish secular school began, they devalued its function and the cultural mission it stood for. They were then attempting to reorganize the consciousness of the immigrants, urging acceptance of the majority and its culture as their main reference group. However, no identity has homogeneous objectives, and theirs was no exception. Conflicts and ambiguities, such as their using Yiddish for self-expression but not promoting its teaching for continuity, were there. However, by being a part of a generation still steeped in Jewish culture, their own individual solutions kept them close to Jewish life in structure, thought, and action.

Glantz seemed pained, surprised, and strongly disappointed by the turn of events in his own family life. His daughters never learned Yiddish, neither at home nor during their brief stay in the Yidishe Shule. The success and fame which he enjoyed at one moment of his life did not carry over into the personal sphere. What he symbolically saw in his own family occurred in the social context as well; and there, too, he felt out of control. In fact, failure and success were two aspects of reality that could not be assessed at the beginning of a project,[31] neither by the actor nor by his audience.

Kahan's reversal of his position was also dramatic. He also seemed surrounded by what was to him "unexpected behavior." He deplored the "lack of moral values," "the extreme materialism," and, most surprisingly, the loss of the Yiddish language. He even scolded youth for thinking what he once promoted, although now considered a mistake: that Spanish should or could be thought of as a tool to express their innermost feelings and thoughts and still retain a connection to the Jewish culture.[32] This was a distant step from his original ideas on integration.

Kahan had undertaken to translate into Spanish the many volumes on Jewish history by Heinrich Graetz. He suggested that Judaism required the possession of "a national consciousness" that could come only from the understanding of the sum of Jewish historical experiences.[33] He worked on the assumption that a Jewish national consciousness could be obtained through the reading of history. His own knowledge of history must have played a special role in his return to emphasizing Jewish continuity issues in the late 1940s and 1950s. History, he thought, provided the necessary (and sufficient) information to form a consciousness. He then offered to contribute to that information in Spanish by translating it.

Ironically, language became the central issue for Kahan. He had opened the lid on what turned out to be at first a simmering cauldron, and when it boiled over, he tried to cover it again. Language—in this case, the ethnic language—denotes a formal intellectual structure but includes a variety of conscious and unconscious references to feelings, experiences, and conditioning from outside the formal intellectual structure. The use of a particular language adds certain qualities and cultural characteristics to any social structure it acts upon, so that thought and structure are closely related.[34] Kahan understood acutely why language was crucial when integration was his objective. He forgot, however, the other culture. By advocating and achieving adaptation and integration through language as the foremost aim, subsequent generations became increasingly estranged from the culture and social structure of their elders.

Glantz's shift can be seen formally in his book *A Kezaies Erd* (A Morsel of Earth). The motto of the book, in the spirit of the Roman poet Horace, says much about his own enterprise: "Does one need to look for allies illuminated by other suns?" But Glantz's own words say it also:

> In whatever happens
> It is to hold oneself into the root.[35]

It is difficult to say to what degree the Glantzes and Kahans of Jewish life in Mexico felt the situation of the 1950s to be at least partially the outcome of their ideas. Their puzzlement and confusion reveals their surprise. These two agents remained "fighters," although the content of their fight had changed. Yet the content of what they were saying had few listeners. They themselves had unwittingly set it up this way. These thinkers had imagined themselves and their ideas as lacking ambiguities and contradictions, but their understanding of themselves was narrow. Their original ideology was based on the illusion of a future without a past; when they attempted to build a future by retaking the past, it turned out to be only an individual and private enterprise. They could "return" to what had been left, and attain some peace of mind. But the Jewish public they addressed could not follow. They had started at a different point. There was nothing to return to.

## A POLITICIAN AMIDST VANISHED POLITICS: BUNDIST TUVIE MAIZEL

The Bundists' importance in building and leading the Jewish community in Mexico cannot be questioned. From their first organizational attempts to their intervention in the process of structuring the community, Bundists participated in the events. However, they did not escape their own ideological dilemmas and conflicts either at the communal or at the individual level. Their ideological view predisposed them to immerse themselves in the new locality: after all, their socialism was particularistic in that it took into account the specific culture groups that were involved in the fight. If Jews were to fight as socialists they had to unite with the local socialist workers—but as Jews.

In Mexico this implied a relationship of equality and reciprocity between Mexican Socialists and the Jews of Mexico. The Bundists had strong connections with labor leader Lombardo Toledano,[36] founder of the Federation of Mexican Workers. These links were so important and impressive that the reciprocity seemed to have been realized even though Mexican workers were never as committed to Jews as their leader was. However, there were other forces within the community that would weaken this relationship. Jews soon distanced themselves from the conditions of the workers by the fact that they were in a working relationship of a different kind. Most were self-employed, a status that changed their solidarity. But there were other problems for Bundists as well. Their original socialist interests and their political aspiration had to come from their local situation;[37] this colored all their activity. World War II challenged them to present an extensive critique of Jewish local as well as international political aims and communal activity. After all, the events of the war and the lack of real support from most, if not all, political sectors was evidence that their ideals had little hope in the world as they lived it.

Their old ambivalences had played a role in their changing emphasis between local identities and their Jewish identity. However, they remained committed to some kind of synthetic relationship between the two. Their unsettled views on this matter and their failure to confront it made the conflict difficult to overcome. During and after World War II, the desire to forge links to a European locality existentially, ideologically, and historically proved to be disappointing and value-shattering. Would a new society be any different from the European one? Could Latin American societies offer any hope for a future for Jews when these societies' policies were based primarily on Western European values? The crisis of the war implied that the Bundists' definition of their ethnic-national identity needed to be reconstructed to meet the new reality. Without this redefinition, they were unable to produce a new affirmative basis for their survival. The worldview they promoted was lost. But Bundists were too shocked to engage in analysis. They had been too attached to European culture, values, and ideals to adjust easily and promptly to one of the most devastating and incomprehensible human and Jewish tragedies.

After the creation of the state of Israel in 1948, the Bundists could have played an active role debating and redefining the needs of diaspora Jews vis-à-vis the new nation-state. But the Bundists were unable to speak, and a complex delimitation of political alternatives also ensued, in which the Bundist were not alone to blame. As a result, diaspora Jews were left without theoretical thinkers and without political venues to express and address their situation. As citizens of other societies, they were left doubly ambivalent—less legitimate than Israelis and, by being Jews, less legitimate than other citizens. The Bundists adopted parts of Zionist thought in this community because of practical politics and emotional conditions rather than out of any intellectual sympathy with the Zionist ideology. In time, Bundists incorporated a self-inhibiting mode of thinking that made it impossible for them to address and maintain a local perspective. It was tacitly assumed that all issues and definitions—emanations from Israel—would cover diaspora reality as well. Despite the unequivocal positive effect of the state of Israel on diaspora Jews, the Jewish ideological accommodation and the loss of its own ideological diaspora profile and authenticity weakened diaspora communal identities.

In general terms, Zionism was culturally linked with the old Biblical Jewish tradition, while Bundism was linked more with a post-Enlightenment historical past. The experience of the Holocaust for the Bund, both directly and from a distance, left wounds and confusion which affected all Jews, though in different ways. For Bundists, the pathos of that reality led to despair; the historical tragedy resulted in a cultural and intellectual grasping to save some linkages to Jewish and secular values, to save and be saved from debasement.

In Mexico, Bundists attempted to respond to the different challenges they faced. After being outside the educational field in the early communal years, some of them moved into it. When the arena of Jewish international politics was closed off to them after the Zionist victory, they channeled their efforts towards local cultural activities. Because they had been involved with education and culture, that became an almost natural arena for their work. Unlike some communists within the community, their relationship toward Israel was flexible, as some became proudly linked to the newly formed state. But, once the communal contours—the political rules of the game—were better defined, enforced, and accepted, Bundists faced a restricted arena of potential control. In the emerging new structural reality of the late 1950s—the Kehillah—it was their commitment to maintaining active a definition of the situation that allowed them to remain dynamic in their previous attachments to cultural work. Undoubtedly, they still had limited success in their endeavors, but if they had planned once for a limitless success, that objective had become severely restricted.

Bundists continued to explain current reality using their ambiguous interpretations of their past identities, which they were unable to change because reality had changed for them so fast and unexpectedly. A change of thinking had not followed. For the Bundists, ideology was a tool of discovery and recovery.[38] They had discovered that the world and its social arrangements needed change and correction, and that the social and political world had failed them in a most tragic way. However, they were using their predefined view of the world to address a new, qualitatively distinct situation that needed mending and change. As a result, they were grappling with the unconceptualized distortions that Nazism and fascism brought into the social world. They knew that change was needed, and that this went beyond "peace" between worker and capitalist. Nonetheless, they could not produce a new conceptualization for a renovated ideology.[39] They were constrained by the very way of thinking that Western society used. Their definition of Jewish identity had always depended on the progressive Western society's acceptance of Jews as partners in a "joint venture." Without a viable and accepting Western society to help legitimize the desired changes, it all seemed futile.

Visionaries do not easily give up their visions, no matter how shattered these may become. For the Bundists, the attempt to sustain meaning meant continuing to be involved in the partial recovery of the shattered European experience. This winding, emotionally charged exercise also gave them a way to recover their shattered selves. While this was done by emphasizing cultural continuity as essential for Jewish survival, they had carved out specific areas of work within the communal framework on which they leaned. Nonetheless, they were unable to create hope in the midst of physical, moral, psychological, intellectual, and cultural chaos. A desire for social life was always present, but Bundists relied on Zionism to attain some respite.

Tuvie Maizel (1897–1984), a Russian-born immigrant who arrived in Mexico as a young man, was able to stand out fairly easily through the layers and conflicts of Mexico. This earned him eventually a major role in the Kehillah structure, with autonomy of action that allowed him to sustain his intellectual and ideological independence there.

Though some Jews came to Mexico fully formed ideologically, many others became ideologically attached Bundists only in Mexico.[40] The organization offered them an intellectual framework. Other immigrants had been schooled in Bundist ideas from the "old home" and had strong ideological sympathies for socialistic ideals. As a movement, the Bund was effective in gaining disciples, mobilizing groups, and offering them a content, even when the content was not precisely defined.

Shmuel Shapshik was, among the early Bundists, the only one thoroughly committed to the establishment of a Jewish school. The school had activist Zionist sympathizers from the beginning, even though it often attempted to bring in and retain the support of all partisan positions. Soon after Maizel's arrival, Shapshik got him involved in education, although most of his colleagues remained outwardly indifferent and even against the school. If the Polish C.Y.S.H.O.[41] schools could not be reconstructed, they proclaimed, then the existing school should give attention to integration with the locality, its problems, and its issues. In time, this position softened as active and prominent Bundists became involved with and had a vested interest in education, becoming each time more identified with general Jewish-Yiddish education and the issues of integration and locality within the school. Shapshik's and Maizel's early interest in education gave the Bundists a grounding in Mexico; this became an area where their work would eventually be most noticed and their influence strongly felt.

Maizel arrived in Mexico in 1926, at the age of 29, with clear Bolshevik sympathies.[42] He had been trained in Russia as a sociologist and demographer. He chose Mexico as his destination because his wife's well-to-do family already had relatives there. Educated, articulate, intelligent, politically active, very able, and soon economically solvent, Maizel joined the Bund and devoted a large part of his time and effort to the cultural development of the community. He vehemently defended the Yiddish language as the language of the community and its preservation; he saw Yiddish as the centripetal force for group survival. Through it and with it, cultural connectedness would be assured. Within his immediate family, however, where his thinking presumably could have best been implemented, this belief was not acted upon with parallel intensity,[43] foreshadowing perhaps some of the ambiguities he would later confront as trends in the community.

In later political confrontations, some accused Maizel of not having been interested and committed to Jewish problems in his youth. They argued that it was the Mexican situation—the foreignness—that enhanced his Jewishness and led him to communal action; they therefore indirectly accused him of lacking intellectual honesty. The accusation was aimed primarily at discrediting him as a leader. Maizel disputed this description of himself. Changing interests or changing emphasis of interests cannot, per se, be considered cause for doubting character. The same could have been said of Glantz, for instance, since he had also changed his original interests once in Mexico, perhaps for the sake of his political expectations. In fact, a change of context often triggers a change in attitude, and should thus not be unexpected. What is truly surprising is that these immigrants wanted to maintain in a different context much of what they had and were as Jews.

Maizel's Russian education gave him a heightened elitist respect for culture and refinement. Though he had studied when the Russian aristocracy and its values were being formally attacked, he both shared that critique and maintained an aristocratic flair for culture. With all his socialist leanings, culture was his major interest and objective. For him culture was more like the German *Kultur*, an intellectual-aesthetic experience. Joining many leftist intellectuals in the thirties, he wanted to offer this experience to the masses and use it as a way to get closer to socialism.[44] After all, culture was a mode of communication.

The sophistication and refinement in his tastes also distinguished him as a personality. He channeled most of his efforts into cultural activities. As other political venues became closed off to a Bundist in Mexico, his having conquered the terrain of culture made him the undisputed king of that arena within the community.[45] He had been active as a teacher and pedagogical advisor to the Yidishe Shule, the Naye Yidishe Shule, and the Jewish Teacher's Seminary. He had gained fame and prestige from his occasional essays. The YIVO in New York published his writings on the Mexican Jewish community.[46] There was, though, another topic to which he devoted his efforts: the linking of the locality with Bundist ideology. He gained political exposure through his connections to Lombardo Toledano of the Federation of Mexican Workers, and organized antifascist and pro-Jewish protests during World War II. This was an activity he would have pursued had he had more of a social base from which to work. Eventually, his Bundist identity was influenced by other political positions in the community; in other words, the identity was defined relationally and was shaped by the power relations among the groups, as other political options gained force and control within the community and Bundists lost force and control. Maizel also incorporated other cultural codes that later became a dominant part of the political culture of the community. Thus, the Maizel of the 1930s and the Maizel of the 1960s were not the same person, even though his Bundist ideology had remained his official political cover. Although his ideology was shaped by the conditions that the community offered him, he remained loyal to himself. While his ideas seemed dated to some, he negotiated and adapted enough of his thinking without changing the political identity to which he adhered, in order to be able to survive within the shifting atmosphere of the community.

Following Bundist ideology,[47] Maizel was initially compelled to change the local conditions of life and the "here and now" of the Jewish community in Mexico. He pursued his political contacts and envisioned the need for political recognition of the minority. For Maizel, recognition of the minority meant "making some room" for the minority and its cultural life. At no time did he or anyone of his party propose the attainment of specific formal (official) "rights" for the minority. Thus, it was always up to the minority to carve out its space; the majority was never questioned as to the appropriateness of its role vis-à-vis the minorities, nor was it asked for concessions.

Maizel undertook to achieve piecemeal changes: He worked for the establishment of formal ties between the Jewish schools and the official educational bodies of the country. He pioneered in the opening of the first Jewish High School (Preparatoria), which few supported because it was not seen as economically viable given the large and always rising school deficits. He also worked with Golomb in the opening of a Jewish teachers' seminary.

In the years that he was the Bund's representative in the Central Committee, Maizel and his party had great influence in shaping the international relations between the Central Committee of Mexican Jewry and other Jewish international organizations, such as the World Jewish Congress. At that time the autonomy of this community was repeatedly emphasized as an essential guiding principle for all interorganizational relations. In 1941, Maizel personally helped 183 Jews who arrived in Mexico without documentation on the ship *Serpapinto*.[48] He joined the Kehillah, representing the Bund movement, but became his own man in the institution, building his own fiefdom as head of the culture department. He was instrumental in the attempted formation of the "Folk Universitet" in Mexico, a center for higher Jewish studies; he also organized a committee for history of the Jews in Mexico. Through his culture department he established and institutionalized many activities, such as the Festival of Yiddish Music and a choir which performed yearly in the national theaters. He organized a small museum of the Jewish Holocaust, and supervised, selected, and controlled all cultural activities of the community which the Kehillah sponsored.

Although Maizel was well respected outside of the Kehillah as well as inside it and was never in danger of losing his autonomous position of leadership in the cultural domain, the Bundist movement was put to the test when the issues of general control and the definition of communal leadership were being debated. The Holocaust and the war itself became the context in which the organizations and ideological positions in this community competed. Bundists dissented from most other groups. On the one hand, they bitterly eschewed the Communist interpretation of the situation. At the same time, they could not accept what they felt was the Zionist "detachment" from Eastern European Jewry. The Bund argued that, ideologically, both positions shared a type of "other directedness": communists expected to change the world following the Russian pattern and were thus committed to the need to change society. The communists were ready to pay any price, and used the failures of other societies (i.e., the Holocaust) to further justify their political objectives. For their part, Zionists were set on Palestine as the only viable Jewish solution, and were driven to establish that society. For them, the European failures also confirmed their political objectives. Thus, according to Bundists, both positions sold European Jewry short. Bundists were attached to European Jewry in exactly the opposite way. Not only were they attached culturally, but European Jewry was the very model from which their ideologically autonomous attempts sprung. Survival of Judaism was linked to the survival of European Jewry. Thus, even when there were temporary alliances between communists, Bundists, and Zionists during and after the war, the rifts were profound.

To emerge as leaders, however, Bundists needed to modify their political interpretation, which required a recasting of their disapora condition in an affirmative light. Maizel's thinking did not meet the challenge: beyond a recovery of the recent past, their stance on the war did not offer a future. A critique of society was needed to address political positions that were so easily complacent on issues of racial cleansing. But how could a group of people, wounded and fearful of their own insecure future, produce a critique of society that dealt innovatively with minorities and majorities just after the World War? Zionism seemed to embody what for most Jews was the "future-oriented" position. Of all the postwar options, it was the only one that offered an autonomous reality. The reworking of diaspora issues required elaborating and reexamining without adequate conceptual tools (1) the notion of diaspora (mixed coexistence) in the light of the Holocaust ( a process which is still going on) and (2) the idea of the state of Israel as affecting and changing the status and identity of Jews and their communities everywhere. For those insights, however, Jews needed intellectual leadership.

Maizel, like other Bundists, was intellectually cramped. He and his group did not look beyond the immediate issues of the war to develop a perspective on the day-to-day political problems of their lives, a situation which had begun well before the war and would continue well after. No theoretical breakthrough was likely, and Maizel attributed the ideological vacuum to a lack of cohesion among the masses, which was in turn linked to new interests stemming from the upward mobility of the younger generations. With this explanation, he exempted himself from further responsibility. He was a "leader," he said, but there was no one to lead.

Although he was partially correct, and the community as a whole had grown more affluent, the lack of interest in ideology had preceded the process of enrichment. Even as early as 1929, there were protests over the inability to reach "wider circles"; after eight years of work, socialist and radical elements of the community despairingly concluded that "very few immigrants came with a party line. Most left their principles at home and kept only the demagoguery . . . organizations got formed and then [disappeared], people are weak and indifferent. It feels like planting in sand."[49] The 1920s were certainly not a time of affluence, yet many were detached from the issues of the time. Perhaps the central problem for them was improving their precarious economic position. This suggests that, in Mexico at the time, economic class did not automatically imply a particular ideological perspective. It may have predisposed one group to "see" certain issues rather than others, but only that.

The fact that certain conceptualizations were absent from the political agenda does not mean that there were no political problems at stake. There were, but the ones that carried communal meaning were those that emerged from the continuing dialogues and concerns of these Jews. In Mexico, the ideological battles seldom became broadly based popular movements. With few exceptions, they failed to capture and engage all the strata of the community. The battles waged by individuals or small groups propelled the communal life and established a structure in which the majority followed. Therein was the crux of the matter: a group of followers had to be mobilized in order for the ideological issue to leave an impact and be incorporated into the structure of the society. There was always someone who found others "apathetic" on a specific issue. The political apathy of the late sixties, seventies, and early eighties was not a totally new phenomenon; what was new was that even the ideologues started to lose their ability to speak ideologically, while the audience had lost the skill to understand them and be concerned.[50]

The inability to address limitations, ambivalences, and contradictions that Bundism faced with respect to Jewish identity made these issues enigmas more than problems to the activists. In this situation, Maizel's practical life reflected the lack of consistency. Any "personality," in an ethical sense,[51] is not a perfectly consistent entity. However, there can be more or less consistency. The diverse and conflicting aims that the movement aspired to were mirrored in the practical aims of the personality, too. The issues of integration and continuity with which the movement struggled, and the losses that ensued, paralleled Maizel's own achievements, failures, and frustrations.

To Maizel, the social behavior of the 1960s, 1970s, and later reflected detachment and discontinuance. The link to the younger generation was lost, and the hope that Bundism would guide them in a specific direction was unattainable. However, the old desire to define the minority as distinct yet integral and involved in the host society, emphasizing only certain secular parts of Jewish heritage, did not attract many followers. From the culture of the minority, they sifted and selected, adhering mostly to secular interpretations of Jewishness and leaving out much that was traditional and religious. For the achieved part of the culture and status they were hoping to earn—their Mexicanness—they targeted the working class as a way of linking and opening the boundary of national definition to which they could belong. They called this "integration into the 'here and now.'"

All immigrants were integrating—not as the Bundists had envisaged it, but still integrating into the country that had given them a place. However, the dual goal was contradictory: were two nationalities to coexist just by toleration? How could the Bund offer a critique of the society that was hosting them, while at the same time suggesting and justifying integration? Becoming a citizen of a society, a member, made them less analytical of their condition: the privilege and responsibility of citizenship inhibited their understanding of the problems that Mexican society faced with respect to the diversity of minorities. That situation, plus the partial reproduction of their cultural heritage, eventually proved to be a deficient socializing force for the subsequent generation.

Maizel represents the silenced voice of a diaspora-conscious Jew, who had a direction but who lost his way because the direction was too abstract and general. He was spurred by intellectual personal convictions and the strong desire to maintain his role and status. He was not easily discouraged. Was it only inertia that kept Maizel at work until the end of his life, or was it an unchanging view of a challenging reality that maintained his internal stamina? Maizel explained his commitment as his way of remaining loyal to his inner voice: "There comes a time when one does things in one's life not because one follows external pressure," he said, "but because of an internal need. I do not know if there are any ears now for my work, but there may still be."[52] This self-description holds true partly for his movement, too. Most of his followers kept their old tasks and roles despite incongruities, and they ignored their political impotence.

Maizel and his movement did not meet the challenge of renovation and innovation; nevertheless, they all worked at their old tasks and roles in the midst of some awareness of imperfect results. They ended up fighting unwittingly for the symbolic retention of a recently disappeared world that had its own value and integrity and that offered a dream—now lost and destroyed, but a dream nonetheless.

## STILL PRAISING WHAT WAS LOST: COMMUNIST BORIS ROSEN

Until the 1950s, Jewish communists in Mexico constituted a small group that had a following and an audience in the general communal debate. Imbued with Marxist theory, they sought to right the wrongs of the world they lived in. They had at their command a then-appealing and often sentimentally expressed set of ideas that echoed the old Jewish ideals of care and social responsibility for the welfare of the poor. However, Marxist theory and ideology included specificities that were not easily compatible with those Jewish ideals. As a paradigm, it had labels and concepts for the failed social structure, for the culprit class, and for "parasitic" social activities; Jews as a group were distinctly defined by Marx as performing a socially negative and distrusted economic role.[53] Furthermore and more specifically, because Marxism was much more than just an economic theory of society, Marxism did not accept the idea of a separate Jewish culture with its traditional religious base. These were deemed obsolete. The uneven application of these beliefs by Jewish communists, who retained diverse elements of Judaism in their paradigm while remaining linked to central international communist organizations, created con-

flicts among the Jews themselves. The Marxist mode of thinking specifically prescribed and proscribed certain behaviors, attachments, and values
which compromised old ethnic values and convictions. Not unexpectedly, some felt that the continuity of the people defined as a religious,
national, cultural group was therefore in immediate danger. At the same
time and despite all this, the interest in the immediate here-and-now,
which the majority of Jews in czarist Russia felt desperately needed changing, led many Jews to espouse or at least sympathize with this new worldview. The new ideology enabled them to face that reality, even when it
threatened their distinctiveness as a people.

Secularized Jews in general had to choose between ideologies, or try
to harmonize the old beliefs with the new paradigms. For some adherents,
it became a choice between a recognizably not fully appropriate paradigm
and the promise of efficient, achievable change. For those Jews who dealt
with this discomfort, what took place was a struggle between two out-
looks: the ethic of social immediate responsibility which pushed toward
*integration*, and the ethic of sociohistorical conviction, which stressed
*continuity* by linking back to Jewish thought that was considered obsolete
by many Jews. Many communist Jews tipped the balance, emphasizing
integration over continuity. However, because they did not discard all of
their attachments to Jewish culture, they faced a tense, complex challenge. Like other representatives of competing Jewish ideologies, Jewish
communists had to justify themselves to their audiences in order to attract
and maintain a group of followers. They therefore had to rationalize
their worldview in terms of their Jewishness to avoid alienating the potential audience to which they were appealing. Jews had allowed ideological
variations to compete for the loyalty of the audience.

However, in a community that had built-in rituals and discourses
and had incorporated continuity into local communal culture, any belief
system that was interpreted as endangering the actual continuity of the
people produced a violent reaction. Jewish communists on occasion confronted other subgroups who reacted negatively towards them, often
calling into question the apparent good faith and authenticity of their
ideological claims. The parts of communist ideology that stressed inter-
nationalism, integration, and unification, for instance, had to be reconciled with issues of Jewish independent culture and particularistic identity.
This remained a constant intellectual challenge for Jewish communists.
Whenever communists were perceived as overstepping from safe criticism of the community to destructive criticism seen as threatening to
other parties or the community itself, issues of their "hidden agenda"
were made public and used as a tool against them.

Communists within the community tended to create their own organizational frameworks; they used other communal arrangements to a

minimum. The only exception was education. Although they did not actively work in the schools to promote their ideas, they made themselves visible in school-related activities and occasionally entered into deep confrontational arguments over educational philosophy. Education became a means to further other objectives; and, if not that, it was at least the most emotional field in which political issues seemed to test their strength, and where they maintained their active voice the longest.

In their attempt to expand their base, communists tried to balance general social issues and Jewish ones. The task was not easy; there was dissatisfaction either with the general society or the minority. Shmuel Maguidin, born in Russia (1905–1993), had strong anticzarist feelings by the age of twelve. In the midst of the turmoil in his country, he suffered at the hands of the Polish legions, and witnessed the anti-Jewish pogroms of 1923 in the Ukraine. He decided he had to leave, and arrived in Cuba in 1924. However, he felt Cuba to be "too militaristic" a country at the time, and could not abide the political culture. He hoped to find in Mexico a political structure more to his liking and perhaps a more socialistic milieu, since he had heard of its social and political revolution. It was also the nearest haven that would receive him.

In Mexico, too, his expectations were soon dashed. If the political system seemed more congenial, his discontent focused on his fellow Jews. The Y seemed to be merely a social center, which to him did not address any of the "real" needs Jews had or should have had. In 1928 he joined a small group that helped create the Jewish Radical Workers Organization with the cooperation of Lithuanian and Russian Jews. After that, he remained engaged in activities that reflected his ideological commitments. Even when the activities and the centers where these took place disappeared, his ideological commitments and convictions remained unchanged.

Together with others, Maguidin attempted to join the then-illegal Mexican Communist Party. But like other Jews who attempted this, he was not welcomed.[54] The Jews ended up organizing their own "cells" and action committees. Jewish communists then organized independently and provided help to the USSR, the Red Army, and a help organization called Socorro Rojo (Red Aid). Most often they established linkages with foreign leftist organizations, sending money, food, or clothing through them. These Jews faced a number of issues that communist ideology stressed and that had to be reconciled with Jewish culture and historical identity. However, the rest of the community watched for the communists' response to the issues that affected Jews: Jewish survival, Jewish settlements. Because they took what seemed to be the "wrong position," they were socially ostracized.

During World War II, communists occupied a highly visible and, to many, a distinguished and respectable position in the political dialogue of the community. World politics took center stage. Too much of consequence was happening in the world not to focus on it. The context provided an occasion to relate the immediate international political dilemmas to the experience of daily life. At the same time, the emphasis on internationalist discourse gave the communists time and leeway to elaborate on communal issues. Although this would have allowed them to sustain leadership roles in the community, this opportunity was never seized. In the meantime, because the Soviet Union had taken a favorable stance towards the Zionists outside their territory,[55] Jewish communists in Mexico could present the Soviet Union as the only real antifascist, anti-Nazi, and pro-Jewish force in the war. Because the World Federation of Trade Unions had also offered the support of the international proletariat for a Jewish national homeland in Palestine, Jewish communists shielded themselves temporarily from the attacks of Bundists and others, and were able to sustain an image of a positive attitude towards Jewish issues. They also found themselves in the perfect position to ally themselves with certain Zionists, who in turn seized the opportunity to make common cause with the communists.

But this opportunistic alliance soon weakened. Communists were forced to take sides on certain Jewish issues. No matter what was said, they were never able to convince others of their unreserved commitment to the Jewish people and nation; they often found themselves having to justify their Jewishness while being accused of being communists first rather than Jews. These internal communal struggles revolved around the salience and loyalty of the multiple roles of a political group; the attackers (communists) did not see these roles as mutually exclusive.

Whatever was said about them, Boris Rosen, Shmuel Maguidin, and Hirsh Minski, among others, led daily lives as part of the larger Jewish community. Maguidin's personal and family lives provide unquestionable evidence of this statement. A comment by Rosen, the longest and most enduring member of the party, for instance, that he had always been "more interested in Dovid Bergelson than in José Revueltas" is not gratuitous. Bergelson (1884–1952)[56] was a Yiddish writer who settled in the Soviet Union in his later years and wrote from the perspective of a Jew within that new society. Revueltas (1914–1976)[57] was a Mexican writer of a social literature that addressed the challenges of communists in the period of Calles and was full of doubts, anguish, and a desire for the clarification of dogmas. But Rosen's rapport to thinkers such as Bergelson, Olgin, and others reflected his commonalities to persons who shared a similar worldview and an objective world that made them feel like historical objects. To the majority, it was not enough just to identify with the likes of Bergelson and claim a Jewish-communist possibility. Was Bergelson not one of the many Jewish writers killed by the system they all supported? Was it coincidental that the killings targeted Jews? How could the Stalinist regime be condoned? These questions were not answered by the Rosens of the party.

Nevertheless, regardless of the communal assessment to the contrary, Rosen feels and talks, even today, of a connection to his birthplace and his ethnic group which he portrays as the experiential, emotional source of his Jewish sensibility, a strong source that his longer exposure to the Jewish community in Mexico did not surpass, but did not erase either. Whatever the source of the connection, the group's insistent claim for it seems real. But claiming connectedness did not ease their joining the community; for them, the story turned out altogether differently. Rosen and his political group were ousted from the official political structure of the community, the Kehillah, neither person nor group can take absolute responsibility. Fights, confrontations, and contentions were the stuff of which communal politics was made—there was nothing new in that. But while there was a dialogue, each political party, no matter how strong or weak, had a voice. Sometimes the voice was louder than the group that uttered it. But because what they uttered was losing meaning for the rest of the community, communists as leaders were becoming less important to the masses. Eventually, communists found themselves without an interlocutor: the dialogue had been foreclosed on them. Further, many political groups lost parts of their agenda in the process of the political structuring of the community. Not one remained politically static. However, in the same way that winners are never equal in their accomplishments nor their style, losers are also diverse. There is a basic difference between losing within the structure and being kept out of the structure. There was a difference between the Bundists "losing" and the communists "losing." In the end, communists gave up their position within the structure, and removed themselves from the communal dialogue. Yes, the community attacked them, their political vision was assaulted, and they were left politically silent; but as they left the dialogue, they became, for communal purposes, politically dead.

Their political vision hovered ghost-like in the early 1970s, when on occasion younger university students picked up their old agenda and attempted a comeback. Some within the younger generation adopted communism as a protest agenda and mainly focused on the indifference of the wealthy to the poor. The small group identified as youth protesters was seen as rebellious, but its activity was seen as an adolescent tantrum. They were politically ineffectual.

While the number of Jewish communists seemed relatively large in the thirties and forties, it all had to do with their visibility; in Mexico, they were always proportionately a small group. Some of them became communists after arriving in Mexico. Boris Rosen (b. 1917), for instance, was an immigrant from Russia from a traditional home, although his father was a secular person. He arrived in Mexico in 1929, just before his Bar Mitzvah, which took place in the new country, although he had been prepared for it in his native Kippel by his rabbi. This rabbi has remained for him a symbolic link to that orthodox past, which has proven to be deep and still evocative, though not active.

In Mexico, Rosen joined the Yidishe Shule in the fourth grade. He lived with an uncle who introduced him to Zionist thought and politics. The uncle's home was a center for colleagues of that ideology, and the young Rosen met Mordekhe Korona, a journalist; Leib Dulcin, a Zionist who eventually attained high status within the central international Zionist movement; Yosef Tchornitzky, a Zionist-activist teacher; and others. As he got older, Rosen became disappointed and disenchanted with what he saw around him. He had read Bundist literature with anti-Zionist ideas which started distancing him from the circle he was in. He read Trotsky. The social context provided by the Cárdenas regime in Mexico was fertile ground for his thinking. After all, in such a socialist atmosphere, socialist ideas had a different prestige and commanded distinction. It all seemed to offer real potentiality. Finally, in his late teens he traveled to New York to study in a Jewish seminary, but quit and joined the Yidisher Arbeter Universitet (Jewish Workers University), which introduced him to Jewish communist theorists like Moishe Olgin and Chaim Zitlovsky.

Rosen had a unique exposure by meeting these intellectuals. Moishe Olgin, a pseudonym for Moishe Yosef Novomiski (1878–1939), was born in Kiev and educated in law, philosophy, and social sciences (1907). He also received a doctorate in philosophy from Columbia University before he joined the workers party in 1921. A prolific writer, he wrote various books and published about six thousand articles and essays. Rosen's second mentor was Chaim Zitlovsky (1856–1943). Though once a Bundist, Zitlovsky had become a socialist-nationalist in a way that bothered even the Bundists of the late 1890s. He proclaimed a synthesis between international socialism and the national forms of culture. He was for Jewish autonomy, a territory for Jews to return to and become productive farmers. He was the first to proclaim the falseness of the formula of the "melting pot" as a theory for the United States. What he wanted was only the "unification of people in the United States."[58]

These thinkers embodied at the time the search for a better society in which Jews would finally have a recognized, equal, just space for themselves among the peoples of the world. Some were caught in the dream in the early part of this century, and Rosen was one of them. Could he convey all that to the Jewish community of Mexico? Would he and his tiny group be able to sustain communist thinking and justify to Jews and non-

Jews alike the need for Jewish nationalist existence, without alienating either Jews or communists in the process? Could he combine his interest of the majority with the minority without losing credibility to his attempt?

As a young adult, Rosen became active in organized Jewish life—in the Y, in the Yugunt Klub (Youth group) (1931), in Gesbir (Organization for Birodbidzhan),[59] and in the Yidishe Folks Lige (the communist League). He served in many capacities in these organizations, and began to publish. He saw then (and still sees) the possibility of creating a Yiddish center in Russia as an independent territory for Russian Jews, along with the Jewish state in Palestine.[60]

In keeping with Marxist thinking, the Jewish religion was for these young communists a reactionary structure. This view separated Rosen, Maguidin, and their group from all institutions and representatives directly linked to any religious and traditional activity. Further, they differed from secularists such as Golomb, who called for the retention of the established Jewish way of life, saturated with religious Jewish practices and tradition. Rosen agreed with the left Jewish refugee Leo Katz in his opinion that Golomb was nothing but a reactionary.

Education was another field in which the ideological confrontation was played out. The control exercised by Zionists and Bundists in education was, for the communists, misdirected. Rosen saw the Yidishe Shule as an apolitical organization, not conducive to the development of political positions.[61] He therefore showed a general lack of support for the school of which he had been a part. However, many well-to-do Jews and the first Bundists acted similarly, albeit for different reasons. Not all communists rejected the school either. But as a group, they did not participate in its day-to-day operation.[62] Rosen's feelings therefore seem to reflect their ideology.

Communists were almost always at odds with Bundists. From the start, communists were more radical and committed to Soviet policy and objectives; they systematically explained away all signs of anti-Semitism in the theory and practice of Marxism. For the communists, the problem with the Bundists was that they did not realize that the theory of Marxism-Leninism was, as they saw it, the only way to fight the capitalist power structure. The espousal of particularism by the Bund and their retention of the cultural idiosyncrasies of the ethnic group did not allow them to fully join the movement for change. But, when communists in the 1950s defected to protest Soviet policy, the Bund provided the political framework closest to their thinking. After the Stalin era, with the uncovering of compelling evidence of Jewish persecutions and the plans for evacuation of all Jews from Moscow in the aftermath of the trials of Jewish writers and doctors, which were cut short only by Stalin's death, some communists were bitterly disappointed and looked for a new structure.

However, they found little or no sympathy and trust among other groups. Those who moved to the Bund in search for the most familiar framework for thought and action were received with caution, and were often reminded of their untrustworthy "repenting" posture. They were often reproached that their change could not erase the past.

This was not the case for Rosen or Maguidin. In general, Marxist-Leninist theory shared with Hegelian thought the ability to explain many of the politically perpetuated social injustices as "extenuating circumstances" of the social structure in the process of change, always connecting the particular suffering to an ultimate positive goal. Rosen shared that belief, which helped him to "understand" Soviet politics towards the Jews: persecution was thus seen as a temporary byproduct which did not require rejecting the ideology. However, following the Prague repression in 1950, when he was a delegate to the Peace Congress that took place in Warsaw, he resisted taking a justificatory, pro-Soviet position. Instead, Rosen resigned: while he could not go against the prevailing "party line," he could not justify the party's actions. In good conscience, he left his editorial position in the *Fraivelt*.

Eventually the communists were ousted: they were deemed unacceptable as a political option within the communal dialogue. They were ousted from the Central Committee in the 1950s, and were no longer seen as a legitimate part of Jewish organized life in Mexico. As an organization, Jewish communists never recovered. Some of the Jewish communist youth in Mexico, who were small in number,[63] eventually left the movement, too; most found their own center of action in their professional or business activities.[64] Few remained true to their original thinking. But Rosen and some others remained loyal to the ideology. In fact, what took place was a further distancing from communal affairs as well as from Zionism. Some communists articulated a pro-Palestinian position not too different from the New Left stance in the United States. By occasionally publicly supporting Palestinian and Arab positions, and labeling Israel the aggressor without ever putting to the test the moral ethos of the Arab political posture, communists were further ostracized.[65]

Although Rosen no longer endorses anti-Israel policies publicly, he explains and defends what he calls the Marxist interpretation of Zionism. For him, Zionism is characterized as by most Marxist thinkers less as a progressive attempt for national recognition than as another national bourgeois movement. Most national movements, he claims, were in essence progressive because they fought against colonial powers, but this could be the case only when they fought from their own territory. But Jews did not yet have a territory when their nationalist movement erupted, nor were they fighting a specific colonial power. Rather, they were forced to use the help of colonialist and imperialist countries alike to achieve their goals. According to Rosen, this made it impossible for the Zionist movement to be truly anti-imperialist, as most other national movements were. Rosen found this characteristic to be the reactionary essence of Zionism.[66]

Rosen concludes that all Marxist pro-Soviet thinkers are against Zionist ideology, but not against the state of Israel. This distinction, however, has never found an echo within the general community, who feel that Soviet politics have never been consistent with Jewish principles. The communal press has always claimed that the defense of Arab interests by communists over and above the Jewish agenda represents more a blind adherence to the Soviet Union than an attempt at constructive criticism; and for communists to suggest that the original Zionist objectives are acceptable but that the process by which they were achieved are unacceptable is to confuse and manipulate their own ambivalences.

Communists offer no suggestion as to what historically could have been done differently. The distinction of levels of analysis and endorsement has always seemed unclear to most and hurtful to the vast majority, who viewed this as a lack of support of the old Jewish dream, a betrayal of authentic Jewish objectives, and the systematic undermining of Jewish-Israeli objectives, without the offering of positive alternatives. Further, the communist complacency with other nationalist movements, accepting their ethically questionable methods as justifiable while holding Israel to higher and loftier standards, was for the community totally unacceptable. The issue in Mexico, then, is not the current Jewish international issue of how criticism of Israeli policies can or cannot be voiced by Jews outside the Jewish state before being labeled anti-Jewish; rather, the prevailing feeling is that Jewish continuity and independent statehood are not at the top of the agenda of communist thought.

These issues, like most, were not resolved intellectually, no matter how much argumentative prowess was shown by the debaters. Communist issues in this case were cast aside or circumvented, much as the community did with their organizations.[67] The socialist vocabulary was not in vogue in the 1950s and did not resonate to a now definite middle class. The challenge of the community to this very small group of people is as follows: to either recast their thinking to be able to continue as trustworthy participants in the Jewish debate, or to address and disclaim their attacks on Jewish ethnicity, culture, and values. This challenge has not been met. Communists could never fight back the faithlessness of the others to them. As individuals, Rosen, Maguidin, and few others remain immersed in Jewishness: they retain their connections, relations, and culture, even traveling to Israel. But as a political group—as a voice and a language trying to define and influence the communal situation—they are absent: they have no followers, no heirs.

The effect of their having been ousted from the structure has left them historically silenced. Lacking the resources required to remain an effective force, they choose to stay outside of the communal network, even when this precludes any possible negotiation or reaccommodation between them and any other part of the left. To lose as the Bundists lost, for instance, meant giving up communal territory and an emphasis on communal priorities, but it gave them the opportunity and the obligation to leave testimony of the issues that were sacrificed, sidestepped, or unaddressed. At the same time, they were able to debate the issues on which they felt the communal wisdom had gone wrong, and to acknowledge those which they either promoted or accepted. Maintaining the dialogue active, even partially, was tantamount to leaving a record of their perspective. Being forced to articulate their arguments, the Bundists left substantive ideas not only for the historical-social memory of the group, but also for a potential reexamination of these issues by other generations.

In contrast, the communist attitude and response to their eviction from the communal organizations largely foreclosed the possibility of a future reexamination of the arguments for their inclusion in the dialogue. Indeed, by not actively maintaining their perspective, they did not socialize and sensitize another generation to their worldview. Herein lies a major difference. The communists' inflexibility led to a notorious lack of creativity. Additionally, the Jewish communist silence was also the result of a relational dynamic: the way others perceived and treated them within the parameters of the Cold War mentality undoubtedly contributed to their being stifled and oppressed. The attitude of the others built an almost insurmountable barrier against them.

Rosen has not yielded, but he has not yet given a satisfactory communal answer either. Further, if issues do not have sufficient intrinsic force to be imprinted upon an organization so that many can think about them and act on them, they also lose politically. Hence communism, a once widespread and widely respected point of view, lost its influence. Once the communal structure took definite form, the power groups and their political turf became bounded. Ideologically, some dialogues won incisively; others were forgotten, obliterated, destroyed; yet others were merely silenced.

## CONFLICT TURNED CONSENSUS:
## SHIMSHON FELDMAN, POLITICIAN PAR EXCELLENCE

Shimshon Feldman (1909–1993) held the highest office in the largest and most important organization of the community for the longest time. He was an institution himself, and had been one for a long time. His power and prestige rested on his role as head of the Kehillah—Rosh Hakahal, head of the Ashkenazi community.[68]

Born in the Ukraine, he lost his mother at an early age, and his father remarried. This uncomfortable situation led him to emigrate after his Bar Mitzvah. In 1923 he left with a cousin for Mexico because he had an aunt already living there. He arrived at the port of Veracruz in 1924 with the help he received from the American HIAS (Hebrew Immigration Association). Starting work as a peddler, he later joined a bakery, peddling bread. Eventually he became a member of the bread workers' union and met people who later became important leaders in the workers' movement. While selling milk, he met Fidel Velázquez, later to become for many years the leader of the CTM (Confederación de Trabajadores Mexicanos), establishing a friendship of great symbolic importance: both became long-lasting authoritarian leaders of their respective organizations. Fidel Velázquez, in his nineties, still serves as the supreme leader of the CTM.

Feldman later worked as shoe salesman, and finally he and his brother began working in the construction business, the field that eventually allowed him to dedicate himself to communal work. He joined the Nidkhei Israel congregation, since most of its members were from Russia. The congregation started as an immigrant benevolent society and congregation in 1922. If any group approximates the form of a *Landsmanschaft*—a benevolent society consisting of individuals from the same village or region—it was the congregation of the Russian Nidkhei Israel and the Polish Agudas Akhim. The former was established first, had a larger constituency, and controlled the Ashkenazi cemetery. Feldman became active in Nidkhei Israel long before he became a central figure in the larger community. He was neither a theorist nor an ideologue; he was a statesman, a practical man, involved in the business of politics.

But if one had to sum up in one word a characteristic that made him unique and uniquely successful at his work, it was his equilibrium. As a politician par excellence, he negotiated with others while always aiming at an equilibrium. In his personal life, he maintained a secular worldview as well as a religious Jewish worldview. He felt this type of combination was necessary to build and sustain the new community. While he was not a rabbi, he respected religious life sufficiently to convince others that lifestyle and identity had to be an active force within Jewish life. As a result, his earlier work within the congregation, his respect for rabbinical knowledge, and his contacts with "authorities" helped him preside over the nonpartisan Kehillah. He united all parties while sustaining the religious, traditional character of orthodox Judaism within the organization, even when there was no majority that lived according to those principles.

In many ways, Feldman's combining of eclectic strands in his personal life mirrored what he imposed and achieved for the community as well. The mixture of secularity and religious orthodoxy, where the former dominates and the latter is subsumed under the cultural life of the group without controlling the individuals who comprise it, was the dominant style in the community until the latter part of the 1970s. Even when later changes raised religious awareness and activity, Jews in Mexico have remained, by and large, a secular-traditional community.

In the late 1920s and early 1930s, the entire political system of Mexico was undergoing a process of centralization, bureaucratization, and institutionalization. In the Jewish community, none of the initial attempts succeeded or progressed beyond the immediate needs that prompted them. The one group that came the closest to unifying the community was the Central Committee (Tzentral Komitet). Their work was certainly first an attempt at protecting the whole community. Ashkenazim and Sephardim united for that purpose in 1938, when the climate against Jews was international, and although Ashkenazim dominated the organization, first by their numerical superiority and later through their indirect control of the Central Committee by the Kehillah, the Central Committee never managed to garner enough support to be an umbrella organization for all Jews on all subjects. Within the communal network, a plurality of visions and opinions coexisted. The multiplicity of cultural and political expressions that were possible for Ashkenazi Jews in Mexico could not be so easily subsumed.

World War II made the issue of centrality salient again. Though the Cárdenas regime had offered in principle the possibility of refugee immigration, in reality all attempts failed or almost failed. Jews organized the Comité Pro Refugiados (1938). Refugees—between twenty to thirty in each attempt—came in ships like the *Orinoco, Iberia, Quanzas,* and *Niasas.*[69] Most were returned. The largest group, 187 in all, arrived in 1941 in the *Serpapinto* and was received only after much negotiation with the government. The extraordinary efforts that were made by individuals or organizations trying to intercede with the government came, pathetically, to very little. The tragic fate of European Jews left most governments noncommittal, and Mexico was no exception.[70]

In 1942 rumors circulated in the Jewish street that 20,000 Jews would be rescued and accepted by Mexico. In reality, only about 32 Polish Jews were taken in out of a group of about 1,400 Polish refugees, while the government opened its doors to refugees of the Spanish Civil War. The Hacienda Santa Rosa, where all the Polish refugees had to stay, became a problem, since the few Jews there were much discriminated against.[71] These experiences highlighted the plight of the refugees and raised demands for the creation of a united front. Thus, in 1943 different organizations, including the Central Committee, ORT, Nidkhei Israel, and Keren Hayesod[72] felt the pressure to centralize their power.

Belief in a strong central organization found general support in the local Yiddish press, too. The dream was to be a more effective advocate by showing some strength. The illusion that a single voice would exert greater pressure seemed to prevail. However, the reluctance to pool resources became a strong barrier to unification. As an issue, it seemed to eclipse the many other beneficial aspects that a centralizing institution would bring. There was no lack of speculation concerning the power that would accrue to whichever organization achieved centrality. However, the agenda of the prevailing organization had to dovetail with the group's agenda. Thus, while the idea of centrality had gathered momentum and the time was ripe for Jews to unite and define their role in Mexico as a community, it was to take at least another decade for this to materialize for the Ashkenazim.[73]

Centralization required effort and communication. As it was, a plurality of visions, definitions, and actions contended with each other. With centralization on the agenda, the status quo and the old style were disturbed; the previous political game was threatened, and a new institutional pattern was beginning to take root. With all these changes, it was Feldman who managed to coalesce the new structure, give it form, and control it.

Although the Central Committee attempted to fill the vacuum and gain control as an umbrella organization to oversee the Jewish subcommunities, it was clear to Ashkenazi Jewry that that group, while more organized, diversified, and trained in communal politics than any other subgroup, could not achieve total control. Internally, there were too many strong leaders—Bundists, communists, Zionists—and their agendas were neither compatible nor likely to be combined into a melting organization of sorts.

From among all the organizations within the community, it was Nidkhei Israel that had, in practical terms, the greatest exposure and experience with the direct internal functioning of the community. They had built a small machinery that managed at least part of the economic resources of most Ashkenazim. The congregation had control over the central area of orthodox ritual by administering the cemetery and offering services to all ritual activities. It also had vested interests and contacts in education. Starting with a Talmud Tora in the early twenties, they financed the religious group which established a modern religious school. The Yavne school began in the forties with the direct help and support of the Nidkhei Israel group. The congregation also collected funds and transferred these to American Jewish philanthropic organizations, thereby gaining some international standing. They also acted as a loan association and an arbitration body.

When the Kehillah was formed and linked up in name and deed to Nidkhei Israel, it assumed a variety of functions, which in turn gave it credibility to oversee the gamut of activities of the community. Though the Kehillah took the form of a democratic effort in which most organizations would be represented, it was not a new organization itself; instead, it was a product of the hegemonic power of the Nidkhei Israel group, which managed to transform itself as Kehillah. With the passive-aggressive insertion of the religious dimension into the later Kehillah through the inclusion of the Nidkhei Israel in name and substructure, a thorough secular institution remained connected to tradition and religion without ever being threatened in its bid for control. This was a direct outcome of Feldman's legendary quest for equilibrium.

The leaders of Nidkhei Israel were therefore strategically poised to take control. Feldman, with his history of active involvement in the congregation, eventually took over the power structure.[74] He was a natural politician who knew how to attract people, coopt them, and provide autonomy for those who absolutely required it. Tuvie Maizel—the Bundist who cooperated with the Kehillah effort—was ceded undisputed control over cultural affairs. Nobody participated in or dissented from his decisions. His cooperation in the Kehillah was earned and exchanged— albeit unofficially—for a level of independence. Maizel was perceived as having significant leadership skills himself. Lacking a strong group to support him, however, he retained his position through his work and personality. This type of political interaction and accommodation became a pattern: many of the encounters between Jewish leaders in Mexico were confrontations between men who were charismatic figures. Feldman's unique ability was to create consensus among them; the clue to his long success was knowing how to include them, keeping them involved in a common task always defined in the most general terms: continuity.

Feldman was an excellent negotiator and consolidator, a quality which helped him avoid the need to divide forces and renegotiate relations of power with new people. This does not mean that Feldman was not an absolute sovereign in the old fashioned way, because he very much was one. He ruled the Kehillah with authoritarian power, as he is said to have ruled his private family enterprises. It was this ability to wield strong central authority while ceding areas of partial autonomy to others that kept him in power for close to forty years. It is probable that an outsider to the community might find this long political control puzzling. After all, in an atmosphere of multiple political postures, visions, and contentions as the Jewish Mexico of the thirties to fifties had, it is difficult to understand Feldman's success at retaining power for such a long time. Feldman's success as the major player is parallel to the success of the whole Kehillah with all its minor players. The use of a vague discourse of democracy and public support to hold on to power seem to indicate a weakness of the structure. So how does one explain this further? Perhaps it is here that we find the best arena in which to make comparisons between the host society and the minority societies and their reciprocal influences, namely, the political structure. Feldman can be said to have experienced a comparative *presidencialismo* similar to that of the Mexican political system. The presidencialismo or extraordinary political power of the presidential figure within the Mexican political system has been widely documented and accepted.[75] It is difficult to call the system authoritarian or democratic since it combines elements of both. For the president of the country as well as for the president of the community there is an unwritten rule of cooperation that all sectors need to abide by. It is crucial that all sectors of society or the community participate in a kind of corporatism. Harmony, for both of these societies, is fundamental;[76] there is an ideological dependency on this value and its use for the achievement of stability. One can conclude at least that the political atmosphere of the country has been conducive to permitting such political rules to flourish.

But Feldman was not only a keen conciliator, he had other political assets to offer as well. His being financially comfortabe allowed him the luxury of devoting all his time to communal work. His availability helped him sustain a degree of salutary involvement and visibility. As a result of his political skills, he was able to consolidate the institution of the Kehillah and give it centrality, hegemony, and prestige within the community and outside it, certainly with respect to the state of Israel.

The personal story of Shimshon Feldman and the General Zionist movement merged, to the benefit of both. The General Zionists increased their prestige and power after the establishment of the state of Israel, and the Kehillah became an instrument to reach continuity, taking on parts of the Zionist rhetoric as part of the guiding ideology of their agenda. The first *Rat* or board of directors of the Kehillah included fifty-six members, of which forty-nine were Zionists or Zionist sympathizers. If the Kehillah maintained some independence, it was due to the factions within the Zionists and to the Bundists and other influences that still exerted some pressure within the community.[77]

The story of the institutionalization of the Kehillah is in great measure the story of Feldman. The consolidation of groups, the centralization and bureaucratization of the Kehillah itself, are part of his story. The international linkage with the then-successful Zionist effort gave prestige to the new organization. The general satisfaction in the Jewish community over the foundation of a Jewish state in Israel, and the need for a formal structure to be able to interact with and engage in relations with Israel gave additional urgency to the creation of a central organization. Even in that climate, however, it was Feldman who served as the mediating force to make it happen. Although the political spectrum had been delimited and the central ideological objectives had been defined, it was Feldman's consensus-building politics that made the new institution the solid center of the community. Feldman lived for politics and made politics his life. He also lived off politics. His prestige and power expanded over time and were further legitimized by the recognition he attained from politicians in Mexico and Israel.

Through Feldman, the Kehillah welded different forces in a manner that gave an eclectically defined identity to the institution. For example, Yiddish was used and supported as the formal and official language of the Ashkenazi community. Most meetings, if not all, were conducted in that language. The cultural activities that Maizel organized and controlled were all carried out in Yiddish. Spanish began to be used in official meetings more often only in the 1980s, after Maizel's death in 1985; before that, it was used only occasionally, when different subcommunities took part in a special event. At the same time, the Kehillah was defined as a Zionist institution, offering unconditional support to Israel. Hebrew, however, never became the official language, partly because the vast majority of the activists, both staff and volunteers, did not speak it fluently. Interestingly, no contradiction was seen in this decision, and no effort was made to learn the "new" language either. In addition, the Kehillah endorsed the orthodox ritual as the acknowledged format for religious observance, without it meaning that all members of the Kehillah—or even the constituent majority—were either orthodox or religious in the traditional sense of the word.[78]

All Jewish daily schools—secular, religious, Zionist—were expected to report to the Vaad Hakhinukh, the education committee of the Kehillah, and all were given support and subsidies. All were linked to Israel. Despite the particular emphasis they chose, they viewed themselves as connected to the national cultural efforts of Israel, the undisputed leader of Jewry.

No channels existed to deal with the questioning of any central tenets of the institution or the system. If any questioning occurred in the political arena, either by individuals or loosely organized leftist university students, it never represented a serious opposition or became a threatening group. Most initiatives for work, projects, or study groups, whether organizational or academic, were dismissed if attempted from the "outside." They were often labelled "amateurish," "lacking in experience," or simply "irrelevant." Furthermore, there was a specifically demeaning style used while dealing with any attempted activist: the systematic infantilization of the doer. Whatever their credentials, the outsiders (young adults with a desire to change or activate a certain department of the Kehillah) were addressed as "child," "youngster," etc. This systematic belittling of others as childish and unable to take responsibility both neutralized their intentions and distanced most of the potential contributors and followers of the dominant institution. Over time, this way of dealing with political outsiders became institutionalized as a surer and more gratifying way to ensure stability.

Feldman remained until the early 1990s the central, undisputed leader; his institution, partly because he was then ailing and older, was headed by one of his sons, who had been groomed for the position for many years and has now taken over. Feldman remained over the years largely unaccountable; the initial democratic effort and process of the Kehillah withered and elections were never institutionalized. Elections were performed with less and less frequency—decades apart—with dwindling participation and with rare changes in incumbents. The Kehillah expanded the body of paid staff, who indirectly legitimized the apparatus with the loyalties and dependencies they developed towards the organization. Order, authority, and legitimization, all wrapped under the more general value of harmony, were part and parcel of Feldman's Kehillah.

Undoubtedly, Feldman's ability and performance until he died have been largely perceived as a success. In fulfilling most of the general objectives the community had chosen for itself, he achieved results that nobody was able or willing to modify.[79] The ideology of the Kehillah allowed only certain things to be communicated, objectified, and discussed. It functioned "expressively" as ideologies function, highlighting issues or problems which are felt by some to be paramount to that group. The ideas of unity, coordination, harmony, and brotherhood were the explicitly achieved objectives.

However, ideology also works repressively, neglecting or eclipsing certain issues or the potential to articulate these issues, denying their communication and thus creating a "public unconsciousness" of them. This occurred whenever anyone attempted to address the local condition of Jews, whether in a philosophically general manner, sociologically, psychologically as identity issues, or politically as interrelation between minority and majority. The Kehillah effectively silenced any professional who saw the communal problems as a legitimate activity that needed to be addressed and therefore challenged. The process of selective nonrecognition not only quieted the professionals, intellectuals, and the young potential activists, but muzzled the issues themselves.

Feldman's closeness to orthodoxy—e.g., Nidkhei Israel—came from his traditional lifestyle. He had no formal education on the subject, but adhered more or less to it. A stronger commitment towards modern orthodoxy came from his personal friendship as well as formal relationship with Rabbi Yakov Avigdor, who in his capacity as co-rabbi impressed him with the wisdom and depth of the Jewish sources.[80] This kept Feldman and the Kehillah close to the orthodox efforts, offering the Kehillah as arbitrator for internal affairs, as *Kashrut* (dietary laws) overseer, and controller of all Jewish ritual through the orthodox paradigm.[81]

Feldman informally exercised veto power over any issue addressed by the Kehillah. His personal approach to dissension was to reach consensus through "persuasion." This approach echoes the old idea of "harmony" that the first American Y Jews upheld and used in the early part of this communal history. Because persuasion was always used, the outcome did not just reflect the opinions of "a majority" but was presented as unanimous: harmony prevailed above all. This consensus should not be understood, however, as the lack of conflict, but rather as the ability to impose a domineering pattern of thought.

The perception of Feldman's success in Mexico seems to a degree unquestionable as measured by his achievement: the establishing of an officially recognized representative organization of Jews in Mexico, as well as a united front against occasional anti-semitism. The Kehillah is both an economic center—offering subsidies to all Jewish daily schools, voluntarily receiving taxation or eschewing it on ritual occasions among its members—and a central religious body always renovating its controls. The Kehillah oversees all activities in the community. The sporadic attempts by younger professionals to examine Jewish-oriented topics that could have opened the door to other groups were dampened. The Kehillah viewed these attempts with suspicion, and either never supported or ignored them.

In its handling of all Zionist youth organizations, the Kehillah revealed the ambivalence and contradictory nature of its objectives. Though supported, any attempt at innovation by the youth organizations was mostly left unaided. The community had not worked out clearly what its relationship and responsibility to these groups was to be: was one objective that they become active Zionists and eventually settle in Israel? Were they groups of future leaders who understood the need for continuity and were trained to take over communal roles? This ambivalence and complexity was not settled in the minds of the elders, nor was it resolved in the minds of the youth who attempted to emerge as potential leaders but often got dismissed before any project was even considered. Indifference and occasional disapproval always meant that any potential young leaders risked being defined as "problematic," identified as potential power threats, and crushed to the point of becoming politically disabled. This method, approved and enforced, eventually became a way to systematically limit and inhibit any attempt by "new blood" to join the Kehillah organization in an innovative capacity. Anyone who could have challenged the prevailing situation stopped vying for positions. It is clear that, once the Kehillah organization obtained centrality and power, it was not interested in sharing it. It never welcomed challengers through its doors.

Feldman radiated a sense of responsibility as Rosh Hakohel, head of the community. His descriptions of his quasi mission of uniting all Jews of

Mexico raised him from the daily routine of politics to a higher level of historical importance.[82] He was respected as an elder statesman until his death. Most of the remaining old functionaries followed him with the force of inertia. But there is no lasting legacy of coherent, articulated ideological elaboration in Feldman's thought or in the Kehillah's philosophy. Feldman's style and leadership leave open to speculation whether the institutionalized structure can survive a change of incumbents, or will become the product of a new authoritarian figure, at the mercy of new politically undefined factions.

This question reveals another characteristic of the Kehillah: it is an institution lacking a historical consciousness that would respect and acknowledge its own activity. The devaluing of the importance of the institution in contrast to the importance the leaders claim for themselves is reflected in the older style of lack of record-keeping and in the tampering with old communal archives. The older sloppiness in maintaining whatever scattered archival material exists is symptomatic of how the Kehillah has operated.[83] Behind it may be a fear of the host society, insecurity, and a desire to keep history blurred. Whatever the reasons behind it, the lack of recording and historiography have precluded a critical self-evaluation. This has made the elaboration of a broader political agenda more difficult, and placed obstacles in the path to an ideological ethnic consciousness. Today, the path may be changed. Israel Feldman, Feldman's son heading the Kehillah, has indicated his intention of changing and technologically modernizing the institution. It remains to be seen if he can inject ideologically other contents too.

Feldman headed an *ancien régime* not on the verge of a revolution, but an *ancien régime* just the same, with its ideological disparities and incongruities, vested interests, and many unrecognized limitations. The structure's positive role while it centralized, institutionalized, and depoliticized its constituent sub-groups is now having other effects: diminished vibrancy, variety, and possibility. Feldman, the devoted politician, basked in the glory of some real achievements, but was oblivious to varied limitations and problems of his social world. He created an institution equally oblivious, but eventually more vulnerable.

## WITHIN THE WINNING IDEOLOGY, THE INESCAPABLE DIASPORA QUESTIONS: ZIONIST AVNER ALIPHAS

There is no doubt that Zionism became the central dominating Jewish ideology in Mexico. Ever-present in the history of exiled Jews was the old longing for a homeland, which created a general, often latent sympathy for the movement. Of all ideologies, Zionism was, once established, the easiest for the majority to follow. It offered a frame of reference and linkage to yet another Jewish community; and, despite its theoretical demands, it allowed Jews who supported the movement only financially to call themselves Zionists without being challenged by all the tenets of the ideology. They were "free" to act on their local issues and were even "detached" from local Jewish social issues. Their position allowed them to retain their autonomy, yet still feel connected.

There were Zionists of different hues in Mexico from the 1920s onward, though they were then very few.[84] However, when Avner Aliphas arrived in 1939, there were plenty of activists in many organizations, and they represented all shades of Zionist belief. Born Mendl Goldman, in Kolne, Poland, Aliphas (1912-1976) joined the Shomer Hatzair movement (left-Zionist movement) at the age of ten or eleven. The youngest of eight children, only he and a sister seemed interested in Palestine. In his teens, he decided to travel to Palestine while his sister remained with their parents. His life there was the life of a pioneer; he belonged to the original group of the Kibbutz Negba and the Kibbutz Chanita, which was erected in an overnight effort, built to meet the "tower and wall" requirements which symbolized property as defined by the British.[85]

At the outbreak of World War II, a visit to his ailing mother left him stranded in Paris. He had three brothers and a sister in Uruguay and a sister in Mexico who hoped to move to the United States. He joined the latter, arriving for a temporary visit in 1939 which in fact led to ten years of work in the community in Mexico.

During the first year of his stay, he thought he would be in Mexico only temporarily and hoped to return to Palestine as soon as possible. He joined the Yiddishe Shule as a teacher to support himself and involved himself deeply in his work. His approach differed from that of other Zionist teachers. He seemed caught in the feverish activity which offered the rewarding possibility of creative political work. He then began immediately to organize and teach youth as potential "Chalutzim" (pioneers), and was active in afternoon activities. For the first time in Mexico, he addressed jointly all subcommunities, establishing centers of the Shomer Hatzair for the different groups. The movement, a combination of Marxist-Leninist and Zionist thinking, attracted increasingly large groups of young people. Aliphas was himself an experienced pioneer, and his personality and message had tremendous appeal at the time. However, rivalries with colleague-teachers arose almost immediately. He had a more emphatic approach to the teaching of the Hebrew language, and aimed to connect youth directly with Palestine and with the idea of Aliya—the immigration to Eretz Israel. This was seen as a significant deviation from the "local" style others permitted. To some,

Aliphas was an arrogant Zionist gratuitously criticizing their efforts.

Aliphas's sharper political inclinations, style, and activity in the educational field soon denied him the support of his colleagues. In an unexpected turn of events, he was fired from his teaching job while he was attending a conference in the United States. These actions exposed the underlying conflict: his views did not allow any accommodation within the school. The school rid itself of him, but Aliphas seized the opportunity to create a new school—Tarbut, a Hebrew school—which he achieved with the support of his relatives and sympathizers. This decision aroused feelings of fear and betrayal by those in the established educational organization. In 1941 Aliphas launched the new school and eventually got the help of two other teachers from Cuba. His enterprising work expanded the school system in the community while the Hatzair youth group became the first truly pioneering movement for Israel in Mexico. Notwithstanding these achievements, Aliphas had neither the support of most Zionists nor the sympathy of all his coworkers.

He married in Mexico and then returned to Israel, bringing to a close the first stage of his work for the community. He had been controversial, but highly productive; parallel to his Zionist influence on the community, he dramatically changed the outlook of the structure of the community.

The return to Israel in 1947 proved to be extremely difficult; now he and his wife had to adapt and practice the life imposed by the ideology they followed. A process of ideological disenchantment began, the result of disillusionment with the Soviet Union's Stalinist policies, and the ideological rigidity that both he and his wife felt was strangling rather than guiding this generation of Palestine pioneers. When they returned to Mexico in 1950—in itself a difficult decision for him—he returned as a Poalei Tzion member (a left socialist member), very much a socialist, holding values of justice and a vision of ideals for Israel, but less radical than he had been years earlier. He took on a job as director of the Tarbut-Sepharadi, but differences over the number of hours of instruction of Hebrew compared to English put him at odds with the board. Losing the fight, he left the school.

Aliphas's crisis surfaced both in Israel and in the diaspora, but because certain aspects were part of the diaspora condition as affected by the new Jewish state, it exposed itself only slowly. Because he did not remain in Israel, his work in the Jewish community was for him paramount. His own experience offered dramatic proof that not all Jews were going to move to Israel. Living in different societies demanded different awarenesses and accommodations. To maintain a connectedness to Israel, to call oneself a Zionist as he did, included feeling uncomfortable with the way the ideology itself looked upon all those Jews who did not move to Israel. Further, to comprehend and work out solutions appropriate to the diasporic condition required a complete overhaul of the ideology and the political condition of Jews in diaspora; this task was well above what he could attempt. He perceived only slowly and agonizingly all the Zionist reactions and pressures. Each angle was a blow on its own, a debilitating blow that made it increasingly difficult to see the gestalt of the political problem, let alone attempt a solution. As a result, the eternal Zionist Aliphas and Zionism were not able to come together.

The history of Zionism in Mexico could be an account of the people that helped spread the ideology, took over institutions, and produced international Zionist leadership—Leib Dulcin. However, this history also needs to focus on the shortcomings of the movement for the diaspora, on the intrinsic problems that the ideology and the diaspora followers faced. The internal definitions of Zionist ideology which touch diaspora Jews and their condition are tautologically negated by that system of thought. The essential ambivalence and contradiction of this polarity has had and still has great consequences for Jews. This difficulty is the one Aliphas experienced in his own life, although he was unable to explain it.

In an attempt to further define and conceptualize the specific diaspora problem, Aliphas found himself becoming an "ideological wanderer," an ironic and difficult position for a Zionist to be in after the creation of Israel. In this second stage, his ideological thought was primarily expressed as a journalist. He was at the margin of the power forces of the then-crystallizing structure, a fact which forced him to rethink his ideology. His intellectual searching reflected some of the inadequacies of the Zionist ideology as a single guiding intellectual line for Jewish identity in the diaspora. Aliphas begun to raise questions. If Zionism was to be narrowly defined, how was the support of Israel going to sustain local Jewish identity? What kind of identity would remain in the diaspora? Was the content of Jewish identity to change because of Israel? Was the definition of Judaism used in Israel acceptable to Jews in Israel and diaspora Jews alike? Unwittingly, what Aliphas began to experience was the intellectual confusion affecting the authenticity of diaspora Judaism. The complexity of the issues and the conflicting loyalties, and the Zionist confounding of the need for aggressiveness to achieve the national goal with the ruthlessness with which internal conformation was attempted left many Zionists in the diaspora perplexed, but unaware of the source of the problem. How could it be that the hoped-for solution for Jews was producing so much confusion, pressure, and internal dissension?

Aliphas's return to Mexico marked him as an outsider from the establishment. Ironically, his alienation was greater than that of the Jews who had never been to Israel. He was judged pejoratively as a Yored—a "returning Zionist," someone coming "down"; this was a label fraught with the implications of inadequacy. This, of course, was an unfair judgment on the part of many Zionists and others who used a double standard in judging those who attempted to live in Israel and those who never even intended to. Besides being a wounding depiction and putting Aliphas in a position in which he had to justify himself, it left him with few friends and collaborators. This distance allowed him, however, to reexamine the different ideologies and the nuances he could potentially endorse, because he had few direct ties with any one political party that could undermine or obstruct his soul-searching.

Aliphas did not find a forum where he and others felt comfortable with each other. What, after all, did he have to offer but questions and doubts? He attempted to organize about ten youth groups over the next decade, but all proved unsuccessful in the long run. Over time, he became more detached from the local youth, their inclinations, styles, and needs. Those who knew him only in his new capacity understood little of him and his attempts at providing guidance and direction. They often disliked his interventions, perceiving them as intrusions. In most cases they rejected the direction and resented the authority, as they sought only a context in which to relate. Unwittingly, he was offering a link to Zionism and Israel, as well as the constraint he himself experienced. Thus he was offering what he was fighting against.

Having been the first to diversify the educational network, Aliphas was so linked to the field of education that he had difficulty detaching himself from it. The combination of politics and pedagogy, however, forced issues upon him that only perspective and time would allow him to address. Left as a commentator rather than an active participant, he radically changed his views on the specific cultural values needed for the reproduction of Jewish identity;[86] this in turn implied a critique of the educational system, the value system, and the lifestyle of the community. From the Marxist Shomer Hatzair, he had gone to the socialist Poalei Tzion, and then included traditions in which even religious knowledge became important. A constant searching and reaccommodating characterized his work.

Though detachment from a specific network allowed Aliphas to change his thinking, he defined himself as and remained a solid Zionist all his life. This position and the relative intellectual solitude to which he was confined were for him a springboard for thought and a source of energy. He had entered politics at such a young age that the centripetal force of power kept pulling him towards the inner circle, never relinquishing the attraction power exerted on him. Forced into intellectual and political introspection, he achieved neither internal satisfaction nor peace. He never fully developed a new paradigm and thus could not establish a platform. He remained unsatisfied and unfulfilled. Between his dissatisfaction with the ideological options he had and his struggles to break through the established political structure to regain some area of control, he never managed to free himself enough to become innovative. That would have entailed detaching himself from all frameworks, and facing the terror of the unknown that comes with such a step when there is no specific paradigm to ground oneself. He would have had to retain some reference or central idea to build upon, but Aliphas did not find the organizing principle necessary for selective retaining and discarding.

He continued to work for Zionist organizations, befriending local intellectuals and politicians such as deputies or senators of the government, extending the support that Israel needed in organizations such as Friends of the Histadrut; nevertheless, his work remained on the periphery of the power structure.

Aliphas's initial enormous contribution to the Jewish community gave him a prominence that he could not sustain in his second stage. His superimposing of what to some seemed to be contradictory meanings, and the unelaborated linkage of conceptions such as socialism, traditionalism, and orthodoxy, caused some to view him as a man of paradoxes, conflicting loyalties, and changing commitments.

The loss of prestige he experienced allowed him to empathize with Abraham Golomb, the pedagogue and director of the Yidishe Shule, with whom he developed a close friendship in later years. What began as a collaborative relationship (they both wrote for *Fraindt*) later evolved into a more personal friendship. There was an underlayer of experience that unconsciously joined them, even though they came from different ideological directions. Both Golomb and Aliphas separated from their networks, though to a different degree and over different issues. This made for a common background that linked them and provided a basis for mutual psychological support. What linked them was a shared conviction that diaspora Judaism needed its own perspective. After all, for different reasons and in different ways, both experienced the reality of diaspora as a condition in need of protection. Golomb expressed this intellectually, while Aliphas arrived at this through experience and his slowly evolving search for a solution from among the existing ideologies to the specific problematics of diaspora Jews. For Aliphas, the intellectual wandering within Zionism was the unexpected consequence of a personal voyage that put him in diaspora rather than in Israel. For Golomb, it was a conscious stand; starting first as a principled fight against the obliteration of diaspora culture in Israel, it developed into a fight from diaspora for diaspora. Both Aliphas's struggle and Golomb's fight were on behalf of the authentic, semiautonomous condition of diaspora Jewry, which, as Golomb suggested, implied a larger and more complex panorama for the content of Judaism for all Jews.

Aliphas's changes reflected his ideological disenchantments and his personal quest for power. However, his changing views cannot be seen as an attempt to establish only a political platform. His was a significant voice that perceived certain limitations, incongruities, and problems deriving from Zionist ideology for Jews remaining in diaspora. His inability to reach a more systematic affirmation of his thought, and a more comfortable position for himself, placed a burden on his listeners. However, he often projected his condition, and saw it as a limitation of the capacity of others to follow him. Although he saw himself as being on the offensive, he was mostly in a defensive position justifying his own changes.[87] He opened the door to reflection, but could not walk through it. Whether he needed greater philosophical grounding or some other type of knowledge or cognitive skill is impossible to assess. He became dissatisfied with Jewish secular thinking and action. The emptiness and distance he perceived in youth continued to gnaw and maintain the unanswered questions: Will the link continue? Will a connectedness of values, culture, and language help us to survive? What will happen if we do not have these links between diaspora Jews and Israel?

He hoped to find the answer in Zionism, tradition, and language. His unequivocal commitment was to Jewish continuity and Israel. He had imprinted and implemented part of his early ideas upon the communal structure; however, the structure he helped build did not prevent the increasing alienation of many, and of youth specifically. Later generations were an indictment of his beliefs: no Yiddish, but also no Hebrew; no common political aspirations; dwindling shared cultural values. Old political issues had been discarded, and no new ones had been articulated. In the 1970s, he was not effective in reconnecting with youth; however, he could not stop wondering about them, and never stopped, it seems, hoping for them.

THE IDEOLOGY OF THE OUTSIDER:
IDEOLOGUE, WRITER, AND PEDAGOGUE
ABRAHAM GOLOMB

Abraham Golomb (1888–1982) arrived in Mexico in 1944, at a later stage of communal life, when the community had a shape, a variety of organizations, and was well into the process of institutionalization. There were clearly defined groups of diverse ideologies and positions. Golomb, a very well known and highly regarded pedagogue, was invited to head the Yidishe Shule. He had experience in Lithuania, Israel, and Canada in educating youth and teachers, and had written extensively about pedagogy, as well as specific manuals on biology, natural science, geography, and psychology (1918, 1919, 1922–24),[88] and of course on his own philosophical/ideological position, which he labeled "Integral Judaism" (Integrale Yidishkait).

Golomb defies categorization, belonging to a category of his own. He was a philosopher of Jewish survival, and was an ideologue par excellence who represented himself only. He had his own elaborated thought and an agenda, and at different moments in time and in different locations he had followers to whom he related as disciples. He was the spokesman for what he would have wanted: a movement.

Golomb, contrary to other immigrants, did not arrive in Mexico with the need to redefine and reorganize his identity. This was all a process he had worked out for himself in his early youth. His orthodox upbringing and training in the Rameiles Yeshiva had offered him an education in traditional sources in which he was steeped; although he was not orthodox, this source always provided an active frame of reference for him. He had visited Palestine before World War I. He had worked in Vilna in a teacher's seminary, which he had to leave because of the anti-Semitic climate of the Polish government. A specific incident triggered his departure. While he was director of a school in Poland, in the anticommunist mood, the government had asked him to identify the communist students. Even though he was not himself a communist, Golomb was a man of conviction and he refused to cooperate. He then feared persecution, and left for Palestine in 1922. He had thought of going to the United States, but there, the Bund had identified him as a "protector of communists," and no jobs were going to be open for him. While in Palestine, he also had trouble finding a job. He taught biology, agronomy, and botany at an agricultural school in Mikve Israel. Later, he worked in Kfar Hanoar–Ben Shemen, the school that was to give him the visibility to be promoted to a top educational position. However, his ideology clashed with the Israeli one.

The period in Palestine was to have a dramatic influence on Golomb; it strengthened the vehemence and integrity with which he defended his thought. Palestine was then in the midst of an extreme anti-Yiddish period, when the languages and its speakers were in constant collision and Yiddishists were literally persecuted and physically attacked in cinemas, on the streets, and elsewhere.[89] This experience of self-hatred that Golomb called "internal anti-Semitism," and the widespread feelings of contempt and scorn for Yiddish and diaspora culture, made him react and protest in an article entitled "Ego-fobie bai Yidn" (Jewish Self-Hatred). He protested against the detachment from one's roots and the dishonoring of Yiddish in Palestine, which he felt stemmed from a blind desire to build links to the geographic area. For Golomb, the Zionists wanted to forget the diaspora and create a new identity. The "new" Hebrew, he claimed, spoken to resemble Arabic phonetics and linked selectively and exclusively to the Biblical period of Jewish history, was symbolic of the ideological and political structures that were being imposed by the few on the many. In his own endeavors, Golomb saw every new opportunity to establish his thought as a fight against what he felt was cultural doom. He therefore protested as the prophets had done long before him. If he was "prophetic," it was because he saw parts of reality to which his generation was blind.

Golomb's Palestinian sojourn represented both the opportunity to occupy a high educational rung and a painful encounter with strong criticism amidst a hostile reality created by Jews against Jews. Once he became a controversial figure in Eretz Israel and found his work confined, he left for Canada in 1938. His handling of these two periods and incidents, in Vilna and Palestine, attests to the firm convictions of his principles.

Golomb's first public speech in Mexico was also the community's first physical encounter with him. Golomb introduced some of his basic notions around which he had developed his conceptual framework of "Integral Judaism."[90] He presented a simpler version of the difference between "Galut, Goleh, and Geulah"—Diaspora, Elevation, and Redemption.[91] He saw all diasporas as negative and explained how Jews had to cope with all aspects of them: political, economic, physical, territorial, juridical, and spiritual. Although he trusted the Zionist attempt to end the political diaspora, he felt the other types were not to be ended or eradicated by that step. For Golomb, the most lethal and most dangerous diaspora was the spiritual diaspora. Neither land nor territory nor juridical "redemption" could alone sustain the people of Israel, he thought. The people of Israel must retake all their culture and way of life, including the more than one thousand years of Talmudically realized shtetl life, and continue to *live* as Jews. He thought that to save oneself from all diasporas, one must guard especially against spiritual diaspora because its devastating effect could be permanent, could happen everywhere, and could destroy without solution.

Golomb did not remain an orthodox Jew. He was secularized in much of his style and education. He was aristocratic by temperament. While fairly young, he constructed a new intellectual synthesis for himself which he thoroughly lived and preached. Golomb commanded respect by his sheer erudition. His knowledge of the Jewish sources, the Bible, the Talmud, Hebrew, Yiddish, traditions, and folklore was impressive. However, the respect and prestige he commanded were conditioned by the uneasy reaction his image and self-definition imposed. Many felt his ideas constituted a demand. When he arrived in Mexico to head the Yidishe Shule and confronted his new audience, he offered not only his pedagogy but also a unique vision of Judaism as a lifestyle. The scope of what he sought to influence made many uncomfortable in the beginning; later, it motivated some to withdraw their endorsement.

This metaphysical understanding of diaspora and the strong urge to retake all Jewish culture, tradition, and religious elements were to Golomb the source of "redemption." The public and writers reacted. Golomb's language sounded familiar, but strange: he was a prophet in a secular world. The words were recognizable but his meaning was obscure. His erudition was known, noticed, and respected by all; so was his intellectual stature. But the content of his work was puzzling. What did he want? Did he come to educate the children or the parents?[92] Was he religious, but not orthodox; was he a Yiddishist, but one who also accepted Hebrew and felt that Jews were losing both?[93] Was he rejecting Jewish hope in Zionism as an absolute and total solution? Was he criticizing all those socialist-communist Jews who fought for changes in their local host societies and in that way were hoping to redeem Jews also? Golomb knew that his position defied categorization. He wrote, campaigned, and worked for it all his life.

"Who am I?" he asked: In Russia, a revolutionary; for the communists, a counterrevolutionary. In Poland, he claimed, Bundists saw him as a communist, and communists saw him as a Bundist; some Zionists hated his socialism, while socialists hated his Zionism. To religious people, he was an agnostic; and the left seemed disturbed by his religious inclinations. Yiddishists in Poland did not recognize him as one of them; in Israel, people saw him as an anti-Hebraist. In Mexico people would want to see his "passport" to know to which "Rebbe" (Hassidic house) he was affiliated.[94] But he was affiliated to none. His extensive and impressive knowledge made his arguments compelling. In Mexico, groups of different persuasions could follow him if they found common elements they could attach themselves to. For some it was his Yiddishism. For others, it was his respect for Jewish tradition and values. Zionists could also, from time to time, follow him because of his knowledge of and connection to Hebrew.

Few understood Golomb in his totality. Whenever his synthesis of thought was translated into behavior and practical life, conflicts surfaced. His broad-ranging approach, which appeared as a redeeming quality at first, became a weakness when translated into practical behavior. The salient quality which had rallied Zionists in his support would suddenly be seen as secondary, because it was overshadowed by another tenet, or treated equally with yet another point (as in the case of Hebrew and Yiddish). Groups were thus confused in their support for him, and could easily turn antagonistic towards Golomb. Not many grasped, liked, or were ready to attempt to practice his programmatic return to a full "Jewish style." Not many were ready to undertake and sustain his demands for Jewish consciousness. Golomb was many things, but he was neither a pragmatist nor a politician. He had no ability or desire to conciliate and negotiate, certainly not on his principles. His thinking had been rationally worked out in many words over many years of intensive work. Nothing was subject to accommodation.

There is little doubt that Golomb was an innovator and was initially welcomed and accepted by all positions because the social structure had a degree of flexibility which allowed for charismatic innovation.[95] The different "coalitions" that he managed to form facilitated the incorporating of some of his thought, until eventually part of it became institutionalized. But only "part" of his thought was accepted. He did not feel satisfied, and could not yield. His philosophy could not, according to him, be dealt with fractionally. It was an organically integrated ideology whose success depended on its total acceptance. Golomb's supporters often turned out to be "partial supporters." Few espoused his entire approach; each group found in his thought some affinity to adopt temporarily. But his demanding and strong personality and his inflexible position vis-à-vis his followers soon alienated him from most of them. His work in the Jewish schools in Mexico marks a stormy period in the history of the community. Every personality disagreement between him and others included some shifting of alliances.[96] His position got increasingly weaker and shakier, and he was forced to leave one job after another; finally, he left the country.

In his many books and articles, Golomb analyzed the effects of general urbanization on the survival of the Jewish communities in the world.[97] He pointed out that the diaspora into which Jews had been forced had changed qualitatively: what had been a "collective diaspora" had become an "individual" one. The age-long "external humiliation" of which Jews were a target had been transformed into an "internal humiliation";[98] in the diaspora, Jews were not only estranged from their land but also (and more importantly, claimed Golomb) from themselves, their culture, their values, and their language. Until recently, he claimed, Jews had lived as a collectivity, and collectively they absorbed their surrounding culture, making it into their own. Aramaic, the language in which so much of Jewish prayer and text is written, was not just the language of the surrounding or domineering culture. This culture and language, Golomb suggested, was adopted and owned by Jewish culture, perhaps differing from the Aramaic of the people they took it from. Medieval sources refer to it as "corrupt Hebrew," already unable to distinguish it as a foreign language.

The diaspora, said Golomb, began only when one "exchanged cultures," not when one incorporated them.[99] These were the exceptional cases of Aramaic and Yiddish. When Vilna in the nineteenth and twentieth century until World War II was known as "Yerushalaim D'Lite"—the Jerusalem of Lithuania—the description was justified, he claimed. Jews lived with Poles, Lithuanians, and White Russians, and no hegemony was imposed upon them. Jews created within their own cultural terms, said Golomb. This, of course, did not happen for Jews in Poland or Italy,[100] who could not call their country Jerusalem. There the process of urbanization, coupled with the loss of "culture," including religion and language, resulted in the loss of the necessary distinctiveness and the inability to maintain one's folkish individuality. "Why do Jews speak in a foreign language to their God? . . . Why do the Jews take on foreign names? Foreign forms of behavior?"[101] asked Golomb. In the diasporas in Europe and America, most Jews had done what they should not have: traded cultures.

But urbanization also brought the loss of the folk essence, the collective spirit or style in which Jewish lifestyles were established.[102] Golomb's Judaism was not an inflexible culture. Golomb suggested that rabbinic interpretation was really folk interpretation which became part of rabbinical commentary. The historical loss of Jewish government, of centralized leadership, of an organized polity, made Judaism an individualized responsibility,[103] though it did not lose the quality of guidance that came from the Jewish collectivity. Therefore, the task should not be simply to concentrate on the "biblical" period as the Zionists did, or only on other selective sacred texts as more orthodox groups did, or live as a self-defined Jew independent of the group.

The task, as he saw it, was to recapture and fix as much as possible on the "all" of it, emphasizing the already long-materialized Talmudic life of the European Jewish experience which had not yet been captured into texts. After all, cultural forms take a long time to gestate and transform, and not all of the later cultural production of European Jewry had been codified. That which Jewish life already lost, according to Golomb, was the link needed to maintain the historic cultural chain of Judaism to insure its survival.[104] The lost treasure of that way of life, a thousand years of practice, had to be retained and regained, since that was the practical life that resulted from a millennium of collective history. To attempt to adopt aspects of Judaism selectively and not historically was to Golomb a false and futile exercise.

To justify his analysis and his methodology, Golomb referred constantly to the historical-philosophical principles that Jews used in order to be able to sustain themselves as Jews. He used the Bible, Talmud, Hagadah—whatever source legitimized his point. He traced assimilation as a process from the very first Jews (only Isaac remains within the group, Ishmael goes; Yehuda stays and Israel goes; the Pharisees remain central and the Sadducees become peripheral; Babilonia remains and Alexandria goes; Ashkenaz remains central and Sefarad became marginal).[105] Each historical case showed Golomb the choices made: between staying within the boundary of the group and dealing with the distinctiveness of the ethnic-religious-national culture-group, or rejecting it for an unclear biculturalism that eventually failed to link itself to the core of Jewish culture and almost always got lost despite the best intentions of many of these actors and their generations. To Golomb, the choice in modern terms was to become a person of the "Mosaic religion" or to be a "Jew." Jews have retained, as other religions have, said Golomb, "Yirat Shamaim" (fear of God), but they have lost all "Ahavat Yisroel" (Love for Israel, for what Jews are, do, and think).[106] Secularization makes Jews "other-directed" and alienated from themselves and their own organic cultural wholeness. If Jews were conducting diverse battles in this world, they should never forget the most important one, the only one that could sustain them: their spirituality. Therefore, Golomb felt, diasporas have to be fought against; the essential path to be followed is spiritual, and not just physical redemption. He recognized the political, economic, and cultural dependency between Israel and other Jewish communities. But mutual help and attention do not ensure the survival of both entities. Added to the problems and limitations of these routine linkages, it becomes imperative, if Judaism and Jews are to survive, to sustain a total Judaism in which each Jew has to work to include all of the Jewishness that has been left out. Only then could one expect continuity. The affirmation Golomb wanted had to come from within Jewish life and thought, not just sentiment; only then could Jews join with the outer world. Without this positive attitude, he felt, there was no hope for Jews as a group.

Golomb's arrival in Mexico occurred well after Glantz and Kahan had expressed their integration objectives for Jews in Mexico. Although there was no direct dialogue with them, Golomb was speaking against any such position and its followers. Golomb's position was a polemic against those early promoters of cultural integration, and it is not an accident that with Golomb the old argument would be renewed in a different form. Here was an offensive that nobody had launched before. More than that, Golomb was attacking any intermediate position that Jews in Mexico had taken, especially those who actively detached themselves from parts of their original culture, language, and religion, retaining some selected aspects of these together with Jewish social relationships in the belief that this sufficed to insure continuity.

Golomb also attacked Bundists, communists, Zionists, passivists, ignorance, and benightedness. In his attack Golomb uncovered the inconsistencies of most positions, ideologies, or Jewish lifestyles. He was difficult to listen to; he was unsettling; he was critical. The reaction to his first public speech was to remain typical. Was he a pessimist or an optimist? Who was he, and what was he for, was not clear to the audience. He defined the life of most Jews as in a *Galut*—a diaspora—in a psychological, not a geographical sense. It was because they were "other-directed" that the diaspora had followed. He defined *Geula*—redemption—as linked to Zion, but wanted it linked to all Jewish culture. Was this a religious hope, a cultural hope, or a political one? a writer asked,[107] voicing the concern of the others. Golomb's fight was aimed at the ingrained way of life and behaviors that the Jews had adhered to by now unconsciously, long before. The desire to adapt and integrate and be at peace, which the Enlightenment had offered as a possibility, was too strong.

Golomb was a man who trod his own path. He looked ahead and went forward, but turned constantly back to his roots, his past, his Jewish sources. And "pasts" were the issue. Being a product of secularization himself, he knew Talmudic Judaism alone could no longer retain the majority of Jews. Only the "Jewish way of life" that was immersed in those old pasts, varied and connected, and had evolved into a living culture could promote continuity and guide the future. The Jewish community in Mexico felt his magnetic presence and he undoubtedly left a profound mark on its educational institutions.[108] But his total definition of Jewishness did not take root. His was an exaltation of all Jewish styles as a way to sustain Jewish tradition, history, and culture in the form of an internal code of folk ethics over and above any immediate situation. The community, however, seemed too removed from that kind of social transcendence.

## CONCLUDING REMARKS

Kahan and Glantz, the early immigrants and the first ones to articulate ideological goals for the community, concentrated on the need to justify their newness in Mexico by stressing their newly acquired hyphen. They felt that it was up to them to develop the new elaborations necessary to define their condition. For them, the language and consciousness of integration had raised to the fore their being strangers while it eroded the common language of continuity between them and the next generation. The problem in its complexity was left unaddressed while communists, who elaborated on the agenda of world-change, took over the dialogue. Eventually, communist inability to keep in touch with the immediate problems and solutions of Jews—internationally with Israel, and locally within the community—rendered them voiceless to the community. Their response, though their numbers as a group had been inversely proportional to the strength and attention they commanded, was retreat. In hoping to change the world system, the community felt they did not address the immediate issues of belongingness, continuity, and survival.

Bundists, as well as socialists of loose affiliations, took over the logical extension of the integrationist position, though in Mexico they remained very active in the cultural institutions of the community as well. This helped strengthen the communal cultural organizations, but it also masked the inappropriateness of the conceptualization they used in their relationship with the majority. In other words, their condition of belongingness was not analyzed but only desired. Taking place in the backdrop of World War II, their own solutions seemed to fall even before they fully took root. Visibly interested in Mexico's problems, Bundists attempted to find the common problems between minority and majority so that "issues," the "class," and the "ideology" could unite the otherwise diverse minority-majority.

In this context, Feldman came to represent the absolute pragmatic politician, the negotiator par excellence. Maintaining himself outside of the ideological fray, he acted upon the daily connections and interrelations between Jews in Mexico and Israel and Jews in Mexico and Mexicans. There was never an overarching ideology, but rather daily responses to the specifics of Jewish life. Each time there was a crisis, pragmatic answers were developed.

Aliphas, our prototype of the left-Zionists, is the first figure to experience in a more or less conscious fashion the specific crisis we here analyze. His was a life wracked by the dilemma of belongingness. The problem became complex as the fact of the new Jewish state of Israel was factored into his thinking and feeling. He always remained at the crossroads. Maintaining clear and strong linkages with Israel, Aliphas experienced the limitations that were imposed on a diasporic community as it imported and submitted to the direct ideological perspectives of Israel. The fact that these did not address nor cope with the multiplicity of experiences and needs of the diaspora was somehow recognized by Aliphas. But he could not provide a different worldview. He lived his consciousness as an internal tortuosity and turmoil. Being symbolically one of the first to experience this crisis, he remained unable to grasp it.

Golomb is paradigmatic of the sharpest, most elaborate, and most open challenge offered. According to him, Jews had misunderstood the problems of internal control, plurality, and continuity of Jewish culture. Because of his personal fight against the Jewish internal control of thought, culture, and identity, and because he never attached himself to a specific diaspora to attempt an explicit reconceptualization of the relationship between minority and majority, he waged a lonely fight that did not become victorious. He remained not only misunderstood within the community, but unable to address and articulate ideas on multicultural living. That, of course, is still one of the most pressing problems around the world today.

If these political solutions were the alternate responses of this diaspora, the community was the experimental ground in which they all confronted each other. Allowed to live in Mexico as individual Jews and tolerated with benign neglect as a minority, Jews themselves were from the 1950s and even now unable to address their condition ideologically. By adopting as general ideology narrow solutions that only partially addressed their conditions, Jews in Mexico ended up barring much of their ability for collective self-reflection.

The Mexican government offered in 1994, for the first time, recognition of its minorities. It remains to be seen whether this new change from the host society will produce a new political accommodation on both groups.

# PART 3

# CHAPTER 4

# *Confrontations That Produced Structural Changes: Five Case Studies*

Each day with our own hands, we make something other than
what we believe we are making, and History backfiring, makes us
other than what we believe ourselves to be or to become.

—Sartre

Ashkenazim in Mexico were undoubtedly fortunate in having been welcomed
by Syrian Jews who helped them to settle and find their way in the new society. The help from the B'nai-B'rith[1] and from HIAS (Hebrew Immigration
Association) was also important. However, what marks the development of
the Ashkenazi communal structure is precisely their break with these sources
of support, help, and direction. This early breaking away and finding of their
own direction was a central characteristic of their structural development.

The account of the evolution of this community is presented in this
chapter by following the various conflicts, confrontations, and breaks
among groups in the community. This section focuses on five specific
cases of conflict that highlight and clarify the specific character and content of the institutionalized life the community was to take on.

In the early 1920s, Ashkenazi communal expansion was partly motivated by what the actors themselves felt and wanted to solve: "not knowing the language of the country, not having access to the local press; [feel-
ing that] the life of the people in whose midst we find ourselves is foreign,
incomprehensible; the same seems true of the meaning and functions of
political and economic life [here]; they are all hidden to us." The changes
that occurred were in part a distinctive *willed social process*. The changes
in the community's organization were to a large degree directed shifts
fought out by contending groups which wanted to establish their own definition of the situation. The outcomes, while "willed," were always both
much more and much less than expected.

The five selected case studies of internal group conflict, and the structural changes that occurred as they were debated and resolved, are: (1) the
process of consolidation and organizational control resulting in the creation of the "Central Committee"; (2) the definition of ideological bound-

aries and political control as fought among communists, Bundists, and Zionists; (3) educational conflicts that aimed at the control of the younger generations; (4) the conflict over language as the reconquering of the control of culture; and (5) by focusing on the politics of interrelation between minority and government and defining the structural condition of the minority as an "incomplete-allowance," these external limitations show themselves affecting the inner life of the group too.

## THE PROCESS OF CONSOLIDATION (THE FIRST EXPERIMENT): THE CREATION OF THE CENTRAL COMMITTEE

The creation of the Central Committee represents the first formal, though experimental, formation of a central political power-center aiming to protect the community from outside threats as well as directing its internal affairs. This attempt must be seen as a social response, with the context of anti-Semitism as the crucial galvanizing force. Some linked the external problems, which were clearly the most important, to the existing internal disorganization of the community. The Central Committee was therefore seen as a mechanism to handle coherently both external and internal issues. It was a reaction to the perceived need for antidefamation activity, as well as an opportunity to centralize power. Responding to these issues, the community became a legitimizing force that either supported or restrained the efforts of the leadership. However, not even the need for protection from external threats was enough of an incentive to allow any organization, in this case the Central Committee, total internal control of the community. Control meant limits on possible action, thought, and lifestyles, and no faction was ready to give up the opportunity it had then, in Mexico, to experiment with its version of Jewish identity.

As the more socialist-minded European immigrants decided to withdraw and form new organizations more attuned to their needs, organizations mushroomed. The repetitiveness and ineffectiveness of the activities of some of these organizations created enough dissatisfaction to give rise to the idea of an umbrella organization in the late 1930s.[2] At the same time, much of what was happening in the country made Jews uneasy about their situation and future; thus, the desire to coordinate internally coincided with the need to create a united front to protect the community.[3] But the theoretical distinction between an umbrella organization or a supraorganizational apparatus, or a federation of organizations in which each member group would subordinate its power to a central authority, was not clear in the communal dialogue. Anything to do with the idea of "centralization," though deemed necessary for coordination and efficiency, brought to the fore the fact that the move implied political subordination and the relinquishing of power for some. This trade-off was acceptable only when outside threats seemed greater than any loss of autonomy.

One threat was the rising xenophobia that Mexico experienced in the early 1920s, when an oil boom attracted many foreigners to the north, especially to Tampico and the surrounding oil areas. Immigrants were seen as displacing the local workers, and protests against foreigners were often voiced. Several organizations against foreigners were founded.[4] The Liga Nacionalista Antichina y Antijudía, the Comité Pro-Raza, the Unión de Pequeños Comerciantes, and the Unión Nacionalista Mexicana all reacted mainly against foreign labor in the country. Though each organization had a different agenda, and some were *anti* specific groups while others were *pro* Mexicans, the social pressures of the time permitted direct and open xenophobic content to flourish. The most virulent racism was aimed at the Chinese in the states of Sonora, Sinaloa, and Nayarit. It reached the point at which the government approved laws establishing ghettos for the Chinese and prohibited marriages and consensual unions of mixed races.[5]

Jews were charged with taking jobs from local workers, an accusation that made Jews feel insecure. The national press published many articles addressing this underlying theme. Jews were portrayed as expendable, though not once were they portrayed as having a negative effect on the troubled economy. No matter how long they had been in the country, Jews were always described as transients, or temporary residents. With the depression of 1929, Mexico's economic problems became even more acute, and the reaction against foreigners and Jews became stronger. Jews were portrayed as "nomadic tribes, collecting wealth, creating a kingdom in each kingdom. Their language is a mixture [of many] and as a result, of lower quality . . . ; [Jews] never want to assimilate, they never like the earth . . . [they have] no interest in agriculture."[6]

The world economic crisis and its aftereffects throughout the early 1930s were accompanied in Mexico by changes in the newly solidifying political system. The regime had plenty of internal and external critics, and antigovernment positions were easily linked with anti-Jewish sentiment. The Sinarquista movement of the right strongly criticized the agrarian policies of the government, the low levels of productivity, and the collectivization of the agricultural sector. Any suggestion of "class conflict" meant that the government was fostering hatred and jealousy between the groups. The Sinarquistas wanted to further the values of order and religious and nationalist spirit. It is easy to see why they sympathized with German and anticommunist ideas; they thus took advantage of the antiforeign atmosphere to give voice to bigotry and anti-Semitism while aiming at the government.[7] The ideology became attractive to some groups of peasants, Catholic extremists, and groups with fascist tendencies. They warned against "racial degeneration" and "the communist Jewish infiltration," and promoted the "expulsion of foreigners from the national economy."[8] Their rhetoric echoed that of others; the different political movements, for different and even conflicting reasons, seized the climate and used the antiforeign, anti-Jewish discourse to further their own purposes.

Anti-Jewish demonstrations were staged in many states of the republic; however, they had great impact and visibility in the capital.[9] The Catholic hierarchy in the country supported antigovernment and anti-Jewish protests through the Cristero movement, which had stirred up bigoted opinions by suggesting that the country rid itself of "Russian, Jewish and Chinese colonizers" to avoid "the decatholization of the country."[10]

The Jewish community was scared. The defenses they often printed in their press were not sufficient to minimize the danger or control the fear. Because of the amount of negative material in the press,[11] they did not know if the government was indirectly supporting these groups, although the prevailing feeling was that the government was not involved. There is no evidence of the government supporting these antisemitic protests,[12] although there is consensus that the government took too long in publicly opposing these public incidents. It is more difficult to clear the local state governments and the police structure, which appeared to sympathize, at least occasionally, with the message of these movements.[13]

Within this climate, communal political insecurity flourished. One limited solution, as the community saw it, was to close ranks, setting aside any issues that had divided them until then. The Tzentral Komitet (Central Committee) was formed in 1938–39 with a sense of urgency and sufficiently strong backing of all subcommunities to take upon itself the role of mediator and protector of the community and the public Jewish image.[14] It is not clear how much protection the Central Committee actually offered, or whether it simply made the community feel protected. In the process of organization and coordination, the Central Committee also attempted to organize the community internally, a move which presumably would increase its strength and its ability to withstand the opposing forces.

The first step towards centralization was to coordinate the major economic activities of the community. To support any organization, its constituents had to produce or collect special funds. The needs for funds varied by organization according to its objective and its popularity. A welfare fund needed different sums of money than a journal, for instance. Funds were always collected to help other Jews; depending on the philosophy of the group, the help concentrated either on local Jews, European Jews, or Jews in Palestine. Behind the monetary goals that each organization might have had was of course the immediate power that such a direct resource offered that organization. Whoever commanded the most resources would also have the strongest weight in directing the internal life of the community. Thus, when an attempt was made to merge the yearly collection of funds, one goal was to control the allocation of monies among the political groups of the community. However, after two relatively successful collections and an attempt to balance conflicting forces, the economic coalition broke down. Zionists wanted control over the money; the Bundists were unhappy with the equal division of funds and claimed their perspective justified a different allocation; each felt its principles had been compromised and its potential limited. The Central Committee then had to limit its activities to the external concerns of the community vis-à-vis the host society.

Without having failed or succeeded, but just lingering as a limited organization, the Central Committee was reactivated during the latter years of World War II. Once again, the increased awareness of an external threat and the growing vulnerability of the community's condition was the catalyst for the move. With Nazi propaganda being distributed locally, the loss of European Jewry seemed to some a more salient issue on which to focus. This time, too, external and local issues were linked, but the extermination of Jews in Europe defied interpretation. Some of the more sensitive minds searched for channels through which protests could be directed. First, they protested against the apparent normalcy with which Jews in Mexico seemed to continue to conduct their lives. Once more accurate information about the mass murders became available, an attempt was made to press the Mexican governing elite into protesting the situation. Tuvie Maizel's efforts in staging national and international protests, linked through the organized labor bodies, were part of these efforts. However, the Central Committee as an organization was tentative and cautious, and lacked connections to lobby for its cause.

It was left to individuals to raise issues and attempt changes. Intermittently, articles expressing outrage would appear, indicting Jewish behavior that offended a sense of propriety. Indirectly, some condemned the lack of public indignation towards the local official political posture: "refugees [are] searching for places to go. For us, it's as if nothing has changed. What can we do? . . . We go on, we do not tear the garment, we do not stop the parties. . . . Why are we so quietly sitting at home, so empty of ideas."[15] And again: "1942 was a year of tremendous catastrophe, physical, moral . . . but has this had an effect on our moral standing?"[16]

Yet the war created an economic "boom" in Mexico. As U.S. industry shifted towards the production of war material, Mexico instituted a policy of import substitution. The manufacturing sector expanded to fill the vacuum left by the decline in American products. This generally benefited the middle classes in the country, including Jews of that class. That, together with the lack of organized communal behavior, seemed to some the reason for Jewish placidity.[17] B. T. Goldberg, son-in-law of the famous Yiddish writer Sholem Aleichem and a well-known journalist in his own right, wrote a public letter to Jews in Mexico reminding them of their "incongruous behavior," and anticipating a further reaction it could trigger from the host society: "if you can be, [as you have been], labeled 'parasites,' you can soon be called 'foreign parasites'; and as false as the parasite adjective may be, it will be covered and forgotten by the truth of the word 'foreign.'"[18] Goldberg's comments were not welcomed. Who was he to criticize the Jewish way of life in Mexico or their benefiting from the general economic advantages of the country? Why suggest that only Jews and that all Jews were benefiting? Why suggest that the host society would reject them specifically? Was he less of a "foreigner" in the United States than they were in Mexico? However provocative, his comments had limited impact. The debate that could have been aroused in Mexico did not take place, and the exchange died down. More important, the idea of foreignness was not challenged at its base; after all, these Jews were citizens, as were the Jews in America. However, the perception of their not belonging to the society was so ingrained that antidefamation, defense, and fear persisted and oriented the Jews' actions.

The Central Committee's specific agenda was not clear, but nobody suggested it could be dismantled as an organization. On external issues, it acted defensively. Nobody suggested attempting to redirect government policy. No public attempts were made to force the government to assume a greater responsibility for the plight of European Jews.

Maizel the Bundist, who was attached to the Central Committee temporarily, coordinated a protest with local workers. This public act was more the result of private ideological efforts among leaders than a stance reflecting social consciousness. The protest was supported by the Bund and the Pro Soviet Union League in Mexico, and won the official sponsorship of the PRN (the National Revolutionary Party), CTM (Confederation of Mexican Workers), CNC (National Peasant Confederation), the teachers' union, the electricians' union, and Spanish antifascist refugees, among others.[19] Nevertheless, much of what appeared to be government support was only symbolic, in contrast to the very explicit and articulate support the politician Vicente Lombardo Toledano offered, for example. Toledano, the leader of the organized worker's movement in Mexico and a sympathizer of the Soviet Union, had offered explicit and open support to Jews and the rejection of prejudice and anti-Semitism.[20] Further, he called attention to what he called the "shared sensibilities of pain and martyrdom" of the two people, Mexicans and Jews, which should orient them into searching for "culture and justice." But Toledano's position was not that of the general government and political elite, nor were his sensibilities the generalized sensibilities of the Mexican people.

Discussions were held to help refugees from Austria and Germany. However, occasional displays of support in the context of an unmoved government meant little locally and almost nothing to European Jews. As Chaim Weizman said in a New York public address: "At this moment, expressions of sympathy without accompanying attempts to launch acts of rescue, [become] hollow mockery in the ears of the dying."[21] The government of Mexico had not changed its detached posture since 1938. In the refugee conference of Evian-Les-Bains, sponsored by President Roosevelt with the attendance of thirty-eight governments, nothing was done for these people. Mexico, together with other Latin American countries, rejected the idea of changing immigration policy to help the Jews.[22] With the adoption of a policy prohibiting immigration to Palestine and the Jewish inability to redress it, the failure of Evian, and the imminent developments of the war itself, the fate of the Jews was sealed.

In Mexico, Lázaro Cárdenas and his policy of nationalizing foreign oil companies created a rift with the U.S. government. The criticism that Mexico faced did not predispose the government to further cooperation with the United States, but rather left it taking a "cold" posture towards its northern neighbor and its initiatives.[23] This was yet another issue in which Mexico tried to establish its independence vis-à-vis the United States. Therefore, the position adopted by the Mexican government on the immigration issue seems, as some analysts suggest, more a response to United States–Mexican relations of the time rather than anything else. Yet, even if such a logic did play a part in the Mexican government's decision on Jewish immigration, one cannot dismiss the fact that there were plenty of governmental officials who justified the government's decision in terms of what they saw as the difficult Mexican economic situation: "the government must observe extreme scrupulosity in the admission of foreigners that in general, do not mix neither spiritually, nor economically, nor consanguineously with our race."[24] In the midst of all this, the Central Committee's activity was tentative rather than assertive, argumentative, or aggressive in exerting pressure on the government to change its policy.

After the war, the activity of the Central Committee seemed less pressing. However, in the later part of the 1940s, before and during the strong Zionist work towards the creation of a Jewish state, when the Central Committee attempted again to coordinate the internal affairs of the community, the different political factions again voiced their opposition to a centralized power center. The Bund felt it to be "too Zionistic," while the Zionists felt it too neutral. Rather than pressing for an elaboration of the internal policy stance of the organization, each political group responded by either removing or changing delegates, weakening the efficiency, centrality, potential authority, and power of the committee.

The threat of the outside world pressed the community to centralize itself, creating the antidefamation center that was the Central Committee. But, once the local tensions eased, the community focused on world Jewish events. In this area, there was not yet a firm consensus, though there had been occasional attempts to craft a unifying position. In fact, two forces were at play: while the need to unite was understood almost viscerally, conflicts surfaced as each group interpreted the situation differently. The diverse modes of understanding and responding to what was happening clearly helped to underscore the differences among the groups.

The Central Committee represented a new path in the process of creating a structure for the Jewish community in Mexico. It was, without doubt, the forerunner of the Kehillah. In specific terms, however, and given the Mexican context, it achieved little for European Jews and contributed very little towards the process of self-definition while assuming the role of representative of Jews in Mexico. It did not have enough influence on the host to define and change its relationship with the minority. This is no small thing: it demands an extraordinary capacity of both minority and majority for the minority to redefine its condition, and the majority to open up the space it is offering. Such a change would require a change of the general definition of the political system of the country as well, to permit a minority—of any type—to have a direct and real possibility of influencing the political system.

The decade of the 1940s and part of the 1950s mark the years during which the sharpest exchanges within the community took place, and in which the most decisive changes occurred. The sifting and sorting of ideas and groups determined who would be acceptable participants in the Kehillah. When ideas and the groups behind them were contested and made unacceptable to the others by the more powerful sections of the community, the contours of power and control were delineated. Certain groups, their proponents, and their ideas were included, while others were barred. Once established, the Kehillah was able to assume power in a process of centralization and control, which occurred only after other organizations and positions were sufficiently weakened and restrained. Only then could institutionalization occur.

The Kehillah, the new organization, became the central controller of the community—as described in part 2—while the Central Committee worked under its shadow. Its agenda had to be, almost by definition, the questioning of the politics of interrelation between minority and majority. Never succeeding in its attempt at control, the Central Committee remained weak. After a decade of maturation of the idea of centrality, with the experience for the community of groups establishing the parameters of acceptable political behavior, something could be expected to change. But it was only after the historical Jewish international context was altered that centrality seemed the most efficient and necessary option for this community internally. The Kehillah was formed in 1956–57. With the new ability to control, the Kehillah extended its control far into the internal decisions of the Central Committee.[25] It was only after the division of labor among them was absolutely established and unquestioned, and after the centrality of the Kehillah could not easily be threatened (1980s), that some independence and separation between the institutions was implicitly worked out.

Even now, the Central Committee has not articulated a position on the interrelations of the community with the host society. Thus the political boundary between the minority and the host society has been neither redefined nor reconceptualized. The work of the Central Committee, though specific, is ad hoc. What remains is a kind of gray area in which Jews find themselves with the political space given to them. Jews are citizens with equal rights and obligations; as a self-defined minority, they seem to be recognized by being allowed to conduct their life from their cultural perspective. But they have not been given nor been able to secure theoretical, intellectual, and judicial space. As a result, any time the government chooses to refer to these groups of citizens as a "minority," and calls them that, an element of insecurity and instability surfaces. While citizens, Jews are also perceived as the "other" (i.e., external to the body politic); their loyalty, their connectedness, and their status are called into question. Jews accept their citizenship, and recognize that as a minority they have dual concerns. An occasional effort is made to suggest that these concerns are not mutually exclusive. But a whole political area remains to be articulated so that the political culture of Mexico and the cultural and religious life of groups that are diverse within that society are viable and complete.

During the decade of the 1980s, the Central Committee's jurisdiction concerned the external contacts of the community and the general society. Though political issues are still its raison d'être, the Central Committee has adopted a philanthropic position towards the general society in the face of earthquakes, tornadoes, and so forth; no other minority seems as driven or as effective in offering this kind of group help when natural catastrophes occur. An aura of elitism surrounds the Central Committee's activities, however, distancing the institution from the everyday activities of the community and of the people in general. It draws into its ranks mostly people for whom the idea and practice of philanthropy are not foreign. It is still directed and financially sustained by the joint efforts of all subcommunities, and it maintains contacts with the political elite of the country in a nonformalized pattern of lobbying that does not follow any preestablished roles and routines. It uses a personal-individual approach towards national politicians and intellectuals in the exercise of "public relations," although the approach is presented as public policy. In other words, public figures are cultivated in the expectation that, if needed, they will show support for the community. Again and again, the feeling of entrusting one's future to others dominates; that, in turn, results in eternal expressions of indebtedness.


## THE IDEOLOGICAL DELIMITATION OF POLITICAL CONTROL: COMMUNISTS, BUNDISTS, AND ZIONISTS

A second case illustrates a different structural development resulting from the power struggles among the three major political positions—Zionist, Bundist, and communist. In this conflict the groups appear as "parties."[26] The three groups were affected, though differently, by the international political scene of the time; similar issues were addressed by their extended political groups. The outcome was determined, though, not so much by the internal merits of each group, but rather by the international events that overwhelmed the existential, material, and ideological resources of these groups.

It is certainly possible to argue that the Mexican political debates of the period provided the context in which communal politics—the Jewish left—could develop. The 1930s in Mexico were a decade of conflict among the various labor unions. Agrarian reform was at the center of the government's agenda. The government encouraged the organization of workers outside the official structure of government itself. Restoration of certain rights—land ownership, for instance—was not simply granted to certain groups but rather was the result of conflict, confrontation, and consolidation.[27] This decade was certainly different from the next, when issues of the left were set aside and the political pendulum of the country moved to the right.

In the meantime, the left had room to work. The Jewish left had a track record in Mexico. In the mid-1930s and 1940s they were perhaps the most vocal of the Jewish groups. Loosely identified, they encompassed socialists, communists, some anarchists, territorialists, and intellectuals with sympathies to socialist issues. Their central focus was examining the activities of the Soviet Union from a Jewish angle. Communists specifically joined the International Communist Party, and had possibly already organized by the 1920s to support the Jewish colonization efforts in Birobidzhan, which began in 1927 in the Soviet Union. Birobidzhan seemed, to those in the Jewish sections of the Communist Party, to constitute an alternative to the Zionist project.[28] The group of Jewish communists was small and was disbanded in 1928, persecuted by President Portes Gil. Most of its original members—communists—were either expelled from the country or sent to "Islas Marías," a prison off the mainland, depending on their national or residential status. During the *maximato* period, as the period from 1928 to 1934 of the presidencies of Emilio Portes Gil, Pascual Ortiz Rubio, and Abelardo L. Rodriguez is called, before the election of President Cárdenas, Mexico had broken off relations with the Soviet Union, and any activities which were defined as subservient to the U.S.S.R. were looked upon as unacceptable and were punished.

The Cárdenas and even the Avila Camacho regimes produced a favorable context for the left.[29] A new Gesbir—Gezelshaft far Birobidjan (Community for Birobidzhan)—organization began in 1934. It grouped publications and again established friendly relations with other left-oriented Jews, even the Bund. Their concerns were progressive; their interests centered on social changes. Respect for the Soviet Union was in those years fairly acceptable in most progressive intellectual circles, and socialist groups in the community were for the most part active devotees. There was hardly an aspect of their work that did not proclaim support for or exalt the U.S.S.R. as on the threshold and forefront of a new social world.[30] This broad spectrum of support and tolerance for a variety of ideologies within their framework of activities made the communists the most influential, sophisticated, and involved players in the community.

The Gesbir group was soon transformed into the Jewish League for the Soviet Union (1936). The main motivation, aside from drawing more people to form a stronger political base, was to fight fascism. Many Bundists, Zionists, and communists cooperated,[31] as anyone who defined himself as "progressive" was to a degree active.

The Molotov-Ribbentrop pact of 1939 produced tremendous confusion among the local left, and signaled the beginning of the fall of communist centrality in the community. This pact between Hitler's Germany and Stalin's Soviet Union attempted to redivide Europe and cede Poland to Hitler. The pact became known by the names of the foreign ministers of each country, Viacheslav Molotov and Joachim von Ribbentrop. What shocked parts of the world was that two archenemies, which to some represented ideological polarities, managed to sign a nonaggression pact that assigned territories into their respective spheres of control. Whatever one thought of the Soviet Union, Hitler's Nazism was clearly anti-Semitic, and a "pact" with Hitler was very difficult to justify. Tensions mounted within communist circles and between communists and others. What were Stalin's true intentions? There was much disappointment and disillusion with the fact that principles were being sacrificed to politics.

Communists in Mexico debated the issue. A broadly attended mock trial on the Soviet policy was organized a few months later—31 July 1940—by the communists, presumably to justify the pact. It was held at the I. L. Peretz Club, a gathering club used by socialists in the Jewish center, on 15 Tacuba street. The activity took the form of an exchange between a defense lawyer who followed the Stalinist position (Boris Rosen), a prosecutor (Dr. Moisés Lisker), and an arbitrator (the late philosopher Dr. Elí de Gortari).[32] While the event meant to appease the left and its sympathizers, it inadvertently showed how the political/ethical questions and requests for accountable behavior were eroding the communist platform. Nobody had offered good reasons for the Stalinist policy. Lisker's support for the communists weakened, true to the role he had assumed at the trial, and his thinking was paradigmatic of that of the majority of sympathizers. The original fragile equilibrium and harmony of the "left" was threatened.[33] Bundists were the most vocal accusers and persistently requested an explanation from communists. The general communist central policymakers launched an effort to restore the severed relationships.[34] Eventually, only the breaking of the pact led some of the detached activists to return to the communist fold.

The left continued to work on its image and representation. The Jewish League changed its name and now became the "Folk Lige," attempting to broaden its platform to attract all groups. The communist monthly *Fraivelt* became a weekly, and was a forum until about 1950. The most unexpected alliance and support that helped the communists in retaining their centrality for some time came from the then-strong relationship between communists and Zionists—specifically, left-Zionists.

The Bund had been linked to the left but was still distant.[35] The estrangement had been latent for years. However, the official break occurred after the execution of their European leaders, Victor Alter and Henrik Erlich, in the Soviet Union in 1941 as they escaped from Nazi Poland. They were accused of being spies. Alter, a leader of Jewish trade unions in Poland, and Erlich, an earlier member of the Menshevik faction in the St. Petersburg Soviet in 1917, were the most important Bund leaders in the 1940s. Always defending Poland, discerning Hitler's fascist goals, and trying to alert the Soviet Union of the fascist threat, they eventually became too prominent for Stalin to tolerate. They were imprisoned, released, and imprisoned again. In an attempt to trace their whereabouts, William Green, president of the American Federation of Labor, was told by Ambassador Maxim Litvinov that Erlich and Alter had been assisting Polish intelligence and had resumed hostile activities, "including appeals to the Soviet troops to . . . conclude peace with Germany."[36] Though the arrests were made in 1941, the confirmatory letter of their deaths came in February 1943. World Bundist outrage was enormous. Local communist explanations did not help; in an editorial in their house organ, Jewish communists in Mexico said: "We do not believe that Erlich and Alter were killed as criminals, but rather as activists-fighters who were against the Soviet regime; the Soviet Union did not commit a murderous act, rather they defended their interests and ideology."[37]

To the Bundists, the acceptance and justification of these deaths was revelatory of how subservient the local Jewish communists were to any policy of the Soviet Union. The Bund felt that the fate of European Jewry was always secondary to the praise and blind hope for the advancements and achievements of the Red Army that communists constantly and uncritically expressed. The politics and diplomacy of the Soviet Union and the Communists had always been distrusted by the Bund. Bundists could not tolerate the extreme reverence, deference, and love with which the Jewish communists related to the U.S.S.R. Following the murders of Alter and Erlich, Bundists systematically questioned and attempted to discredit what to them seemed the unquestioned positions that communists took in relation to Jews in the Soviet Republics and elsewhere, especially the treatment of other Bundists and even Zionist leaders who also met a harsh fate at Soviet hands.[38]

In 1943, two Soviet Jewish leaders, actor Shloime Mikhoels and poet Itzik Fefer, were sent to Mexico, the United States, Canada, and England by the Jewish Anti-Fascist Committee, an organization supervised by the Soviet government. The purpose of their trip was to maintain, enhance, and repair some of the still very necessary support that was weakening. This was part of the general communist policy and it was applied to Mexico too, but it appeared to be an effort made by Jewish-communists to justify Soviet policy and strengthen the eroding sympathy toward the Soviet government and its policies. The visitors highlighted the benefits to Jews from Soviet policy, suggesting that the Soviets sought to make Jewish issues, even nationalist Jewish issues, central to their political agenda. They therefore proclaimed the Soviet Union's interest in Jews and in the protection of Jews and their needs. In addition, Constantin Umanski, a Jew who was then the Soviet Union's ambassador to Mexico and had previously been ambassador to the United States, was also an important liaison between the groups; he had clear political authority, skills, and linguistic tools to reach his audience. Notwithstanding all these efforts, the rift continued. Yet, the communist movement survived. The communists continued their activities and succeeded in sustaining their centrality at least for a time.

The solidarity among these groups had not been limited to the press;[39] many activities were involved. Umanski was an often sought-after guest at Jewish communal public meetings. The Mikhoels and Fefer visit was handled and hosted not only by local communists, but also by Zionists; a reception was organized in the Zionist school Tarbut with the presence of forty-five presidents of diverse Jewish organizations. Ambassador Umanski addressed the meeting.[40] The next day, a meeting with thirty distinguished Mexican and Latin American artists was organized for the visitors; the guests included painter Chávez Orozco, playwright Alfonso Gómez de la Vega, Chilean writer Pablo Neruda, composer Carlos Chávez, and philosopher Alfonso Reyes. The Central Committee received the visitors separately; Jews tried to make it a Jewish event, while Mexicans regarded it as a Soviet-Mexican exchange. Whatever the success of each group in appropriating the event, its ample visibility and interest illustrate dramatically its importance and the acceptability of the left at the time.

The fissures of 1941 eventually escalated to an absolute confrontation, an open war between Bundists and communists. But the first years of the conflict were eclipsed by the linkages and political relationships that obscured the context. In the early 1940s, the Jewish communist circle received an enormous boost from two sources: (1) the left-Zionist group, which joined them in recognition of the fight of the Soviet Union, and used their forum to express their views in exchange for close contact with wider circles of the community; and (2) the exiled communists of Europe, primarily from Germany and Austria, Jews and non-Jews who arrived up in Mexico as temporary guests.

In 1942, these refugees formed in Mexico the "Bewegung Freies Deutschland" (Movement for a Free Germany) in a pro-Soviet climate. Following a period of detachment from communist efforts because of what was called the "Wall Street influence" on Mexico, or a stronger attachment to the United States, in 1942 Mexico joined the allied countries in the war. After that, it was only logical to reestablish relations with the Soviet Union. This took place in 1943.[41] This made it easy for communists to express their thoughts, which were mostly of an antifascist character.

Local Jewish communists and refugees shared not only Marxist-Leninist ideology, but also, as part of the official international communist movement, the desire to establish and widen "popular fronts" of support.[42] These intellectually sophisticated activists offered much more than just their political affiliation. They brought to the forefront two issues of general Jewish concern that helped them establish a link with the general Jewish community: Germany's responsibility towards Jews because of the Nazi regime's systematic policies against Jews; and the idea that Jews, a minority, had a right to express themselves nationally. This was an indirect recognition of political Zionist ideology. These intellectuals therefore gained a double entry into Jewish communal life: as communists and antifascist fighters, and as vocal advocates of the Zionist position and defenders of Jewish civil rights everywhere.[43]

Given this favorable atmosphere, the refugees and the Jewish left—communists and Zionists—created a network, exchanging ideas and audiences. Refugees such as Paul Meyer, Bruno Frei, Otto Katz, and Theodore Balk cooperated in communal activities, and some of them even published in the Jewish journal of the B'nai-B'rith, *Tribuna Israelita*. However, the most important "broker" in this relationship between the Jewish sector and the communist exiled refugees was the writer Leo Katz. With a distinguished career in the German, Austrian, and French communist parties, Katz was an indispensable link between the groups. He was deeply versed in Jewish culture and used Yiddish, which allowed him close surveillance of the Yiddish press and the activities of the community, and gave him access to that medium. The experience of returning as an adult into a mature, thriving Jewish environment, where his issues and agenda were public issues and had a meaningful context, awakened in him ideas that were dormant or nonexistent among his exiled Jewish colleagues. Katz is, in many ways, paradigmatic of the atmosphere of the time for these Jews: Jewish issues were the prism through which international politics could be understood. More than any of the others, Katz intervened in internal communal affairs that touched on other arenas, too. He was the only one of the Jews in this group who, after leaving Mexico, seemed to have felt an unbreakable bond to Israel and Judaism that almost superseded his previous communist activities.

Although Mexico was the first country in the world to experience this collaboration between left-Zionists, Jewish communists, and general Communists alike, this alliance did not suffice to keep Jewish communists at center stage of the community. A countervailing center of power, the Bund was not at ease and often attacked. It had forfeited in the sharing of the communist platforms, but could not build a sufficiently large membership to compete in the power game. As things stood at that moment, the communists seemed to be in a much more powerful position. The Bundists lacked a local socialist base. However, the communists soon suffered the same fate. Not only did their base not widen, but it actually decreased very soon after. However, while they celebrated, Bundists had a sense of being excluded from the main ideological discourse, a sense that socialists were really losing communal territory altogether.

The Bund's attacks on Jewish communists and communism were systematic. The interference of an "outsider" in the protest elicited a vigorous response from the communists and turned the confrontation into a war. Golomb, who was nonaligned, publicly raised his objections to the discriminatory treatment of Jews and Judaism in the Soviet Republics. He was immediately considered an "enemy" by the communists, while the

144 ASHKENAZI JEWS IN MEXICO

Bund strengthened their ties to him, further polarizing the situation. The communist response came from a powerful figure who felt himself to be a match for Golomb. Leo Katz presented not so much an intellectual defense of the Soviet position, but an attack on Golomb. He was vituperative in his attempt to discredit Golomb's ideas.[44] Golomb did not get into a full fight. He made his statement as a protest, and left the arena of the political groups. His educational work suffered indirectly from the confrontation, yet he managed to deliver a dramatic blow to the communists.

The Bund, still without a defined constituency, sharpened its attack and also turned against the left-Zionists and their coalition with the communists.[45] Analyzing their ideology, the Bund found inconsistencies in Zionist activity. "Where should we help: Palestine or Poland?" asked the Zionists. For the Bund, the question itself revealed a total lack of perspective, a false dilemma. As they saw it, millions of Jews in Europe were in need of protection. How could anyone compare Poland to Palestine then? For the Bund, the Zionists' answer to the question made clear their political interests and intentions. The Zionist position, the Bund asserted, was clearly and uncompromisingly for Palestine; for Polish Jewry, they only "shed a tear and offered a Kaddish."[46] Did this mean an interest in the Jewish future? Dr. Nachum Goldman, the great international Jewish leader, founder of the World Jewish Congress, who among Zionists fought openly for support of diaspora Jewry within Zionism, was criticized for doing too little, too late. In one of his visits to Mexico with his colleague Rabbi Stephen Wise, solid communal support was shown, but the tension did not disappear.[47]

Zionism in Mexico had organized its base around the Keren Kayemet, the Jewish National Fund, the land purchase and development fund of the Zionist organization. Internationally, the organization was formed in 1901, but it started its work in Mexico in 1925. Its activities were organized around festival celebrations and memorials, a practice that gave it an opportunity to collect funds for Eretz Israel. The public was becoming used to this form of support.[48] The Zionists had also been trying to organize their diverse groups into a federation[49] while left-Zionists—Mordkhe Korona, Avner Aliphas, Kalmen Landoi—all worked with the communists publishing in *Fraivelt*. The group was willing to "forgive" the Soviet Union and communists because of the antifascist role the Soviet Union was taking on. Whatever the accommodation, Zionists gained access to a wide audience through a ready-made platform.

Adopting a different style from that of the communists, who had fewer representatives participating in the various organizations, the Zionists were directly involved in communal internal affairs. As teachers, writers, journalists, and other professionals, they took part in and used the services of the community. This proved to be useful, as the community felt that the Zionist ideology, positions, and principles were unquestionably prestigious. Like scattered seeds, once the environment was adequate the Zionists' ideas could grow and flourish. The Bund ridiculed the alliance of "Zionists, with the Reform Rabbis of the USA, the wealthy Jews and the progressive Communists."[50] This criticism, however, did not undermine the association these organizations had with each other. The questions, however, raised doubts, and the Bundists' questions were at the time very pertinent.[51] What the Bundists picked up in their political analysis was the ease with which issues were sold out to political expediency.

But the Bundists' criticism was not only aimed at in-house politics. They questioned general communist policy too. And what exactly did communists stand for? Did they want to help Jews or not? they asked. Using a cultural case to illustrate the pressures that a communist society exerted on Jews, they asked why an Ana Berkovna, for example, needed to become Ana Borisovna in Russia? Even a name, a Jewish-sounding name, presented problems in a society that disliked Jews. The communists did not want Jewish ethnic identity, nor Bund politics; could one think that communists were for Zionism?[52] And, if communists were not to be trusted, what was happening with the Zionists? Was a political goal worth all the Zionists were ready to sacrifice?

Among the communists, not all types of Zionism found favor. When Nahum Goldman and Baruch Tzuckerman, for instance, world leaders of Zionism from the World Jewish Congress, visited Mexico (as Zionist representatives periodically did), the communists criticized the visitors' seeming lack of interest in and attention to Jews in the Soviet Republics: on their agenda, Goldman and Tzuckerman did not include anything on Soviet Jewry.[53] Communists felt that the lack of support from the General Zionists was something they had to address. They saw the Zionist position towards the Soviet Union as opportunistic rather than based on a shared belief system. This, they thought, paralleled the behavior of Jewish orthodoxy, which was now sympathetic but made common cause with the communists only to express vengeful feelings during the war.[54]

The awareness of possible political problems between the groups was latent. Local communists began criticizing the local communal organizations for not being "cemented." Maybe, they argued, it was the "lack of communal democracy" which made them so vulnerable,[55] focusing their criticism on the internal political structure. It was, however, not democracy per se that they were interested in, but in a mechanism that could secure their shaky structural future.

In the efforts to retain leadership and authority, *Fraivelt* continually publicized the achievements of the Red Army, specifically pointing out the accomplishments of Jews in the military field. At the same time, the communists claimed that the journal always sought to "respect all Jewish positions even when not in accordance with the Soviet Union, . . . to be a nonpartisan organ, with a platform against Fascism." After 1943, when these tenets were published, the communists openly attempted to be part of a larger unity and still maintain their position. *Fraivelt* continued to propagandize its "synthetic approach to all Jewish life," presenting what it felt were the major Jewish needs. To prove the point, it often quoted the early experiments of Jewish settlements in Crimea and Birobidzhan as examples of the advanced and responsible thinking of the Soviet Union towards Jews, regardless of their failure.

The communists made repeated attempts to retain their centrality and prestige. A 1943 description of Russia and Jews provides an example. The communists suggested that the structure of society in the Soviet Union had changed, and with it the Jews had changed too. The metaphoric characteristic "hump" of Jews, referred to in Jewish literature, was gone, they claimed. "It is not surprising that the Jew in Russia has stopped missing a personal country. Can one want another mother when one has a perfect one? This could only occur when one has a stepmother, as is the case everywhere in the world but not in the U.S.S.R. Further, even the Jews of Palestine feel that whatever they want to achieve, the Russian Jews have achieved already."[56]

But what was one to make of the Bundists' claims of the persecution of the Bund movement and Bundist leaders and even their claim of the persecution of Zionist leaders in the Soviet Union? To make their point, the Bund launched additional attacks, publicizing the liquidation of Zionism in Rumania,[57] for example. Because communists' answers were not forthcoming, the attacks became increasingly frequent, direct, and daring. And something did happen. A reconfiguration in the power structure of all political factions appeared to be taking place. Once the war ended, it was not a Bund versus communist confrontation only. The Bund attacked the left-Zionist alliance as well as the General Zionists. The communists in turn protested what they called the Bund's lack of "political vision," and went on to criticize the larger Zionist body. Zionists rejected the Bund's political positions. In other words, all alliances were weakened, and the political vulnerability that was in the air manifested itself.

After the tremors with which the war had left Jews in diaspora, the agitation did not die down. The anger and frustration among the groups continued. The Bund openly requested the general organized community to ban communists, closing the door on them and withdrawing any tolerance for their organization.[58] Heretofore, limitations on political alternatives were imposed by partial authorities supported by a diffuse though general desire to retain an undefined ethnic centrality. The Bund clearly sensed that the centralization of power was now imminent. The request of the Bund was politically timely and accurately targeted to yield results. In the end, the community did unify, and the communists lost centrality, but not because of the anticommunist request. Zionism became the dominating force. The communists lost ground not because of the Bundist attacks but because the Zionists found them to be too far out of line as a group and had the power to enforce their view. Other factions which were linked to the Zionist position supported the developing structure and helped enforce the new boundary. When the Soviet support to Israel eroded in 1951, the Central Committee debated the communist position on the issue, since local communists sided with the Soviet Union and attacked the imperialism of the United States. Added to this was the fact that the communist leaders of the community had also just been denied visas to visit the United States, as the country was at war in Korea and all communists were suspect. The personal frustration of communists was mounting. They therefore grouped Israel, the United States, and the local communal structure as enemies. In response, the community applied a "Cold War" attitude towards them. Thus, two blocs had formed, the "we" and the "they." "They" were seen as negative and subversive.

The future of the communists was sealed then; they were immediately ousted from the joint organizations, and they left. The dialogue between the groups, and the political, moral, and cultural questions that they asked each other, were part of an established method of communication and self defense. No group other than the Bund asked so many public questions, all of which were insistent, persistent, and piercing. The questioning process gave the Bundists the perception of power, and every answer, or its absence, forced the communists into greater submission.

The Bund's "final purpose of questioning [them was] to dissect";[59] and their intention may have been double: to dethrone the communists from their privileged public position, and to gain control of the communal public domain for themselves. The Bund inadvertently achieved the first goal but failed in the second. The political changes for Jews, the establishment of the state of Israel, made all the Zionists unspoken allies. By the early 1950s the communists were a much weaker group, almost a destroyed group, yet there seemed to have been a kind of "fear of the dead" attitude towards them.[60] Nobody was sure of their absolute defeat, and people wanted to see them vanish. In the end, the now definitely stronger Zionists used the communists' inability to recognize Israel's function for the community to deliver the final blow. The last communists of the community did not retaliate; they just withdrew.

But how did Zionists establish their hegemony? No confrontation had given any one subgroup a clear victory. How did the Bundists lose their grip on the situation? A shift had occurred, and the left had lost out.

The sharp debates among the groups resonated in the community. Bundists never stopped protesting what they called the "double standard" of the communists: their criticizing Nazism while silencing criticism of the Ribbentrop-Molotov pact; their praising Zionism, but supporting the Arabs. The communists had retaliated by presenting issues that the Bund could not easily refute. They claimed that the Bundist defense of Polish Jewry when Polish Jewry was no more was politically and ideologically hollow.[61] They saw the Bundist positions as short-sighted and unable to deal with the political crisis the war represented. The Bundists to them seemed too focused on the war issues.[62] Bundists felt that the communists used the Marxist paradigm to understand World War II, while ignoring the Jewish question. The Warsaw ghetto uprising, for instance, was portrayed in *Fraivelt* as a step taken by "subjected people" influenced by "the historical battle of Stalingrad."[63] To use Marxist ideology to suggest that the battle against the Nazis was a protest of the subjected against a power structure, as if this were a protest like any other, was for the Bund not only a misconstruing of the "war against the Jews,"[64] but also a distortion of reality to highlight the tangential political accomplishments of the Soviet Union. Ideology controlled most explanations, the Bund contended, while history was sidestepped.

The intellectual support of the Communist Folk League weakened. After the war, key refugees, including Leo Katz, returned to Europe, most of them to work in regimes that led to their unnatural deaths.[65] The support of the Soviet Union to the new Jewish state was eroding. Communists who followed the party line distanced themselves from Israel and Jews in general. This behavior tested the limits of communal toleration. The vast majority of the community, even the least politicized ones, turned away; the undefined coalition between communists and the left-Zionists was lost, and even some of their own loyalists abandoned them. After the Holocaust, there was little tolerance for attacks against the new Jewish state, especially when no other political "solutions" seemed to have worked.

The creation of the state of Israel was a balm to the suffering survivors of the war, and the oldest dream come true to most Jews. Regardless of ideological differences, the birth of the state of Israel offered the most independent of political solutions available to Jews. The "Jewish street" in the community was in a mood of intense and heartfelt euphoria. In this frame of mind, Zionist work and activity were irrevocably legitimized. With the founding of the state itself, the acquired gains of previous struggles could and would be used in the institutionalization process.

Whether or not the Zionists actually conquered audiences, as the Bundists claimed,[66] or whether the general sense of elation and accomplishment was linked to the materializing of the shared biblical dream, is unclear. Still, feelings of happiness and hope suffused any activity linked to the newly born state. The joy of Zionists was indescribable, and that spirit was shared by most Jews.

A fundamental change had occurred. Zionism, a most effective vision, was now a reality. The power of that reality was being recognized. Zionists became the undisputed winners in the struggle that gave all Jews an international political victory. The Bund conceded victory to Zionism before anyone else; they recognized that the Zionists had offered a viable answer to the Jewish reality of the time.[67] However, from the perspective of the diaspora, an essential ideological problem lingered as active opposites: the new reality of the state of Israel and the old diaspora remained as two contradictory, persistent facts. After all, the failure of the one was the justification of the other. The fact that the diaspora remained a reality was neither a limitation nor a failure of the new Jewish state. Rather, it highlighted the essential social contradiction that beset multicultural interrelations throughout the world, including Israel. The problems of interrelations between diverse groups—the political incompleteness to which minorities were and are subjected—required (and still requires) a new ideological articulation.

Jews, however, lacked the ideological tools to work on these problems. For Jews in Israel, the politics of survival took precedence over the politics of interrelation. For Jews in diaspora, Zionism became the reigning ideology; but for their immediate condition, they had no ideological tools with which to fight. Though the political world had changed dramatically for Jews, the world had ironically remained essentially the same: the extraordinary tension between diverse ethnic-religious-cultural groups had not been addressed, and the current political accommodation represented a new standstill rather than a new qualitative ethico-political beginning.

The persistence of diaspora, then, required new analyses. For Jews in Mexico, these lingering issues surfaced all too soon. A new confrontation within the host society brought this problem to the surface. The United Nations vote for the recognition of the state of Israel, for instance, resulted in ten abstentions. Mexico was one of them. The seemingly silent stance of the government, which spoke loudly while trying to conceal, affected Jews in Mexico more than it appeared.

Nothing had changed the ambivalence of the Mexican government towards Jews: not the Holocaust, not the state of Israel, and not the local accomplishments of Jewish citizens after four decades of productive exchange. The "moral necessity" for the state of Israel had not been understood or accepted by the Mexican government.[68] The abstention revealed not so much the claimed neutrality of the government as the thoughts it still harbored about Jews.[69] Regardless of which group gained control over the community, this issue had to be addressed. In fact, it should have been on the agenda of the dominant group.[70] Local concerns did not disappear. Instead, they became the subtext of most ideological thinking, in the perpetual efforts of the dominant groups to remain powerful and central.

## CONTENT LEGITIMATION AND CONTROL: EDUCATION AND THE GROWTH OF THE SCHOOL NETWORK

The third case study belongs to a different arena: education. It illustrates how politics permeated other spheres of communal life. Viewed as a second front, it replayed the ideological conflicts in the organizational struggle the community was facing. Educational conflicts reenacted and restated the political positions and alternatives of the period. Interestingly, the same pattern of winners and losers reasserted itself. First there was conflict that produced "structural growth," and new schools were developed. However, the conflict became much more. Because education appeared to be a self-contained field in which politics could be put at the service of seemingly nonpolitical objectives, it was an easier arena in which to further political objectives intellectually. As a result, the conflicts paralleled and magnified the more general political exchanges. These confrontations highlight the specific choices the diaspora community had to make, and the consequences it had to pay, once it subscribed to a single dominant ideology. This was a fight to control the young and hence the future of the community.

Education is the arena where issues of how to shape and integrate the young are discussed; thus, even in its philosophical and sociological forms, education has always been essentially political. Confined to a specific domain of society, educational issues and schools can become "repositories for values that nobody cares to try at large,"[71] or that are more easily introduced through a limited part of the structure. Theoretical politics can therefore lead to practical confrontations. This was certainly the case in Mexico, where the educational arena became the theater in which the ideological conflicts of the community were played out. The fierceness of the fighting was only a partial proxy for a general communal confrontation; it was, even more, emblematic of the passions and importance of the issues raised and what they meant. The parameters of the fight, originally confined to the educational sphere, spilled over to involve the whole community. Use of the media and the convening of open communal meetings made the masses participant-observers of the debate; this broadening of participation transformed the placid masses into a group acquiescing to the changes that were taking place.

The educational conflict epitomizes the struggles that molded the modern society of Jews in Mexico. It was not just a simple fight among teachers, but a deep-seated ideological confrontation. It was at the same time a crisis of ideology, a crisis of principles, and a crisis of authority. It unexpectedly reopened the issue of identity for this community: local identity, international identity, and shifting loyalties. The solutions that were adopted contain most of the ideological choices. While appearing as pragmatic negotiations, these solutions implied the consequences, the dilemmas, and the unanswered problems that this community was to face. So what may appear as a stage of adaptation, resolution, and peace is in fact the mirage of a renewed social crisis.

Historically, many individuals who did not participate directly in the broad, overtly political confrontations of the community felt comfortable taking an active role in areas that were more limited and confined, less threatening and visible. From the earliest time in Mexico, the education field fulfilled that role and offered that possibility. Although the issues discussed were clearly political and philosophical in nature as well as technical and pedagogical in content, the educational arena veiled its political character by transferring the abstractness of the problems into a narrower field. This quality, and the tangible immediacy and directness of the field, attracted many nonpedagogues who felt linked to and affected by education. This was particularly true during the early years of communal life. It was less so in the 1940s, when the roles of the actors were more directly defined and the education debate more explicitly combined ideology with pedagogy, the subtext of a major communal change.

The first twenty years of formal education in the community[72] were characterized by the dynamic changes and possibilities of the educational field, in which the different ideological positions were all viable possibilities. The school, which began activities as a "Kheder"—an old-style Jewish school—was soon the forum for fights over control, in which Zionists, attempting to reform the old educational style, wanted to introduce Hebrew into the curriculum. The use of Yiddish was questioned; the use of English in a Jewish school was questioned; the teaching and practice of prayer as a compulsory activity was for a time enforced and then eliminated. Different educational packages were frequently put together and modified.

The first and by far the most influential decision of the community was to choose among what seemed economically determined options: either to continue to build a comprehensive daily school or to limit the communal educational efforts to an afternoon program, as a supplement to the formal education. The government had allowed the formation of private schools, though not parochial ones. Although the relationship of the government to minorities in the area of education deserves further investigation, we know that individual deals were made on occasion, as the case of the Mennonites shows. The Mennonites managed to work out an agreement which defined special waivers; these were signed by President Obregón in 1921. The agreement included exemption from military service, far-reaching rights over their religious rules (including their practice of polygamy), and authorization to found their own schools. These accords, however, were not generalized practice by the government, and did not extend to other groups.

Most of the time, the government chose not to enforce stringently a constitutional article dating to 1917, establishing that education must be free and nonsectarian, as well as democratic, nationalistic, and committed to social equality.[73] The article had been used primarily in the twenties and thirties as a strong governmental anti-Catholic stand against parochial schools. In the forties, however, the government adopted a more lenient attitude, from which minorities benefited.

Because the Jews in Mexico wished to maintain their cultural distinctiveness, the idea of a private school made immediate sense. The government did not intervene, either for or against, and the school had to be built with limited communal resources. The content of the education lent itself to competition and conflict. But the contention was not limited to Jews of Mexico only. Jews there were receiving help from American organizations, which felt they had the right to impose their views on how the money was to be spent. The American organizations of B'nai B'rith, and HIAS and the local Jews—Bundists and Zionists—became entangled in what appeared to be a simple budgetary problem that in fact masked a philosophical identity issue: the school that was going to be financed would reflect the type of Jewishness that Jews wanted to promote.

The Mexican community decided to develop a comprehensive Jewish school instead of an afternoon school. That decision was crucial; it separated Jews in Mexico from their American helpers. It also challenged, albeit indirectly, the American definition of a distinct ethnicity. The Americans favored an afternoon school as means to "connect [faster] to the local culture and the group." This implied that the definition of ethnic culture was subsidiary to the educational process. The local Jews felt that this approach presented ethnic culture as either transitional to youth's development or of marginal importance, limited to religious distinctiveness (as is the case of American Sunday schools). In rejecting the afternoon or supplementary education idea, the community affirmed its desire to maintain a more central ethnic definition of themselves in the formation of youth.

Equally revealing were the conflicts concerning the content of the curriculum. Some wanted the school to include English as a subject. Some wanted to use Yiddish as the main language of instruction, while others did not; even the issue of how much Yiddish would be taught became part of the confrontation. English as a subject was postponed for later years, for older children. Religious instruction was limited to prayers and eventually eliminated, since secularists comprised the vast majority of the community. Finally, three groups, each with its own approach, crystallized in the fighting to control the curriculum: (a) the religious-biblical approach, (b) the Yiddish literature and Jewish history approach, and (c) the Hebrew approach.

Meyer Berger, a leader among the teachers and later a director of the school, espoused the Hebrew agenda. Fearing that he would prevail, the supporters of the other positions called for a general meeting. This resulted in a compromise between the Yiddish and Hebrew approaches, with secular subjects taught in Spanish, as requested by the government. The school stabilized between 1927 and 1929, and the inclusion of both Yiddish and Hebrew became a trademark of this institution and of local Ashkenazi Jewry. The religious element of the school was phased out because of lack of support. The school was called in Yiddish "Yidishe Shule" almost naturally, because the majority knew and used Yiddish. But Hebrew was included as a connection to core Judaism. Zionists highlighted the importance of the language for their project, and, though the balance was tipped in favor of Yiddish, a collision on the subject of language was avoided. Both these sectors concentrated in those years on modernizing the school and distancing it from the "old-fashioned" linkages to the Kheder. Hygiene and discipline became central issues. Bundist, Zionist, and Yiddishist ideas coexisted for a time. The school had close to six hundred children by the early 1930s.

*The First Conflict: The Fight for a Voice*

In 1940, Avner Aliphas arrived and joined the teaching staff at the Yidishe Shule. Having always been an active left-Zionist, he immediately aimed to change the balance and emphasis of the school's curriculum. That soon put him in a difficult position among his colleagues: some felt personally displaced and criticized by the emphasis required by this "new Zionist" (as if they had not done their job well), while others did not feel altogether comfortable with the increased emphasis on Zionism that Aliphas brought to the school. Aliphas had created a second area of work for himself—the youth movement Hashomer Hatzair—where he was in control of the group's education and where he channeled much of his energies. He organized this as an after-school and weekend youth group and gained rapid celebrity. Within the school, however, his position seemed increasingly shaky. On the one hand, he had neither the freedom nor the authority to direct activities and control changes, as in the youth Zionist organization;[74] at the same time, the school staff was getting restless with his educational approach, which did not abate even when he had the youth organization as an outlet. Aliphas had the enthusiasm and charisma of a practicing Zionist: after all, he had just come from Palestine, where he had been involved in pioneering work. As he conveyed his enthusiasm and ideas, he was given a chance to speak, but he made too many uncomfortable by his advocacy for changes in relative emphases, authority, and prestige.

In 1941, not long into his job and while on a trip to a Zionist Youth Congress in the United States, Aliphas was suddenly fired from his teaching job. He attempted to protest the school's action, but was unable to reverse it. He claimed that the school had no grounds to dismiss him. He alleged that he had not missed any school days, and that the action was totally unjustified. The school claimed that Aliphas had not asked for permission to travel and should have been available for school meetings. The authorities indirectly expressed the view that both his trip and his behavior within the school defied the school's central authority. Undoubtedly, the occasion was seized as an opportunity to take a "safe and needed" action to separate someone deemed threatening from the school.

The result of this incident was unexpected. Aliphas did what no communal member had done up to then. Less dependent and less committed to the established network of teachers, less engaged with the unspoken agreements and views of the community, Aliphas seized the opportunity to break the educational status quo and challenge the existing educational monopoly. If he was leaving the main school, he would create his own Zionist school. With the support of his relatives and some followers who respected him and trusted his ways, he quickly established a new nationalistic school, Tarbut.[75] He did not rely on the central Zionist movement to finance the enterprise, but rather used the resources of his followers. To everybody's surprise, the Tarbut school opened in early 1942. Aliphas succeeded because a significant part of the group accepted these changes, and he could draw on the quiet support of the masses.

In addition to the specific variations and emphases in the subject content of the two schools, the Tarbut marked a general reversal in the relative importance of Yiddish and Hebrew. While the Yidishe Shule maintained the dual Yiddish-Hebrew program, with an emphasis on Yiddish, the new Tarbut school, with its Zionist emphasis, shifted the established relationship. While Yiddish was part of the program of the school, emphasis was on the role and function of Hebrew. This, then, was a Hebrew school that included Yiddish, while the old school was a Yiddish school that included Hebrew. In the midst of the conflicts and awareness of the differences, neither school did away completely with the "other" language. Only later, in the 1950s, did Yiddish wane in the Tarbut school. For that, no major battle was enacted.

In this assertive mood, other sectors in the community came forward to establish their views. The orthodox group organized its own school, Yavne, with support of the Nidkhei Israel congregation. The school of the congregation had functioned until 1941 as a religious Talmud Tora, supplementary to their regular schooling, with forty children.[76] At the end of that year, it became a full day school. The possibility of such educational fragmentation was facilitated by the arrival to Mexico in the late 1930s of well-trained European teachers, who had been specially invited or arrived as immigrants by chance, joining in the great already renowned modern experiment of Jewish education launched in Mexico.[77] The influx of newcomers fortified the central Yidishe Shule, while allowing certain teachers to possibly break away and teach in the other schools.

The new triad of schools did not jeopardize the survival of any of the schools, although this was feared by the original incumbents. The argument that the lack of resources would weaken and destroy the institutions (although accurate in its economic assessment, since the schools seem to have been in perennial deficit) never affected other aspects of the schools. Soon the Sephardic community organized its own "Tarbut" school, also with the help of Aliphas. Within two years, the whole educational structure had so grown as to have modified the entire panorama of the community. To the surprise of most Jewish communities, the small communal experiment in Mexico created a network of day schools which was not matched by most of the larger and more sophisticated communities in the world.[78]

The expansion of the school network indirectly produced a further refinement of the ethnic ideological elaborations. Each school offered a rationale to justify itself, and the established political groups had to carve an intellectual territory to justify their alliances. Aliphas of course advanced the Zionist perspective by developing Tarbut as a national Jewish school engaged in the active support and education for Eretz Israel. The Bund claimed that Tarbut saw in the Hebrew language the beginning and end of Judaism, and so justified the Yidishe Shule as broader in scope: it was a school for Bundists, Zionists, and right- and left-wing thinkers, offering languages, literature, and culture in a secularist frame.[79] Some Zionists, however, remained attached to the original school, and never allowed it to be redefined as Yiddishist only. The fact that not all Zionists joined Aliphas made it harder for him and the Tarbut, but this same fact also left open the possibility of reconquering the Yidishe Shule, since both sectors had not been clearly separated. The next move for the Yidishe Shule was to invite Avraham Golomb to help it grow further.

As a "general" school, the Yidishe Shule, which combined Zionism, Yiddishism, and general Jewish culture, could be defined variously depending on what was going to be highlighted. As the largest and oldest school, the Yidishe Shule was neither small enough to be ignored nor weak enough to be forgotten. That school was almost a natural battlefield among the competing forces interested in control. The lesson was not limited to schoolchildren. It was a political lesson for the whole community, and the conflict was waiting to be staged.

*The Second Conflict: The Fight for a Speech*

The last confrontation in the Yidishe Shule produced an institutional change. The importance of the conflict was a result not only of the aggressiveness with which the groups fought, but also of how the conflict affected other areas of the community beyond education. The debate should not be dismissed as yet another fight that produced a coexistence between an old and new school. This was a fight that sought absolute control and a definitive rearranging of roles, status, prestige, and authority. Thus, although the community still lacked a central enforcing power able to impose absolute limits on undesired alternatives, this was a fight to control the content of political (qua educational) alternatives. Because there was no formally defined political territory for the ideological conflict, the conflict was fought in all the domains where ideology could manifest itself. This confrontation became a test of the "best" ideology and of authentic ethnic loyalty; it was therefore a tool for the establishment of what were to become entrenched principles.

In 1944, when the world-renowned pedagogue Avraham Golomb was invited to head the Yidishe Shule, an open reception was organized in which most organizations were represented. Although some mistook Golomb for a Bundist, the Bund complained of not having even been invited, a move that later proved ominous. Somebody wanted to separate Golomb from the Bundists and to avoid any impression that Bundists were gaining strength with the appointment of Golomb. However, the Bund was represented in the reception anyway, endorsed him, and wished him success. Golomb was introduced to the general public as an original educator, a man with a spiritual personality. He was surely a man to leave a mark in the community.

Golomb was unique, the exponent of a precisely elaborated view of the educational process he was going to head. He believed in a comprehensive definition of Judaism by which people had to think and behave; in other words, a *Weltanschauung* by which Jews had to live. His position suggested that ethnic culture was made up of ethnic language, tradition, folklore, and so on, all of which had to be used in daily life as essential elements that defined the identity of a Jew. Nothing that Jews had produced that had been incorporated into the group's way of life was seen as negative; it was all part of the continuing wisdom deployed by Jews all over the world and in different periods. It was all an integral part of the definition of Jewishness that was transmitted from generation to generation.

Golomb was uncompromising in his positions and a strict enforcer of their implementation, and teachers found themselves very quickly polarized either for or against his positions. The demands Golomb was making on every teacher about every action, and the level of self-awareness of identity he himself had and expected of the teachers, immediately created a strain. His scrutiny included both the private and public selves, and covered school-based as well as out-of-school activities. This created great tension. But to those for whom this made sense, Golomb represented a "total" person-philosopher. Those who followed him, followed a prophet/leader.

By 1947, only three years after his arrival, Golomb was at the center of the school disputes that extended into the local Yiddish press. There were three strains of conflict that affected Golomb's position in the school between 1948 and 1949: (1) a conflict with the communist Leo Katz, which arose after Golomb published two letters of a Rumanian colleague criticizing Soviet policy; (2) a conflict between Zionists and Bundists, in which Bundists appropriated Golomb; and (3) a conflict between the Zionists and Golomb, which was the final stage of the dispute once ideological groups had solidified and inserted themselves into the conflict.

The conflict with Leo Katz was one in which the personal rapidly became political. Rumor had it that Leo Katz, an antifascist refugee and new activist, had aspired to a teaching job at the school, but that Golomb had blocked his appointment. However, animosities between Golomb and Katz openly erupted over a strictly Jewish-communist issue. In 1947 Golomb publicized two letters he had received from a colleague in Rumania concerning Jewish persecution there. The letters specifically described the closing of Jewish schools by the government and the imposition of prohibitions on the use of Yiddish and Hebrew.[80] Other minorities did not seem to be affected equally, these letters said, as the Serbian, Bulgarian, and Hungarian cases showed. Whatever Golomb's motives in publishing his friend's letters, he did not seem to have planned a broader campaign to discredit the Soviet Union, nor to attack the local communists. It was the promises that communism and communists were making to Jews that he was questioning.

Katz confronted Golomb directly. Erudite himself, Katz was Golomb's intellectual equal. Katz therefore launched a barrage of attacks against the teacher. *Fraivelt* followed up Katz's accusations with provocative articles against Golomb and the school.[81] Calling Golomb's Rumanian letters "lies," the communists took this opportunity to discredit Golomb.

158    ASHKENAZI JEWS IN MEXICO

At the same time, Bundists found this to be the perfect opportunity to further their anticommunist dialogue. They therefore supported Golomb even though they often disagreed with what they called his "mixed nationalism-Zionism." They supported his "Integrale Yidishkait" theory, which Katz mocked. Although Leo Katz left for Israel in January 1949, the stage was set for continuation of the fight. Zionists who had accumulated resentments against Golomb and felt displaced as far as the control and direction of the school went were stimulated to find their own way into the fray.

While the communists and Bundists focused their debate on Golomb, the others had broader agendas. The Zionists had not expressed their full views in relation to Golomb's work. The opportunity for their participation presented itself soon enough in the tense atmosphere that prevailed. In a school meeting, in what was probably a discussion about Golomb and the general situation of the school, Yonia Fain, an artist and teacher who had previously repressed his resentment and dislike of Golomb, became very aggressive during an argument with Shmuel Shapshik, a Bundist colleague who defended the director. Fain was expelled from the school, probably by Golomb, for the use of physical force, and the board supported the decision. However, seven teachers identified as Zionists struck, defending the Bundist Fain against Golomb; they managed to obtain Fain's reinstatement.

Soon the confrontation started to change qualitatively and build on its force. Groups were willing to cross party lines to further their immediate goals. Zionists were arrayed against Golomb, using the Bundist Fain who opposed Golomb; most Bundists aligned themselves in favor of Golomb. Though Golomb was at the center of the dispute, it was not clear who was attacking; because so many were attacking, the conflict appeared to be too diffused. However, the volatility of the confrontations and the variety of the sources that sparked them were premonitions of the structural tremor that the community was to experience. Pressure built as reports of these incidents were discussed openly in the local press, informing the whole community about the school situation. At the same time, the opportunity for change seemed within reach, and the possibility of dethroning Golomb appeared imminent.

For a time, the fight turned personal rather than substantive. Attacks appeared in the Yiddish press against Golomb's family and his character. Derogatory descriptions were made. Questions and accusations of mismanagement surfaced,[82] but remained undocumented and unproven. The few who questioned Golomb in the press, questioned everything about him. These were not gratuitous questions; each one had a deliberate aim.

By then, all political groups had become active participants in the crisis: communists, Zionists, and Bundists, each for their own interests, used Golomb according to their need. The Bund asked Fain privately to resign from the party. In the meantime, the board which had initially supported Golomb's actions began to falter when it was attacked by the Zionists—teachers and outsiders alike—who were active in the school and wanted to control it. As the board further weakened, Golomb's attackers gained. The symbol of Golomb was either pulled in or out of various alliances according to their political objectives. In such a fight, Golomb was being "de-formed" by all the groups, even by his supporters, who played their own cards and not his.

Letters of protest against the treatment Golomb was receiving appeared in the American Jewish press,[83] as well as in Canada and Argentina. Distinguished writers wrote to the Yiddish press protesting the treatment given to Golomb and pleading for an end to the affair. Nothing, however, could quell the fury of the fight. The *Forois* quoted Emile Zola and called the crisis a "dreyfussade," alluding to the Dreyfus affair in which an innocent Jew was convicted. Golomb was being used as a scapegoat to be destroyed. Everything he stood for was being distorted.

The third set of issues raised against Golomb, although entangled with and building upon the others, attempted to interpret some of his behavior as anti-Zionist. Unsubstantiated, irrelevant, and humiliating gossip reported that Golomb would not eat chocolate from Israel,[84] and that he answered a student's "Shalom" greeting with "Gutmorgn," emphasizing Yiddish rather than Hebrew.[85] But the most acerbic criticism centered on Golomb's refusal to allow the "Keren Kayemet" collection boxes of the National Fund in the school. This was taken to be clearly anti-Zionist. Golomb, however, had a particular explanation for his decision; he was not opposed to the teaching of the Hebrew language and literature, nor was he opposed to Eretz Israel as a central fact of Jewish life. His ideological position acknowledged the need to teach *Tzedaka* (charity) to the children, but not in a partisan manner. If money was to be collected, it had to be done for all Jewish causes—a folk collection—among which Israel would be distinguished but not separate. He would not allow favoritism for this charity or the control of all charity work to fall in the hands of the Keren Kayemet. Whether right or not, Golomb's position was used by the Zionists to call into question his alliance with Israel and the nature of his relationship to Israel and Zionism. It became a test of his loyalty. The Poalei Tzion party in Israel[86] suggested that the Mexican affiliate negotiate with and defend Golomb if and only if Golomb recognized and acknowledged the source of their support by allowing some Israeli Zionist symbol in the school. Two representatives then attempted to negotiate a solution with Golomb: if the collection boxes were not to be used in the whole school, perhaps he would at least allow them in the lower grades. Then Zionist support would be forthcoming. Golomb, however, did not yield.[87]

By November 1949 Golomb's opponents were calling for his resig-
nation.[88] A series of meetings took place amidst quarrels between the
board and the administration of the school. The board resigned in a
meeting which was later not recognized as legal. The Central Committee
stepped in, attempting to reinstate and replace the board. No agreement
was reached, but an open communal parents meeting was proposed in
November of that year, the school year not yet being over. The dispute
had already become a community affair, the Central Committee stepping in, and the school groups feeling attacked and without sufficient
power to defend Golomb and his followers. The board's weak position
reflected Golomb's own loss of political strength. Yet to the opposition it
seemed that the active pro-Golomb people still had a chance to control
the school; at least they so argued in justifying their next actions. They
coopted the Spanish department of the school, the maintenance staff,
and the school-bus drivers in an effort to finally overcome the Golom-
bists. These groups threatened to write to the National Ministry of Education, they informed the Central Committee, to tell them that Golomb
was an "undesirable element," "an enemy of the country." If Golomb did
not resign within a few days, a general strike would be declared and the
letter sent. Scaring the administration with the threat of possible government intervention and plainly hinting at expansion of the conflict,
the administration resigned voluntarily and were followed by the board
and Golomb, too.[89]

The conflict had focused on a variety of issues, but it was mostly a
conflict between Zionism and a nonconformist force in the diaspora. For
those Jews in diaspora who wanted to define Judaism and the practice of
Jewish life differently—though not necessarily independently—from the
definitions worked out by Zionists in Israel, this conflict constituted a
milestone. It was a fight for and against the hegemony of Zionist ideology. From the Zionist point of view, it was a battle that had to be won if
Zionism was to become the dominant viewpoint. From Golomb's point of
view, it was a battle to retain a diaspora perspective different from the
Zionist-Israeli one. Nevertheless, his view did not prevail.

The confrontation in this educational front was so bitter and
extended partly because of what was at stake and partly because of what
Golomb represented. He was a symbol, not an easy entity to topple.
Golomb rebelled not against Zionism, as the opposition suggested, but
rather against attempts of the Zionist leadership to control all facets of
Jewish culture-identity. According to Golomb, the plurality, multi-
facetedness, and richness of Jewish culture were not to be shaped and har-
nessed to fit the immediate narrow needs of Israeli Zionist leadership.
Judaism was not going to be "remade"; if Golomb had his way, it had to

remain a long complex chain of events, a history and a culture worthy of being sustained, irreducible to one dimension. Zionists, like all Jewish ideological groups, had always been aware of rival alternatives that competed for public support. Parts of Zionism had long ago opted to deal with this fear by making it an either/or choice for people, rather than trying to solve it intellectually and politically through coexistence. In Palestine, Golomb had experienced the consequences of the immediate political extension of this unidimensional kind of thinking. He could not fight against it there, and was determined not to compromise. In the diaspora, he hoped to counter this perspective by rallying others to his beliefs. At the very least, he hoped to clarify to others the enormous consequences of the internal cultural destructiveness stemming from the Zionist political position.

Golomb, the Yiddishists, and the Bundists who followed him, as well as some teachers who adhered to his leadership and inspiration, established a new school, the Naye Yidishe Shul, out of this conflict.[90] To all appearances, this was a "solution" based on tolerance and coexistence. But this was only a mirage. Golomb and all he stood for had lost. The established school he had wanted was gone, and he had to start a small new school with his group. He may have felt he now had another chance to build on his principles, but, within a few years, dissatisfaction with him by the new board, or perhaps the erosion of his prestige given the devaluation of all he stood for, pushed him out of this school also. He then left Mexico altogether.

During the conflict, Golomb never answered any accusations directly; he never justified his position in writing (though it is known that he did not have very many opportunities to publish).[91] Thus, Golomb did not fight his battle conventionally. One can only speculate on the reasons why. Possibly he felt that he spoke a platonic truth transcending the cacophony of emerging political opinions. Even if he had so desired, Golomb was no politician; political charm and negotiating skills were not part of his personal make-up. During the conflict he was politically ineffectual. He absented himself while much was at stake, and did not participate in any of the factual discussions. Golomb neither acknowledged nor disputed any statement. The factual debates, which were related to events and circumstances and constituted the crux of the political debate, were not important to him. Not only was he not a politician, he actually chose not to be one. Most probably he felt it demeaning. Yet factual truth that is based on testimony, witnesses, and opinions is political by nature and exists only to the degree that someone speaks about it.[92] Golomb, however, refrained from entering into petty arguments. His only truth went beyond politics; he attempted to behave rather as a philosophical truth-teller, and tried to convince by example rather than by persuasion.[93] But this battle was a battle of politics within politics. Golomb's silence may have been a weapon, an extreme form of defense. Through it, he avoided giving himself away, but he also appeared to be more dangerous than he was. His enemies fought him till they saw him vanquished. His "persistent silence [led] to cross-examination and to torture";[94] it also led to his defeat.

Zionists were on the ascendant on all fronts in the late 1940s and 1950s. Political success as exemplified in the establishment of the state of Israel had a profound meaning for Jews over and above their own specific dialogues. The Zionists' newly recognized position had particular poignancy in the context of historical Jewish despair. Any failure to celebrate this achievement was not regarded with complacency by most in the community. Most recognized the achievement and extraordinary meaning that these political changes had for Jews.

However, two realities remained—Jews in diaspora and Jews in Israel—and with this, intellectually and ideologically, there appeared to be a contradiction. For the Zionists the diaspora was a constant reminder of the need for their existence as well as a lessening of their legitimization. Given the complexity of the relationships, a pattern for interrelations had to be worked out. Patterns of control similar to those that united or neutralized the factions within the new state were also applied to the diaspora. The complex interrelations among the Jews were not perceived as a problem by any political party at the time. The inability to solve and deal with pluralism and cultural tolerance within the Jewish subgroups was to affect Jews everywhere, leaving unsettled the issue of the political interrelation between minority and majority. Thus, while the practical-political Zionists and their local followers recognized that they needed support from the diaspora[95] and used all means to secure it, it is still a valid question whether the Zionists had to fight in such an all-encompassing way and cause such internal cultural turmoil in order to achieve their aims.

Jews in diaspora and Jews in Israel shared, unwittingly, a common political truth: states are made up of mixed ethnic-cultural-religious populations. For Jews in diaspora, this political reality emerged constantly as a gray area of political indetermination, and is still as much a challenge in the 1990s as it was in the 1950s.[96] Further, the pragmatism with which internal political and cultural differences was handled among Jews themselves dampened their ability to improve the political condition of interrelations in diaspora. More than anything, Zionist political control in diaspora left Jews in diaspora without a political language with which to defend their political status. Again and again, the only method was political improvisation. Again and again, the challenges of double loyalty, legitimate political association with Israel, and public cultural differentiation within a state were left as latent political problems of minorities in the diaspora. Not knowing how to deal with pluralism from within (among Jews themselves) has added to their inability to deal with external pluralism (between minority-majority relations).[97] A conflict that appeared to be the most internal of communal conflicts, and that did not seem relevant for the larger minority-majority relations, later began to show its full consequences.

Contrary to popular myth, Golomb was not fighting the basic tenets of political Zionist ideology. He never denied the importance of Hebrew, biblical sources, or, most important, the state of Israel. But he could not accept the corollary held by political Zionists, who saw modern Hebrew culture as the exclusive carrier of Jewish ethnicity. Golomb did not subscribe to the cultural requirement the Zionists were imposing, nor was he convinced that this was necessary for the creation of the Jewish state and for all Jews. For Zionists this was a chosen and justified political path. For Golomb, the choice was an insurmountable ethical and social mistake. He did not argue the practical and political implications of his position anywhere. Neither Golomb nor any other Yiddishist or diaspora-culture defender in Mexico appeared to be aware of the political dimension of their fight. What Golomb and all partisan non-Zionist groups lacked was a philosophical understanding of internal ethnic politics. By not articulating his position in the press during the fight, Golomb weakened his political standing. He felt it was degrading to answer each complaint. However, he misjudged the power of politics and his opponents' ability to use his silence as a political tool. Further, neither group saw the international political consequences of this internal behavior.

In the short run everybody won, though some won more than others; the Yidishe Shule was left to Zionists, maintaining the old double Jewish curriculum but without Golomb and what the Zionists saw as his dubious loyalty and cultural emphasis. Golomb created a new school, where he also preserved, true to his principles, a double Jewish curriculum. The general communal message, however, was that Zionist principles had triumphed. Yet, something else was nebulous and implicit in the dominant message: the loss of prestige and apparent lack of need for diaspora Jewish culture.

The establishment of Zionism in the world arena required the internal elimination of any competing group or system of thought that was perceived as threatening to this ideology. With the Zionist ideological triumph, the diaspora obtained extensive political benefits. The creation of a Jewish state was perhaps the only way for Jews to proclaim their opposition to "moral discrimination."[98] But it also entailed institutionalizing the intellectual alienation and cultural detachment of part of the diaspora culture. To achieve this, part of the unwanted culture had been identified and labeled as politically subversive. Very soon, the shedding of diaspora culture occurred in the daily life of the community at different levels: in the schools, in other organizations, and finally, in the choice of ethnic language.

Golomb's personal shortcomings, if overcome, could scarcely have changed the long-term outcome of this trend, long in process. All Jews were affected by an older and now deeper trend: "Enlightenment had blinded these Jews to the beauties of their own civilization."[99] The ambivalent ethnic identity helped Zionist ideology to return to the source, the "good" part of Jewish history, and, at the same time, to separate it from other ideological alternatives. What secular Jews lacked was, ironically, a strong and total vision of ethnic affirmation and continuity. Whatever the form of Jewish nationalism, it never became a theory for restoring total Jewish culture. Jews had become, as a group, ambiguous about themselves: unclear, unsure, and unsettled about their culture and future. This was evident in their chosen actions as well as in their chosen silences. The extraordinary triumph of Zionism was the victory of an ideology that was at once the product of such ambivalence and an active promoter of it. Zionist success was clouded by its own violation: victory in the geopolitical realm was implicitly linked to the inability to restore the Jews' lost source and culture—ironically, in a way, their *raison d'être*. Somewhere, the nonfulfillment of a promise and an obligation was being enacted.

## THE CONTROL OF FORM: THE LANGUAGE CONFLICT

> Language policy is politics by other means.
> —Sigmund Diamond
> paraphrasing
> Clausewitz on Warfare

The language conflict between the Yiddishists and Hebraists illustrates the ideological and practical consequences of the school conflict. Both symbolic and real, this fight over what may appear to be a diffuse territory of thought is an example of the power intrinsic to language, as well as of the power plays that the seemingly unpolitical issue of language can mask. The bilingual confrontation in Mexico echoed the older language confrontation in Eretz Israel at the beginning of the century; both, no doubt, were cases of "politics by other means."[100]

In the midst of Zionist (and Jewish) rejoicing over the creation of the new Jewish state, the bilingual issue among Jews surfaced in Mexico at an unexpected moment: just when the structure of the community was a step away from its "final" institutionalization. Most communal organizations had been using Yiddish. The issue was effectively depoliticized; it was a commonsense part of local life, not disturbed and not disturbing. Nonetheless, the problem of bilingualism was suddenly raised in the context of the educational conflicts.

Three issues need to be reconstructed in order to understand the ramifications of the problem: (1) the Zionist reenactment of the bilingual conflict in Mexico, using language policy as a means to further their political aims in the community; (2) the loss that the Yiddish activists experienced during the Hebrew-Yiddish language confrontation in Mexico; and (3) the lack of a political agenda in the position presented by Golomb and other Yiddishists. The conflicts between Yiddish and Hebrew had had a significant history internationally, but it seemed initially less consequential at the end of the 1940s and 1950s in Mexico in the midst of the other political conflicts. The language issue, however, was soon reenacted and fully repoliticized.

The period in which this occurred, which coincided with the Golomb-versus-Zionism controversy, illustrates that, while the dynamic of ideology affected organizational centralization, this in turn led to the establishment of a strict "party line," with clear rules of compliance. The result was an atmosphere that enforced obedience to the ideology. As a result, Israeli practical political Zionists were unable to adequately address diaspora cultural issues, and the diaspora leadership was unable to politically address its internal problems. Like all other confrontations over structural control, this conflict was fought as a political conflict.[101] The loss of an ethnic language and the attack on it by a competing ethnic language represents philosophically the tension that exists between continuity and integration, by proclaiming surreptitiously the existence of a profound desire in most Jews, perhaps openly articulated since the Enlightenment, for an identity transformation of their Jewishness, for which Zionism—in diaspora—became a functional response. This was at the core an identity conflict and a power conflict. This conflict thus became yet another stage in the internal political war. How did it happen?

Since the mid-1940s the "proper" ethnic language was an issue in the local community. When Aliphas started the Tarbut school, the problem for him was not only language but also the general atmosphere and "chalutzian enthusiasm" (pioneering enthusiasm) that he felt the Yidishe Shule was lacking.[102] The Tarbut school included Yiddish in its curriculum until the 1950s, after which it languished. However, Golomb's arrival in Mexico and the expectation that Yiddish was to flourish intensified the Zionists' arguments for Hebrew in their effort to offset his aims.[103] Others were also examining the consequences of selecting or favoring one of the two languages, especially the divisive effect that this could have on the community. In Eretz Israel this problem had slowly become associated with political parties, and with their changing fortunes. In the Mexico of the 1940s, however, there was no systematic advocacy for or against either language; rather, sporadic articles appeared on each position, keeping the issue "fresh" and potentially politicizable. Occasionally, someone protested the increasingly common use of gentile names and the restricted use of Jewish names. Suggestions for the use of Yiddish came almost in passing.

In 1947–49, not long after these initial, scattered events, the language issue took on momentum. These were the years of the crisis concerning Golomb's school. Beyond his educational views, Golomb represented the potential growth of Yiddish. Once the language issue began to get attention, the potential reassertion of Yiddish was seen as a threat (a) by those who favored the language's disappearance and (b) by those who feared its potential to oppose the central (Zionist) power in the community.[104] In reaction, pro-Yiddishists argued that most pro–Eretz Israel organizations used Yiddish; hence, there had been no political conflict around the issue. The question was thus raised: why was Yiddish now associated with "opposition"? At the end of 1947 the Bund was organizing a Folk Universitet where youth were to receive "Yiddish instruction in a serious and systematic way."[105] Maizel was attempting to expand the Yidishe Shule school to include a high-school level; the teacher's seminary, headed also by the same active teachers, was being formed. These steps may have seemed to some to be very threatening expansions.

It is unclear whether these initiatives increased the perception of Yiddish as a political threat or whether they were already responses to a language under attack. What happened was the crystallization of three positions on the subject: one group that "suddenly" started to perceive the fact that Yiddish was being used less; another group that ignored that fact but yet remained active in the language and attempted to expand its domain; and, finally, those who protested the use of Yiddish because they claimed it contained much anti-Zionist innuendo. Salomon Kahan, for example, was vociferous on the spiritual denial that accompanied the denial of Yiddish.[106] He protested against the lack of status and prestige of the Yiddish—and Jewish—teacher, and the demise of the language. At the same time, in December 1947, the Bund was organizing a specific youth branch to "further their socialist ideals" and to "spread secular Jewish culture and its creations." It was also a move to oppose, in their view, "the youth taken with Zionist illusions" that they felt were false or limited. As an important defining point of the group, they emphasized that Yiddish was their official language.[107]

Golomb became a lightning rod for all groups during much of the uproar. Although Golomb's stance did not coincide perfectly with the Bund's position, the Bund appropriated him as a leader. While he avoided being linked exclusively to them, he could not afford to alienate them either. Bundists and Yiddishists could appear politically threatening to those who were sensitive to the issue and ignored the demise of the language. After all, language contains conditioning elements that can foster a variety of loyalties. If language can evoke, it can presumably provoke. And so the Zionist attack was launched directly against Golomb in the school system, since every educational system is a political means of maintaining or modifying a discourse, its language, and the knowledge and power it brings.[108] Zionists thus felt that, if their intuition on language was right, Golomb and Yiddish were two forces to be feared and expunged.

Many avenues were explored during the conflict, some more aggressively than others, but all aiming to achieve the same result. Zionists were on the offensive and all Yiddish culturalists seemed always on the defensive. A less aggressive suggestion was that Zionists unite both schools (Tarbut and Yidishe Shule), promoting the same ideology in both. The idea, which never reached fruition, was that both ethnic languages be kept in the schools to make sure that "a positive spirit to Israel" would reign.[109] But, because political control and not language per se was the real issue, this did not become a viable alternative.

The language struggle in Mexico opened up a lot of unresolved conflict and opposing ideas.[110] Furthermore, the issue illustrated that, at least for diaspora Jews, the Zionist cultural-political solutions of the early part of the century remained unresolved; that not all the political and cultural commitments that Zionists were demanding for all Jews were acceptable commitments. These Zionist "solutions" evoked political coercion, as well as undesired limitations on definitions of identity. For the Zionists, however, the issue presented the opportunity to exert political control and extend the status quo, that is, conflict. Though less physical than in Eretz Israel, the conflict in Mexico involved the coercion and imposition of the practical-political Zionist paradigm, which already had prestige and standing and now carried its own force.

Jews had long recognized the importance of language for retention of group identity.[111] The political confrontation that developed between Hebrew and Yiddish in this century reveals the way language can be used to retain control. Although the language was separate from the realm of religion and traditions, it was always inclusive of these: "The struggle (now) was not on behalf of traditional Hebrew, but on behalf of modern Hebrew."[112]

Since distinct positions coexisted, neither one had become a sectarian movement. The period allowed for space, coexistence, and relative tolerance to groups with their different language approaches when they would not and could not attempt general control. Over time, however, a conflict for power unfolded, because all the groups defined themselves as the most authentic and legitimate way of being Jews: Yiddishists, dual-language advocates, and Hebraists. When new definitions of identity were suggested as mutually exclusive and the parties acquiesced to the new rules of the political game, new boundaries for ethnic inclusion or exclusion were drawn.

If language is the "single most characteristic feature of a separate ethnic identity,"[113] its sociological importance is obvious. That alone would justify focusing on how language became politicized for this community. This conflict, however, adds another twist to the complexity: the groups involved—Hebraists and Zionists—wanted to change their identity and self-awareness, as well as to remain in control of that process. The process, of course, was self-fulfilling: once the language was changed and with it their sense of themselves, they were a changed group. The unmet agenda was the political fight. The fight over language within the community was pragmatic as well as philosophical and political, a fight to extend a new mode of consciousness and being. The act of rebelling against one's language can be interpreted as the search for an exit from a condition of captivity. This ambivalence to group identity seems to have been ingrained in the spectrum of the Ashkenazi population.[114] The inability of the Yiddishists to mount an effective offensive and to transform the situation from an individual to a mass conflict is linked in part to the tacit acquiescence by the masses of the other opposing stance, and a deep desire to change.

Yiddish had become a symbol of "everything that kept Jews from entering the civilized Western society."[115] If Yiddish had once been an emancipatory and developmental force in the symbiosis between Yiddish and the Ashkenazi group,[116] it was no longer perceived as such by many. The tensions between Yiddish and Hebrew were old, with the latter being seen as the holy language. In the nineteenth and twentieth centuries, pro- and anti-Yiddish sentiments took on an intrinsic existential character. Among the modernizing Jewish elites of Warsaw, Vilna, Lodz, and Odessa, the linguistic arguments were well known.[117] Some Jews attributed the external prejudices facing Jews to the Yiddish culture and language. The language issue therefore deflected the animosities directed at them.[118] Some embraced Yiddish to escape from what they felt to be the oppression of religion, and then Yiddish itself became the reflected image of cultural oppression imposed by Western culture. Thus, a reason to reject it was raised. When Zionists added their rejection to this complex context, they were using a symbol that had been erected for rebellion but was now used to rebel against.[119]

*The Older Conflict in Eretz Israel: The Model*

In the effort at renovation, Hebrew and Zionism could be linked: modern Hebrew as the renewed language and unique link to what was presented as the authentic root, and Zionism as the political activity to retake and rebuild the lost sovereignty.[120] At the beginning of the twentieth century, however, the Zionists faced an uncertain future. In the early years of the century, there was nothing to predict either the creation of a Jewish state or the official adoption of Hebrew. In Eretz Israel, political groups were bidding for control of the emerging structure. Among them, two are important for our story because they were the strongest groups in the dispute. The Poalei Tzion (Workers of Zion)[121] was a radical socialist group with powerful branch organizations in Europe and the United States, as well as in Palestine. The second group was Hapoel Hatzair (The Young Worker),[122] the first indigenous Jewish labor party in Palestine. The most characteristic confrontations between these political parties took place primarily during immigration periods. With each wave of Jewish immigration into Palestine (1907, 1914, etc.), the Zionist leadership doubted if any group could retain political power in the country. This was especially true for the Poel Hatzair group. The issue of language catalyzed the struggle for power.[123] It became important for each immigrant to know that solidarity with the emerging body-politic was expected, and that political competition would not be tolerated. Because the political structure of Eretz Israel was still undetermined, the struggle for compliance on the issue of language was at the same time a struggle for ultimate political control. Yiddish became the focus of political contention, being seen as an anachronistic symbol of the world some wanted to leave and as an aberration in any new, authentic definition of the Jew in the world that some wanted to build.

As early as 1905, Yiddishists began their search for a way to defend the Yiddish language and redefine its status, elevating it from jargon (dialect) to language. In 1908, Tshernovitz, a town in the Austro-Hungarian monarchy with a population of only 21,500 Jews, was the site of a language conference where all current views on Yiddish were debated.[124] Four views on the language collided there: the ultraorthodox traditional utilitarian view, for whom Yiddish was the daily secular language and a barrier to further assimilation; the modern utilitarian views of Maskilim, Zionists, and socialists, for whom Yiddish was the tool to reach the masses; the view that saw Yiddish as a natural outcome of Jewish national expression and culture; and, the most radical, the view that saw Yiddish as the sole or major expressive vehicle for Jews. The real conflict was between the last two positions. At the same time, Hebrew had to be recognized and included somewhere. In an attempt to preempt the confrontation with Hebrew, a statement was issued declaring that "Our national language is Hebrew, our folk language is Yiddish."[125] With this equivocal statement, the moral debt to Hebrew was acknowledged. However, the reciprocal feeling, the moral debt of Hebraists to Yiddish, remained absent. Whatever the intent of the conference, it brought about a perceptual change in Yiddish, viewing it as a political-economic force rather than just a cultural symbol.[126]

While these debates were taking place, the fight over the use of Yiddish in Eretz Israel became violent, extreme, and coercive. It is difficult to say if all believed in the eventual triumph of making Hebrew a living language. Almost nobody in the secular camp rejected the attempt, though putting the idea into practice required an extraordinary effort. In daily life, when it was made to appear that the success of the one language depended on the elimination of the other, the confrontation between languages became sharper. In Eretz Israel attacks against Yiddish erupted as soon as the language was perceived as a cultural and political threat to Hebrew hegemony. Publications were silenced;[127] conferences and lectures in Yiddish were attacked in Yaffo, Haifa, and Jerusalem. There were systematic refusals to rent conference rooms to Yiddish speakers, refusals to print Yiddish material, attacks on kiosks selling Yiddish newspapers, and attacks on films. The conflict escalated to the point that an explosive was placed in the publishing house *Liga*.[128]

Certain factions within the Zionist camp, taking their cues from the Hapoel Hatzair, aimed to consolidate a new body politic with new principles and new ideas, and with them, to institutionalize a distinctively Zionist approach. The linguistic change that these groups were eagerly promoting, monitoring, and coercing implied a definition of the "proper" way for Jews to express loyalty. The struggle between Yiddish and Hebrew was thus a deeper struggle over the definition of Jewishness, and how this definition reflected a specially defined ethnic solidarity.[129] The defenders of Hebrew rejected bilingualism as a cure for the pathology which they felt the diaspora had inflicted on Jews. They also sought to change and break down old loyalties,[130] using language for all that it connoted and was linked to. The Poalei Tzion of Palestine sought to attain political hegemony through the supremacy of Hebrew. These Zionists thought that a single language (along with other homogenizing forces such as the army and a new culture) would create a new consciousness, a new consensus, and a united body politic. They knew that language is imbued with the past, and that linguistic change could erase this past.[131] Yiddish, an effective link to the past, thus had to vanish; otherwise it would remain a source of competing loyalty. Yiddish was therefore imbued with the prejudices held by both the outside world and, later, large parts of the Jewish world, making it the "medieval, primitive unassimilable language" that some despised, or learned to do so.[132]

The aggressive controversy and exchange that occurred between the two in-group ethnic languages therefore became a social struggle over a new historical structuring and the definition of a nascent body politic which aspired to be radically different from all older Jewish centers of power. The Zionists' rejection of Yiddish and renewal of Hebrew left them with no paradigm to lean on, but gave them the expectation of creating a new one: utopia. For the Yiddishists, the change implied a personal rejection and the undermining of their cultural paradigm, a situation they neither understood nor wanted.

This no doubt marked an identity crisis for the group; however, it was also a power struggle in which language was used as a test of legitimacy to govern. Zionists attempted to erode previous moral commitments, loosening the institutional roles that linked people to that older culture: this was done by cutting off a language.[133] Ben Gurion, who was always aggressively for Hebrew and against Yiddish, expressed the aim of Zionist policy through the use of language policy. At a conference in 1907, he supported the decision that all party activities be conducted in Hebrew by saying: "if this means to some that we are distancing ourselves from the Galut (Diaspora); well yes, that is the aim with which we came here."[134] More than a decade later, the political use of language was less subtle. In Eretz Israel in 1918–19, the right to run for office and to vote in the assemblies of the Yishuv (community) was limited to Hebrew speakers, using a census to register the elementary knowledge of the Hebrew language of voters and candidates.[135] Obviously, this was not only a linguistic preference, but a clear expression of the political use of language to control the body politic.[136]

The move to limit privileges and rewards to the Hebrew-speaking population over the Yiddish-speaking one was a move to solidify a particular political structure against competing ones. It also furthered a version of the nationalism that the former group promoted. In that version, Hebrew and Eretz Israel were one, with no room for anything defined as diaspora-fed. To support Yiddish, they claimed, was to support "a cult"; the language was deemed deviant and had to be expunged. The language requirement thus emerged as the best criterion for full membership in the developing polity. Language became the test for determining allegiance to a set of beliefs seeking to shape the social order. Language, like faith, "was used as the evidence of things unseen"; it attested to the acceptance of a new secular creed, basic to a new political agenda.[137]

*Mexico—The Language Conflict Forty Years Later*

In 1944, reminiscing on twenty years of school work, Meyer Berger, the first director of the Yidishe Shule, criticized that celebrations of the school were thoroughly empty of Jewish content: they presented Mexican dances, Spanish poetry, and used no Yiddish at all. Despite these occasional awarenesses and their linkage to specific agendas of groups in the community, they represented the struggle to accommodate with the surrounding culture and the various ways Jews adopted to deal with it. Nevertheless, until then, the goal of continuity had dominated the community dialogue and was affirmed, albeit imperfectly, through most organizations and activities of the Ashkenazi community. The ethnic language was included as an essential part of the communal structure. This did not mean, however, that tensions about language were settled or that these could not reemerge unexpectedly as a political point of contention: Yiddish was by no means universally accepted as the language and symbol of continuity.

What the renewed conflict of the late 1940s and 1950s showed was that, even when institutionalized structures exist to further and reproduce an ideology, the process is never perfect and other forces may change whatever seems structural and reified. The variety of forces impinging on the structuring process led to a constant relinking of past and present and contained the motor for change. Other cultural and political agendas, including the integration vision, also played a role even when they were not an explicit threat to the prevailing social structure.

The diminishing use of Yiddish in daily life was not imposed or coerced, but chosen. The primacy of one ethnic language versus the other was not an issue. After all, bilingualism was being obliterated by the languages of the countries where Jews lived. It only became an issue when Yiddish had to defend itself against Hebrew; only then was the fight transformed into a cultural internal struggle.[138] The fight for Hebrew suddenly created an awareness of the weakening of the Yiddish position in general. In fact, the same eroding of identity that was masked by the Yiddish problem in Mexico was the one used by the nineteenth- and twentieth-century Ashkenazi Jews when the old Hebrew language itself was revived, and the project made a success: Jews choosing to speak Hebrew expressed a desire to change.[139] The same latent forces for and against Yiddish were active in Mexico, and Zionists in Mexico trying to reassert their hegemony benefited from the lack of will to defend Yiddish in the diaspora, too.

In 1947, the fight over language was emblematic of the last major battle of the war for political control between the old forces imported from Europe. Because it echoed the exact arguments that had been used in Eretz Israel in the early part of the century, the language debate became a way for Zionists to reaffirm and solidify their identity and territorial control. For the Yiddishists, among whom the Bundists composed the largest but by no means the only contingent, this became a symbolic fight to retain the cultural roots of their thoughts, acts, and being, which they saw destroyed by the Holocaust. It was philosophically and temperamentally incomprehensible to them that, after the war, Zionism would be furthering the destruction of Jewish culture. Moreover, the clearer it became that Zionists had established a state and prevailed over other political options, the more difficult it was for Yiddishists to understand the Zionists persistence in their attack. For the Yiddishists, concessions on the political front did not imply acquiescing on the language issue. They were therefore lulled into thinking that language was a discrete topic, and grounded their position on sentimental and philosophical arguments rather than political ones. The combination of thought wrapped in nostalgia only made the Yiddishists weaker in a world that required political thought and action.

An anti-Yiddish letter published in *Der Veg* epitomized the argument on language:[140] Yiddish, the writer suggested, could not be valued because it was diaspora-linked, a dialect, Germanic, lacking in authentic value. The article caused a reaction in Mexico and in New York.[141] Yosef Rotenberg, a Holocaust survivor and Bundist activist, writer, and teacher, called it "a vulgar kick to our folk-language, a kick to our folk-soul, a mean profanation of our holiest feelings." In what was a typical statement in defense of the language, he added:

> Yiddish is today much more than just a language. Yiddish is today a symbol, a symbol hallowed in martyrdom. Yiddish is the groan from our suffered ones and the song from our lost ones, those that perished "al kidush hashem" (sanctifying His name). Yiddish is our consolation and hope; Yiddish takes us further into the battlefields of our history. To detach oneself from Yiddish is to detach oneself from a living Jewish people, it means detachment from hundreds of years of folk-creation.[142]

But these thinkers failed in translating this cultural plea into a political demand. The cultural argument was not convincing enough to the masses who then and now did not see it as rewarding as the Zionist project was made to be.

The institutions that sought to retain, rebuild, or promote Yiddish and Jewish culture, were, aside from the schools, the Teachers Seminary and the Folk Universitet. "The Folk Universitet will be the place," according to Rotenberg, "where an authentic folkist intelligentsia will be forged."[143] There, he felt and hoped, the sensitivity and consciousness for folk values would be nourished. Occasionally, *La Voz Sionista* would publish an article against Yiddish,[144] based on the local Zionist platform; but the fact that the Tarbut school then taught Yiddish was publicized too.[145] This showed that the community could not so easily politicize the language issue; there was resistance.

Yiddishists, in the midst of the school conflict, often referred to the Zionist attacks on language as they had taken place in Israel. In Mexico, as others had done in Eretz Israel before, they asked for guaranties on the formal and political status of Yiddish. They protested the fact that most diaspora organizations that held Yiddish as essential but supported Israel were now thought of as not thoroughly Zionistic; they had been first accepted and now pushed to the side. Again and again, the negative attitude towards Yiddish by Israeli organizations, government, and press was commented on in Mexico. The defenders of Yiddish were puzzled by the fact that Israel allowed and produced two German dailies, one English, one French, one Polish, one Rumanian, and one Bulgarian, but none in Yiddish. There were only two Yiddish weeklies. The Yiddishists in Mexico requested, as had been done forty years earlier in Eretz Israel, that the "Ivri" (Hebrew) should not be separate from the "Yehudi" (Jew), meaning the Israeli from the diaspora Jew. Both languages were referred to, metaphorically, as part of one culture, "like two eyes of one head."[146]

In 1949 it seemed that some Jews of Mexico had attained a clearer political understanding of the unequal bilingual policy.[147] This understanding was articulated, but much too late: it was articulated only after Yiddishists confronted it all as an irreversible reality. The conflict was then acknowledged as a political maneuver used to measure Jewish solidarity with Israel. Yiddishists understood that the fight over language was also a fight over a discourse and a style. Language was represented as potential power, and language control represented actualized power. The fight therefore determined who could speak, how, and why. For a moment, then, it seemed that this understanding could produce at least a political agenda. But it did not. The struggle in the cultural realm became the tool to establish a boundary demarcating one side as legitimate, the other as expendable. Further, the fight was not about discourse only; it also encompassed behavior that signaled loyalty to a specific group.

However, Yiddishists came out with nothing more than a request and a hope for mutual brotherly understanding: the Leshana Haba B'Yerushalaim, they said ("next year in Jerusalem"), goes together with the prophet Isaiah's view of the future in which "the wolf shall dwell with the lamb." Neither a political posture nor a strategy, this stance precluded a frontal attack and a choice between mutually exclusive options. The Yiddishists were both guarding against the break, and suffering the repression of the break. In their position, the Yiddish defenders clearly recognized the importance of Israel. Even if these groups had initially seen Israel as just "another" community, the reality of the new Jewish state had changed the international political structure dramatically, and Yiddishists granted and conceded that in their thinking. They had understood the moral necessity of the state, and they supported it. Part of their tentative position derived from this premise. If diaspora Jews had been instrumental for Israel, Israel was now recognized to be instrumental for Jews everywhere. But the losing of this cultural, intellectual, and political option for Jews was not just a matter of losing part of the "unnecessary" past. It unexpectedly and unforseeably meant losing part of the future. In failing to address diaspora culture politically, Jews failed to address the political context of the diaspora itself. Diaspora never became an understood social program, neither in Israel and nor in the diaspora itself. But the diaspora never ceased to exist, and it became a phantom problem for Zionists as well as for diaspora Jews. The language to address itself had been, if not totally vanquished, at least severely wounded.

## Political Aims through Language Policy

The Zionist rekindling of the language conflict in Mexico was a reenactment of the language policy conflict that took place in Eretz Israel between Yiddish and Hebrew speakers. Yiddishists in Mexico were reluctant to ignore the Zionist policies, which broadened the conflict beyond the confines of education and extended it to the wider community. Golomb's loss of the Yidishe Shule, the Tarbut's becoming a Hebrew-only school, and the wider attack on the Yiddish language all signaled the modification of the communal structure in its content, if not in its outer form. The declining prestige of Yiddish and its dethroning as the main language of communication of the Ashkenazim represented the acceptance of the dominance of the Zionists and their attainment of political hegemony. Zionists used this to secure diaspora support and establish their presence in the organizations, using either negotiation or force, as the failed deal with Golomb and the language policy show.

The declining prestige of Yiddish and diaspora culture was not followed by the quick adaptation and change of all existing social arrangements. It was part of a historical process, linked to an international pattern; it formally confirmed the change in the political system.[148] At the same time, the rank-and-file did not react. Had the leadership not clearly articulated a posture for them to follow, or were they acquiescing? Or had they really longed for change and seen Zionism as the "solution" to their conflicts? Ethnic language cannot erode in just one generation, becoming a hollow cultural-religious ceremonial reference point, without affecting the group dramatically. There was astonishment: as if by seeing the present conflict, a piece of the undesired future was revealed.

The activists' astonishment[149] once they realized the diminished stature of Yiddish in education, politics, and culture reveals the unexpected success of integration compared to continuity in the community. The passive acceptance of the use of Hebrew as more rewarding by the supposedly large Yiddish-speaking public may be interpreted as a type of opposition to Yiddish. Those who saw the Yiddish language, culture, and identity as an imprisonment weakened it by escaping into another world; the group thus legitimized the outcome of the conflict, and, at the same time, attained further integration.

The Yiddishist leaders could not have been so detached from the masses as they built a network of organizations based on the principles they were defending. These principles had been addressed and debated openly as part of a political agenda. So, the question is, why did the public not participate actively in the language issue? Why were more persons not willing to fight for their own language? Was the public so changed, or did the leadership assume that their public aims were not going to be affected by the private agenda of each individual? Why did they assume that the two sets of goals were consistent?

Golomb had suggested that identity was shaped by language, culture, and tradition. He also suggested that the lack of language fostered not only social loss and detachment but also profound internal and social anomie. The only solution, Golomb claimed, was to retain the past through interpretations. The loss of the language was the symbolic loss of a whole world.[150] For Golomb, Yiddish, Jewish culture, and the Jewish way of life, including Hebrew, contained the elements of continuity required for the successful process of transmission and to modify and develop what was transmitted. Culture was never static, but an essential core had to remain for the identity growing out of it to be recognizable.

Yet Golomb's ideology, like that of many other Yiddishists, was less a pragmatic political agenda than a code and a language for cultural-ethics. Culture and language were to be understood within moral parameters. Culture, Golomb argued, should not be treated merely as a tool for esthetic entertainment devoid of ethical considerations. Esthetics had to be superseded by ethics. If one could only be present to the world and others through language, then ethnic language and culture were constructs essential for the group's existence.

At its best, the Yiddishist response was presented in emotional and philosophical terms. First and foremost, the Yiddishists responded to the devaluation of the language itself as if they were still elaborating the agenda for the language conference at Tshernovitz (1908), where the legitimization of the language was an issue. However one defines the response, its timing, linked to the political events of the 1950s, limited its effects.

For Golomb, the intellectual object and the practical project was to think and live one's own history, not to free oneself from it. Only then could one think creatively, live connectedly, and build a future.[151] Only by affirming continuity could the collectivity restore, recover, and build. Golomb, however, never provided collective guidance for addressing and countering linguistic politics. He spoke to the individual and his consciousness, not to the group. While one party, in its aim to secure organizational and ideological hegemony, used language policy as a means to an end, the other group, the defenders, addressed and explored only the unthreatening character of the language: survival, culture, identity. These were two distinct discourses, but one lacked the other's power, immediacy, and practicality. The Yiddishists, feeling helpless, analyzed their ideology of survival, while the Hebraists, feeling hopeful, practiced the politics of survival. Ironically, Golomb, the defender of shtetl life and culture, was unable to break from the philosophizing and toleration that were essential to ethnic ideological accommodation. He was concerned with the subjectivity of culture, while practical Zionists were oriented by the objectivity of politics. Although Golomb's thought was affected by the reality of the new Jewish state, he was unable to react and incorporate that reality; the experience of grief and loss evoked in him and others like him a desire to retain rather than let go.

In the 1950s, Zionists in Israel concentrated further on how to consolidate that success. This coincided with their battling against Yiddish in diaspora, while they eased their stance in Israel. Only after power was secure did Israel make minor concessions to cultural diversity. It was then that Yiddish was given some recognition: in 1949 the Histadrut launched the journal that became and still is the most prestigious journal in Yiddish of its kind, *Di Goldene Keit* (The Golden Chain), headed by the renowned poet and writer Avraham Sutzkever. The Hebrew University of Jerusalem, ending a long and bitter battle that begun in New York in 1927, opened a Department of Yiddish in 1951. The height of Zionism's prestige in Mexico coincided with its attempt to impose a cultural homogeneity rooted in the Zionist perspective. This, ironically, occurred at the same time that the official Israeli policy began allowing some pluralist expression. While Jews in Mexico were experiencing the imposition of a cultural and political pattern which defined identity and communal life, Israeli policies were moving in the direction of greater tolerance.[152]

In Mexico, much had been culturally lost. The loss through language and of language is extremely difficult to assess. Yiddish for this generation cannot be compared to the loss of any other social "fact" or "thing," or even made parallel to other languages (e.g., Ladino, Judezmon, Judeo-Persian, Judeo-Arabian, Targum, etc.). There is an immediate historical, generational, and biographical connection to Yiddish that the other languages lack. The community in Mexico had its own experience with this cultural loss. Whatever the definition of Jewish reality in the 1950s and 1960s, it did not come about as a Hegelian synthesis of opposing forces. It was a result of visions and forces that fluctuated in their weakness and strength. Golomb and the Yiddishists in Mexico, departing from the earlier attempt of the either/or position, wanted a synthesis. Sadly, they were unable to articulate it politically.

In Mexico in the 1990s, a very faint conversation between these visions is still heard. An attempt to offer courses in Yiddish for teachers and other professionals is fighting with the inherited values of the 1950s. It is too soon to know what the next generation will want and do with what it has heard, but this generation is engaged in the continuing debate, whether it recognizes it or not.[153]

## INCOMPLETE ALLOWANCE:
## THE POLITICS OF INTERRELATION

> Once the inevitabilities are challenged, we begin gathering our
> resources for a journey of hope.
> —Raymond Williams

Citizenship was the most important issue determining relations between Mexicans and Jews in this century. By allowing Jews to become citizens, even in the absence of a definite immigration policy, Mexico unexpectedly became host to a Jewish community. There is now plenty of evidence to show that the interrelations between the minorities and the government in Mexico were uneven. There was always an incompleteness in the political possibilities allowed to any group that was persistently seen as the "other." Citizenship, theoretically a form of equalization, can in fact reproduce other forms of inequality and repression.[154] When a society that opens its doors to "others" does not, in turn, allow them to openly maintain their otherness through political channels, a type of cultural violence is committed. While the minority may experience discomfort from this symbolic violence, it often mistakes it for an unachieved equality, the imperfect functioning of the system, or some internal communal problem. It seldom sees it as the result of limitations in the political space offered. Though the minority defines itself and is defined as such by the government, citizenship fosters a condition of political atomization.[155] The result of such interrelation is a mutual identity crisis stemming from the mismatch between the expected behavior of the self and the imposed conditions of that society. Because no pluralism was expressed within the formal Mexican structure,[156] minority distinction has been invoked by the government in an ad hoc fashion. At the same time, minority communal response has always been politically undermining.

The result is a structural political condition limiting the possibilities for minority self-expression, an "incomplete allowance." This concept refers to a specific type of political violence which limits the rights of a minority to live its cultural difference fully—politically and philosophically. The concept also suggests that the government continually manipulates the boundary of political incorporation.

The condition of political incompleteness started as a structure which the majority imposed on the minority, reproducing itself as the minority struggled to fit into the mold offered by the majority. But because the condition persists under the explicitly equalizing formula of citizenship, it is difficult to identify the source of the particular violence the minority experiences, and it, in turn, becomes unwilling to challenge the situation. Incomplete allowance refers to the government's actions vis-à-vis the minority as well as to the political and philosophical incompleteness of the minority. Further, incomplete allowance also affects the majority, which in defining itself as an open, free, and democratic society, deceives itself and misrepresents its own image. Thus political misrepresentation is used and imposed in a society, with consequences on a minority. The autonomous individuals who have rights of citizenship find themselves in a problematic situation when they decide to act as an aggregate. The state can shift its position on their inclusion into or exclusion from the body politic. Their loyalty and legitimacy always have to be proven. The problem of incorporating diverse political cultures and perspectives into a single social unit remains largely unresolved, resulting in arguments about loyalty and unity between and among groups that must coexist within a larger, often hostile world.

In their quest for some autonomy, the Ashkenazi community had to deal with two forces: with the Mexican government, because of its territorial location, and with any organized Jewish group to which it owed cultural-religious alliance. Inside the country, the connections of the Jewish community with other international Jewish organizations had always been regarded with distrust. After all, those multiple alliances proved to the Mexicans that this population was not fully commited to its newer political status as citizens of the country. Yet international Jewish organizations such as the American World Jewish Congress (WJC), which was a voluntary association of representative Jewish bodies, communities, and organizations from all over the world, organized to foster the unity and protection of the Jewish people.[157] The contacts of the Jews in Mexico with the local politicians were too few, their lobbying was too weak: from the perspective of the WJC, these Jews were not helping the Jewish cause. In 1948, when there was intense Jewish lobbying to create a Jewish state, the WJC found Jews in Mexico contributed little to their efforts.[158] But the inneffectual attempt to further Zionist goals[159] by forging links between the Jewish community and general Mexican society was not only the result of communal disorganization, as the WJC representative suggested. The constraints that Mexican society imposed on this minority made it very difficult for them to act as a minority. Having accepted citizenship, and lacking channels to justify collective minority action, Jews in Mexico were not interested in being seen as a group linked to an outside entity, for this interest in a "foreign political body" would allow their hosts to label them as disloyal to the Mexican state. This kind of activity or lobbying, in the context of a government that ignored the minority condition as a facet of the political life of the group, appeared to be unwise.

World Zionist leadership strived to get world opinion to sympathize with the need for a Jewish state, but the Mexican government remained undecided. A campaign was launched to gain the Mexican vote,[160] and, though nothing was promised to them, Jews expected results. Much of the activity was initiated by and directed from the central international Zionist body. In the end, however, the Mexican government abstained in the United Nations' vote on the partition of Palestine. In explaining itself, the government sought to be even-handed vis-à-vis both Jews and Arabs. In a statement, Ambassador de la Colina stressed Mexico's sympathy for the Jewish people and explained the active stance that the government had taken against the "barbaric procedures" of Nazism; he also reminded Jews that Mexico had opened its doors to "thousands of refugees." At the same time, he praised Syrian and Lebanese citizens who had made their home in Mexico, devoting themselves "to work" and offering "their love" to the country and its people. But the ambassador's attempt at balance revealed a curious difference in his treatment of Jews and Arabs. When referring to Jews, it was Mexico's actions that were highlighted, and even exaggerated; in referring to the Arabs, it was their giving actions that were acknowledged.[161]

The incomplete allowance of the Jewish political position was exposed: the Jews in Mexico had been neither sufficiently active nor successful in securing Mexico's affirmative vote for the Jewish state, nor were they comfortable in their internal status within the country. The abstention of the government was then doubly wounding. As a Jew suggested in the local Yiddish press, "It hurts me as a Mexican Jewish citizen. . . . We, Mexican Jewish citizens are sure that we have helped very much in the local economic development of the last 25–30 years."[162] The repetition of the fact that they were "Mexican Jewish citizens" flew in the face of the government's attempt to destroy the sense of belonging they felt they had rightfully earned. The Jews in Mexico felt inadequate in their role as advocates of the state of Israel; yet, seen as a minority by the Mexican government when they acted as individual citizens, they also felt threatened.

After this tension in the relationship between majority and minority, Jews began to focus on themselves, their condition, their political space. But this introspection also took the form of self-punishment. Jews seemed to need to prove an exaggerated and compensatory loyalty that could not be effectively expressed through government channels. This resulted in a bizzare incident within the community. When Israel was declared a state, celebratory activities were organized. The community did fundraising for the young state as before, but now there were Jews for whom the pressure of this effort seemed excessive. A group of eleven members of the community, headed by Dr. Abraham King, a territorialist, and Jacob Abrams, an anarchist,[163] formed a Defense Committee to ward off what they saw as undue pressure from communal leaders. They protested to the World Jewish Congress in New York, suggesting that WJC representatives in Mexico were engaging in what they considered to be "illegal practices." They explained that money in support of the Jewish state had already been sent, and protested that the most recent drive had been characterized by intimidation and the use of coercive methods. The Jewish press in Mexico, they said, had announced that those who "refuse to contribute" or failed to do so in "large sums" would be judged in an open trial. They therefore wrote on 23 June to protest the fact that such a trial had taken place on 16 June 1948. They described further that a hand-picked jury was "imposing prearranged sanctions," and that there was a "lynching spirit," as the newspaper *Di Shtime* termed it. Seven sanctions were imposed, even a type of *kheirem* (ban).[164] A list of the "accused" would later be given to the government of Israel, which would presumably impose its own sanctions. The protesters deemed these actions both illegal under Mexican law, and reprehensible as a moral violation of basic religious Jewish principles. Their counterthreat was to use the Mexican and American press to their own advantage.

This imposition of what was defined as acceptable political and economic behavior is an account of rules applied by a dominant sector that is frightened about the possibility of being displaced by individuals they would rather see in the periphery. It is also an example of the exaggerated display of solidarity and loyalty that ostensibly asserts connectedness to the ethnic group while other connections remain loose. It may be suggested that the internal violence experienced by the community when its legitimacy was undermined by the government precipitated the harsh imposition of sanctions within the ethnic group. Thus, the minority searched for ways to legitimize its condition as a minority while affirming its different relationship with the majority. In the process the Jews did not question the majority but themselves, thereby limiting their capacity to analyze their political condition. Hurt by being perceived as "not so loyal," they turned inwards "to prove" their loyalty.

The condition of incomplete allowance is always present but becomes sharper in moments of crisis. In such situations, Jews expose more clearly the political incompleteness in their thinking and their actions. At the same time, the extent to which the minority was subjected to a policy of incomplete allowance by the government is revealed.

This episode demostrated the condition of political exile of the Jewish minority and its unstable status as members of Mexican society. It is in the interplay of discourse and power between the groups that we see most clearly the nature of the political space given to "others," specifically to the Jews in Mexico. As citizens, Jews did not relinquish their right to be different; this fact was implicit in their understanding of their identity, though there were no available political channels through which they could exercise or assert it. Minority difference was maintained by the majority as a convenience that was highlighted or not at a chosen moment. This symbolic exclusion which is imposed on Jews by their being unable to participate in the political definitions of the country is merely the "reverse of the effort to impose a definition of legitimate practice";[165] in other words, it represents not a move towards democracy, but away from it. In a way, it is as if Jews as minorities have not allowed themselves to use the power of identifying or challenging that which represses them, and choose to live their condition confused, while neither the majority nor the government recognizes the fact that they silence the other.[166] This particular form of violence can only be practiced on subjects who know and feel, but who also endorse this form of domination with their own actions.[167]

This is not to suggest that conflict among groups—whether cultural minorities, religious minorities, or other—can disappear. We cannot expect the goals of different groups to be compatible all the time; there will always be conflict. What is proposed here is the possibility of avoiding "morally intolerable" actions without at least offering the possibility of a communication about alternatives to those involved.[168] If pluralism as an overall value is rejected within a group and between the groups, we are condemning people to live a fragmented internal existence under a totalizing society with but one truth.[169]

The increasing moral dilemma faced by Jews in Mexico having to juggle their loyalties and cultural attachments has not been solved. The fact that "acceptable" Jews exist today—using *acceptable* as a definition imposed by the other—and that they are occasionally received by the government, is a function of time, adaptation, language assimilation, and other acculturating factors. The structural condition of incomplete allowance in which Jews find themselves forces them to be ambiguous on "who are they": Jews, Mexicans, Jews of Mexico, Mexican-Jews, etc. Each of these labels represents a transitory identity: it provides guidance on how to act in any given situation but does not contribute to a coherent identity. Jews, as any minority or any other group that is defined as the "other" in society, should be able to express and defend their own conduct through channels which do not cast doubt on their qualifications to be included in society. The doubt and fear that arise from persistent questions such as "Is he or she one of us?" and "Are we one of them?" are evidence of the site of crisis. As John Shotter has stated:

> To live under terms set only by others is always to feel not just different but inadequate in relation to these others. It is, I think, a sickness or a tiredness in having continually to live a life not of one's own, [with] a desire to have a voice and to be listened to seriously as of *right* . . .

The incomplete allowance of citizenship is but a form of conditional membership for the minority. In Mexico, the minority lives in peace as a group within a space; yet it remains within its political space as people living in a room, but a room with no view.

*Afterword*

If this section is read as the description of the establishment of a dominant ideology, it must also be read as a description of some of the effects that the group faced once cultural homogeneity was enforced. Though one can easily understand the desire of leaders to retain power indefinitely and the bureaucratic inertia which favors a dominant ideology over a plurality of world views, it is nevertheless difficult to explain why the limitations on plural thinking and acting that were so subtly introduced became so readily accepted by the masses. Furthermore, it is difficult to understand how this community, which nourished a diversity of opinions and styles, can hardly recognize its current condition.

The cultural distance between pioneers and later generations, as well as the cultural alienation and estrangement that came to characterize younger cohorts, were most evident during the fight over language, when the survival of only one ethnic language was at stake. With the loss of language, the possibility for sustaining a culturally attached and examined life has been limited. This political and cultural trend within the community is an awesome social fact. Undergirding this conflict was an ideology which in effect redefined reality. Zionism accepted the rejection of Jews by much of Western civilization; other secular Jewish ideologies either ignored this, circumvented it, or attempted to change it. This fact gave Zionism an undisputed force and a sense of reality. It strengthened its power once the state of Israel became a reality. As legitimate and grounded as its international policies may have been, Zionism fostered internal policies which foreclosed to many in the diaspora the possibility of anchoring themselves in this ethnicity.[170]

These diaspora Jews have lost a great part of their grip on the past. They did not lose all their past, nor all access to the past. But they lost a large portion of it and, what is more important, the ability to return systematically to it to be able to direct their future. If to hold a meaningful view of the future requires an anchor in the past, Jews in this diaspora, now detached, have further removed themselves from that possibility.

In offering such a critique of the current condition of the Ashkenazi Jew in a diaspora, it is the future which I would like to retake. The fact that certain political choices have foreclosed the cultural possibilities of the group is not only a problem for those who are directly affected by the imposed limitations and restraints, but also an existential Jewish problem which needs to be addressed by all Jews. In fact, this problem encapsulates a general current social condition. Part of the modern Jewish struggle has been a fight for the possibility to be able to live as equals with cultural and religious differences in any society. The inability to attain that functional condition in most of the world gave rise to the Zionist agenda for a national solution for Jews. Yet, given that solution, the world has not subdivided into internally homogeneous groups. Modern societies continue to be extremely heterogeneous, still unable to deal with that condition. Citizenship has not offered a positively secure solution to minorities, as most of what has happened in this latter part of the century has proven. The conditional character of living as a minority has not been done away with. To be able to live openly with one's culture, in the broadest sense of the word, has been, to a degree, the Jews' political agenda. As a result, the internal fights that have limited their cultural plurality are as important as the external fights that threaten the cultural plurality of minorities everywhere.

The social problem we are addressing is not just a political issue but a moral one. The two levels of restrictions must be addressed in the future if we are to overcome the internal and external oppressions of society. If the statement that "Man must realize himself morally"[171] is not a commandment, it must at least be an aspiration. The future may be different from the past, and this may even be desirable. However, if nothing of the past is acknowledged in the future, we are condemning group life to be contingent and without meaning. The future must offer, at the very least, a way to recognize certain meanings of the past. It is not then the ambiguity offered by multiple cultural loyalties that we want to escape. Ambiguity is built into the condition of minority/majority as well as on all social living, and if social difference with equality is the goal for the next century, it must be addressed and recognized as an ethical-political demand that all men and women have upon each other.

Cultural pluralism and the coexistence of different groups has been a world political problem for a long time, but the infamous history of this century, and the current economic and political restructurings of the regions, seem to demand coexistence as an even more urgent goal. For Jews, in Israel and the diaspora, these were the two options, not mutually exclusive, although much of the debate assumed they were. Zionism accepted the reality Western civilization had often tried to enforce; for the

Zionists, Jews could survive only in their own land. None disputed the need for a Jewish land: but its corollary, the inability for Jews to live in diaspora, not only did not make practical sense, but contained a terribly dangerous philosophical premise. It ignored or overlooked the fact that the condition of intercultural living is universal and unavoidable.

All Jews then lost culturally essential elements. But Ashkenazi diaspora Jewry lost more: it lost the possibility to affirm its own condition, a prerequisite for its own cultural renewal. To lose parts of one's culture and to lose one's language is no small thing. This quiet and almost unnoticed loss is, however, symbolic of an even greater alienation: the losing of access to one's culture for the renewal of its meaning.

# NOTES

## CHAPTER 1. THE REESTABLISHING
## OF AN ACQUAINTANCESHIP

1. Though that is a style of argumentation often heard, Jews can either be described as the worst or the best; both cases make them unusual subjects. See Manuel Payno's description in 1889 of a Jew, Nathaniel Davidson, whom he characterized as "the best and most amiable subject I have ever met in the world" (in González Navarro 1994, 2:426–27).

2. One must highlight that immigration still occurred in New Spain as well as in Brazil, despite the difficulties. See Anita Novisky, "Jewish Roots in Brazil," in Elkin and Merkx 1987:43.

3. Gojman 1991. She traces a network of cripto-Jews who were persecuted; see also her *Trujillo-Indias, una ruta de conversos,* vol. 2 (1994).

4. See Cosío Villegas 1988, vols. 1 and 2.

5. For the French case, see Nichols Barker 1980.

6. See Margalit and Halbertal 1994, as they make the argument for the right to a culture in the case of Israel.

7. Zoriada Vázquez 1988.

8. The current population estimate of Mexico is about 90 million inhabitants.

9. See González 1988.

10. Ibid.:"para unirse y confundirse con los hijos del país."

11. González Navarro 1994, vol. 2.

12. The same argument was later used against Mexicans in the United States.

13. Notice that this kind of treaty never came about for the Jews, as there was no political entity sufficiently central that could represent them.

14. Turner 1971:261. In the state of Sonora in 1923 and 1930 there were laws against marriages between Mexicans and Chinese.

15. Turner 1971:93–95. See also Mishima 1985. Later, President Díaz (1880–1910) also sponsored immigration of foreigners and repatriated Mexicans; about sixty colonies were created, thirty-seven by foreigners, of which thirty-two were privately financed by French, Belgian, Spanish, Boer, Japanese, Russian, Puerto Rican, and American sources. Mormons also came, after they received their Privilegium, the guarantee of their right to polygamy. See Sawatzky 1971:53.

16. Lerner de Sheinbaum and Ralsky de Cimet 1976.

17. Chalmers 1977:29, 41.

18. This statement, already part of American folklore, needs qualification. The U.S. immigration policy was not just a good-hearted policy of the govern-

ment. As Steinberg (1981) suggests, America needed immigration as much as the immigrant needed America: 32 million people immigrated between 1820 and 1930; they constituted cheap, mobile labor, taking "for the most part exploitative jobs at the time when American capitalism was in its most rapacious phase" (38).

19. Soyer 1986. Soyer illustrates the monetary connection between the Landsmanschaftn and European Jewry. See also Anita Brenner (September 1926), for the *Jewish Telegraphic Agency*, on the smuggling of Jews from Europe to the United States through Mexico.

20. Zárate Miguel 1986:78–79.

21. From the A.G.N. Dirección General de Gobierno, Circulares de la Secretaría de Relaciones Exteriores; see Carreño 1994:73–74.

22. See Leff 1979.

23. Turner 1971:65.

24. Meyer 1973.

25. See *Excélsior* (Mexico), Dec. 1919, Jan. 1920.

26. *Der Veg*, Yubilei Oisgabe, 1940, p. 203.

27. The Alliance Israelite of Paris was the first modern Jewish international organization (1860), organized by French Jews "for the emancipation and moral progress of Jews; to offer effective assistance to Jews suffering from anti-Semitism." It did not work on behalf of minority rights and Zionism; rather, it was begun to provide assistance to Jews who wanted to leave countries where they suffered. See *Encyclopedia Judaica* 1:647–54.

28. González Navarro 1994:90–91.

29. Krause 1970:327–28. Krause explains that attempts were made in 1907 to bring eighty thousand Russian Jews to colonize part of the state of Jalisco. The experiment failed.

30. As reported in *Freeland*, the Jewish-American Territorialist journal, there was as late as June 1957 a Jewish agro-industrial committee that was attempting colonization in Mexico, with (as they reported) the sympathy of the government. However, problems with the immigration laws and lack of money made it a failure. See *Freeland*, April–June 1957, p. 5.

31. *Freeland*, Dec. 1955.

32. Lesser 1972; González Navarro 1960.

33. Zárate 1986:61.

34. See *Freeland*, 1945 (vol. 1, no. 3).

35. Important on the subject are also Manuel Gamio and Andrés Molina Enríquez, among others.

36. Shabot 1990. In 1940, Vasconcelos created the magazine *Timón*, and showed himself to be a pro–Hitler-Mussolini Catholic who, while deprecating most of political life, expressed a visceral, racist anti-Semitism.

37. Hansen 1971:22–23.

38. Bazant 1977:162.

39. See Ashkenazi 1982.

40. See Bokser 1992.

41. See Berliner 1936.

42. Brenner 1924.

43. A. Gojman, *Wizo*, July–Sept. 1984.
44. *Fraindt*, Sept. 1962, p. 11.
45. J. Belkind, *Undzer Vort*, May–June 1927, p. 5.
46. Anita Brenner, *Jewish Telegraphic Agency*, 1 August 1925, Archive Amigos de la Universidad Hebrea de Jerusalen, Mexico.
47. See Brenner 1928:30.
48. Ibid.
49. Available statistics are very weak on this information. The one and only internal study of communal demography was conducted in 1991 (and came out in public in 1993) by a joint effort of the Hebrew University of Jerusalem and El Colegio de México.
50. This is probably different for the case of the United States and, for instance, Argentina in Latin America. There is and has been a long on-going discussion over whether Jews have attained a kind of hyphen or not with other cultures/nationalities. There is a lack of agreement as to whether the term *hyphenated Jews* (paraphrasing Sosnowski) is an unproblematic reality. See Elkin and Merkx 1987, especially section 5. Senkman (1987:236) finds that the integrationist project in Argentina did not allow for a continuing loyalty to Jewish ethnicity, and Jews, paradoxically, persisted in double loyalties. Sosnowski (1987) interprets the minority-majority relations as fairly accomodationist, especially achieved through a literature that "bridges these worlds." However, Senkman's view differs, since for him Gerschunoff, the writer "whose literary achievements were rewarded with special acceptance, was unable to translate this personal achievement into the acceptance of Jewish culture by Argentines" (269); that, for Senkman, is a better test of the cultural exchange.
51. Sosnowski 1987:297. See also Sosnowski 1986. The discussions in Mexico on the issue were developed in the First National Jewish Conference, Kehila, 1973, where it was suggested that the hyphen is not a new hybrid but rather an amalgamation of multiple loyalties. See also Moshinsky 1977:4 and Coriat 1979:39.
52. A new generation of Jewish writers, mostly women writers, has emerged in Mexico. They are not included in this study since this analysis aims specifically to trace the thought that had direct impact in the building of the communal network. Their efforts, produced later in time, have remained peripheral and have not achieved consequentiality in communal terms, the requirement to be included in this study.

## CHAPTER 2. THE DEVELOPMENT OF THE COMMUNAL STRUCTURE

1. *Der Veg*, Nov. 1936.
2. Merkx, in Elkin and Merkx 1987.
3. *Undzer Vort*, no. 16, 1929, p. 2; also Jan. 1931. Gojman, *Wizo*, July–Sept. 1984; *Der Veg*, 25 Sept. 1936.
4. Meyer 1978; Medin 1983; Gojman 1994, with Gloria Carreño (see vol. 1 for demographic information, and vol. 7).

5. *Der Veg,* Yubilei Oisgabe, p. 140.

6. *Forois,* no. 25, 1944, p. 4.

7. Dr. King, *Freeland,* April 1956.

8. *American Jewish History* 79.1:320.

9. Feingold 1981. See also Goren 1970, who concluded that "most Jews remained interested in the minimum of separation necessary from the larger society for maintaining their Jewish identity" (252).

10. Bartra 1987; Lafaye 1974; Pérez Ruiz 1992.

11. Ashkenazi 1982; Gojman, "Migración" (n. d.); Martínez Montiel 1988; Gojman, *Conversos* (n. d.); Gojman et al. 1987; *Tribuna Israelita y Multibanco Mercantil,* 1987.

12. Hamui de Halabe 1989.

13. Merton 1976:164–65.

14. *Der Veg,* 15 Sept. 1936. Notice that 15 September is National Independence Day in Mexico, and it is then that analysis of the Jewish presence in Mexico is presented.

15. Attacks occured in Yucatán, San Luis Potosí, Guadalajara, Monterrey, Mazatlán, and Mexico City. Anti-Semitic material appeared often in *La Prensa, El Nacional, Vanguardia Nacionalista,* etc.

16. Abruch 1971; Gojman 1987.

17. Meyer 1973, especially vol. 2, "El Conflicto entre la Iglesia y el Estado, 1926–1929."

18. De Romano 1978; also my interview with Glantz.

19. Zárate 1986:152.

20. *Der Veg,* Yubilei Oisgabe, p. 142.

21. J. Glantz, *Hilf,* 1950, pp. 22–25.

22. See Sennett 1978.

23. See Goren 1970; also Hyman 1979, Endelman 1983, and the recent chronicle by Calvin Trillin (1994) of the conflict over the "Eruv" (demarcation line) in northern London. In all of these, one finds descriptions of the tensions between "newcomers" and "established Jews."

24. Differences in reading style of the Megillah text in the Purim holiday resulted in a fight.

25. The list of publications is as follows: *Oif Der Vokh* (1931; two issues only), edited by Verbinsky; *Meksikaner Yidishe Shriftn* (1932–1934); *Farn Folk* (1932; Zionist leanings); *Oifboi* (1935), from Gezbir, edited by J. Glantz; *Land un Arbet,* pro-Palestine, with Mindlin and M. Rubinstein as editors; *Meksikaner Shriftn* (1935–1936, monthly for about four months), edited by Glikovsky; *In Kamf* (1936), edited by Kahan; *Baitrog* (1936), edited by Glantz, with all writers in the form of a book; *Undzer Ruf* (1936), antifascist presentation; *Di Tzait* (1936, biweekly until 1938); the opposition to *Der Veg, Di Shtime,* which evolved into the second-largest paper, with ex-personnel from *Der Veg; Undzer Vort* (1936), edited by Glantz; *Undzer Vort* (1937), edited by Corona; *Ershter Mai* (1937); *Yugunt,* a children's newspaper, edited by Berger; *Undzer Shul* (1934), celebrating ten years of school; *Almanak Fun Hilfs-Farein* (1935–1938), edited by Glantz (two numbers); *Undzer Shtim* (1936); *Tribune* (1939); *Yidishe Tribune* (1939); *Gama,* edited in Spanish; *Yidishe Bailague; Nosotros* (1939).

26. See introduction by Parsons, in Weber, *The Sociology of Religion*, 1964.

27. Few old records were kept in order. Only in 1994 did the Kehillah establish a documentary center, where it stores its materials and offers informational services to the public.

28. *Der Veg*, Yubilei Oisgabe, 1939–1940, p. 44.

29. Habermas 1972.

30. *Der Veg*, Yubilei Oisgabe, p. 109. For an update on Jewish actors or writers in the last thirty years, see Malkah Rabell's "Presencia Judía en el teatro en México" and Nedda Anhalt's "Los Premios" in Gojman et al. 1987:69–85.

31. Levine 1987:81.

32. No archive material is to be found on this. The information comes from the Jewish press recounts made by writers, especially Glantz, Kahan, and Bayon.

33. There were also, by 1929, *Meksikaner Yidish Lebn, Undzer Lebn, Di Vokh, Der Fraindt*, and *Undzer Vort*; in *Undzer Vort*, no. 15 (1929), p. 2.

34. Bulletin YMHA, Sept. 1927.

35. *Der Veg*, Yubilei Oisgabe, p. 158.

36. See Cuddihy 1974:205 and chapter 19.

37. In the United States, particular Jewish problems have often been expressed in universalistic terms, gaining strength and legitimization. This helped Jews to present and mobilize many issues. See, for example, the case of Meyer London, the founder of the Socialist Party of America in 1900 (Sorin 1989): "London recognized the legitimacy of ethnic demands and class needs, local interests and interests of the general proletariat; the reality of particularist oppression with the broader context of economic exploitation." Even orthodoxy has shown in the United States, for example, some degree of "secularization." In the attempt to follow the immigrants in their wavering from their native tongues and cultures, orthodoxy also searched for a way to Americanize. The Jewish Theological Seminary was one of those attempts. See Davidowics 1984:56–57. In Mexico, orthodoxy also attempted to reach out by being less critical of the nonobservant population.

38. It had become a question of "how much of a Jew should one be." See Meyer 1979.

39. For an assessment of formal Jewish education and identity in the late 1960s, see Ralsky de Cimet 1972. See also the only census of the community.

40. Kahan assumed that the formula "Jew in X" (any country) should be problematic for Jews. However, other host societies were unwilling to accept Jews on the terms Kahan wanted, something he did not consider Mexico doing. The phrase "Jews in Germany," for example, was used by Rabbi Leo Baeck in the Jewish Organization he headed, and was imposed by the Nazis, who prohibited the use of the term *German Jews* (*Encyclopedia Judaica*, 7:491). Hyphens then are social statuses which have to be granted, as well as wanted. It seems, though, that both the minority and the majority view the hyphen as a type of dilution of the original minority, a distancing of sorts. For a different view of the issue of hyphens, see Sosnowski 1987:307; he suggests that hyphens produce unease, but that they are a successful synthesis, "composites against assimilation." See also Goren 1970:215, for the suspicion of the Jewish hyphen in the early 1920s in the United States.

41. Both authors fought against others and others against them at this time. Their change of position was not immediately understood or accepted, and perhaps was rather distrusted. See *Forois*, June 1948, p. 22.

42. Glantz, in Kahan 1951:206–7.

43. Kahan 1946:95 .

44. *Der Veg*, Yubilei Oisgabe, p. 160.

45. Zionists such as Zevuln Berebiches, Chaim Lazdeisky, Kalmen Landau, Mordkhe Korona, and Avner Aliphas are examples.

46. Avni 1987a:45–70.

47. Porter 1966:16–20.

48. See *Fraivelt*, Aug.–Sept. 1944, pp. 16–18.

49. Leibl Bayon's writing is unusual in his frequent analysis of the Holocaust and the stilted reaction of Jews in Mexico. Though strictly speaking he was a Territorialist, he worked with the Bund very closely. See also Mordkhe Korona, *Fraivelt*, Feb 1944, pp. 10–14.

50. Notice that visits of major Zionist leaders (Nahum Goldman, Baruch Tzukerman, Stephen Wise) occurred only in the 1940s, when they were negotiating political and economic support and counteracting communist support. For the case of Argentina, see Schenkolewski 1988.

51. Goren reports, for American Jews, a similar cause-effect description, though for a different period. The shifted interest was affected by international events after 1917—e.g., America's entry into the war, the fall of czarism, Britain's recognition of Zionist aspirations, etc. See Goren 1970:214 for the case of the brief Kehillah experiment in New York.

52. Zadoff 1988.

53. See Kahan 1946: "A new type of person is being created in Eretz Israel. Free, proud as a Jew, as a person, and Histadrut its creator . . . aiming for a world with social justice in Eretz Israel and everywhere. His arms? Culture, culture and more culture" (112).

54. *Der Veg*, Yubilei Oisgabe, p. 159.

55. Oral-history interview with Shmuel Maguidin.

56. His first book in Mexico was printed four months after his arrival. *Forois*, June 1947, p. 29; July 1947; Jan. 1948, p. 45.

57. Kahan 1946:167–68.

58. Fain recalls the positive reaction of Joaquín Gamboa, director of Bellas Artes. Margarita Nelkin, a Spanish refugee, wrote exaltingly about Fain's work.

59. It is interesting to note that Deborah Dash-Moore also reports a delimitation of political alternatives or acceptable postures within the Jewish communities in the United States. However, this process got solved by what she calls "secondary migrations." Different cities took on a particular stamp; for instance, Chicago and Cleveland were Zionist, and Baltimore and Philadelphia were orthodox. In Rischin 1987:112.

60. For a variety of Jewish responses after emancipation throughout the world, see Birnbaum and Katznelson 1995.

61. In his book *Zakhor: Jewish History and Jewish Memory* (1982), Yerushalmi analyzes the ahistorical qualities of Jewish thought and its role in forging ethnic memory. His argument points to the systematic (political) use of

selective parts of the past. It is here argued that a very similar pattern has been used in contemporary communities: power positions use ideology that is based on selective accounts of the past.

62. Menachem Mendl was a character created by writer Sholem Aleikhem to describe a person full of imaginary, intangible, unachievable ideas and economic plans.

63. See *Der Veg*, Yubilei Oisgabe, p. 160.

64. Golomb, in all anthologies; or in Golomb 1946.

65. *Undzer Vort*, July 1929, p. 3.

66. Aliphas (n. d.).

67. A. Zacharias, *Undzer Lebn*, May–June 1929; I. Abrams, *Undzer Lebn*, May–June 1929.

68. Simmel (1964:15) referred to it as "pure unification," or "*Vereinigung.*"

69. Coser 1964:80.

70. Elazar 1977.

71. Elazar 1977:21.

72. Other Jewish communal arrangements in other countries have been modeled after the French Consistoire, which limited its function to religion and social welfare, or the German Gemainde; all were variations of the Kehillah framework.

73. Meyer 1989. See also Friedlander 1990:38, who quotes Richard Marientras describing the French case: "The liberating forces of freedom destroyed the cultures of the French provinces through assimilation, reducing the traditions of the people living there to a kind of folklore, turning their languages into a shameful vice. In the spirit, these forces of freedom offered the defenseless Jews a deal they could not refuse: Emancipation at the expense of their Jewish national dimensions. To become citizens, Jews would have to give up their collective way of life."

74. Elazar 1977:40–46; see also Birnbaum and Katznelson 1995.

75. The case of the United States is different; see Elazar 1977:50. The Kehillah quest succeeded only temporarily; see Goren 1970.

76. Tuvia Maizel, *Forois*, March 1948, p. 2.

77. *Forois*, Jan. 1944, p. 32.

78. *Yidishe Velt*, no. 2 (1945–1946), p. 2.

79. *Yidishe Velt*, 1 Dec. 1945.

80. *Undzer Vort*, Oct. 1929.

81. Sh. Litman, *Forois*, 1940, pp. 26–28.

82. Avni 1987a. Mexico was practically closed to Jewish immigration of refugees. The case of Santa Rosa was not one of Jewish refugees only; in fact, there were only about twenty-five Jews there and the camp was a symbolic exception to the rule of Mexican refugee immigration policy. Jews were not made welcome and this type of immigration was not encouraged. The work for refugees in Latin America was handled by James G. McDonald, high commissioner for refugees from the United Nations (1933), and Dr. Samuel Guy Inman. Avni concludes that there are four patterns of attitudes toward refugees in Latin America: (a) anti-Jewish policy (Brazil); (b) vagueness coupled with political barriers (Argentina); (c) conflicting tendencies (Ecuador); and (d) humanitarian posture without any implementation (Mexico).

83. Carreño 1994:87–105.
84. *Forois*, Jan. 1948, p. 12. Parallel attempts in the United States of organizations could have had influence on Jews in Mexico. In Chicago, for instance, the American Jewish Conference changed to the Assembly and National Jewish Council.
85. *Forois*, May 1947, p. 26; Jan. 1948, pp. 1, 40.
86. *Forois*, Feb. 1948, p. 22. The Central Committee had the following representation: 8 Zionists, 2 nonpartisans, 3 communists, 2 Bundists, 3 Sephardim, 4 Syrian Jews, 3 German Jews, and 2 Hungarian Jews.
87. *Forois*, 15 Nov. 1949, p. 3. The argument is highly complex: how else is a minority to be heard if only majority votes are the path for decision making.
88. Yosef Zakharias, *Forois*, Jan. 1948, p. 11.
89. *Forois*, Jan. 1944, p. 10. See also the specific episode on the increased internal pressure during this collection of funds in the last section of this volume, "Incomplete Allowance."
90. *Forois*, Feb. 1948, pp. 20, 22.
91. Pozniak, *Forois*, Feb. 1948, p. 20.
92. It is interesting to note that the money that is raised for communal funds is sent to Israel first, which later returns parts of it for local usage. At different times, but especially during critical economic times, when local issues need more economic backing, this arrangement is periodically questioned, but has not been changed.
93. *Forois*, 18 Dec. 1948, p. 1.
94. Eventually, after Kadima, they added Kapai (1927–1933), League for Workers of Israel, Poalei Tzion, Pioneer Women (1935), Keren Kayemet (1926), Noar Hatzioni (1939), Naye Tzionistishe Organizatzie (1936), Brit Trumpeldor (1937), Mizrachi (1939), The Zionist Federation, etc.
95. In Mexico, the main work of the Keren Hayesod started in 1940–1941. In the late 1940s it went in and out of the joint communal campaigns. After 1954, the organization became more central. See Austri-Dan 1957:30–41.
96. Even the Tarbut school effort did not receive funds from the Zionist movement in 1941.
97. Austri-Dan (1957) suggests that when school and local organizations had trouble covering their expenses, campaigns were initiated to get help; later, this system was also to be used for Eretz Israel purposes. However, for the purpose of the individual movements, the inability of the community in Mexico to buy the necessary *shkalim* (shekels) because of straitened financial circumstances prevented for a long time the possibility of their participating internationally. The shekel was the fee and card of Zionist membership, as well as a voting certificate for elections to the Zionist Congress. Until 1960, the number of shekels sold defined the area-delegates to the Congress.
98. Shapiro 1971.
99. This was certainly not always so for all Zionist groups. Austri-Dan (1957) reports difficulties in forming a Zionist Federation in 1949–1951, due to the "disruptive dominant stronger interest" in local issues (10). Schenkolewski (1991) shows that in Argentina, Moises Kostrinsky, president of the Zionist organization, concerned himself strongly with local issues, too.
100. "Poalei Tzion" was a movement that tried to base itself upon the Jewish proletariat and combined Zionism and socialism for its ideology.

101. Cemaj Portnoy, *La Voz Sionista*, 23 Sept. 1943, pp. 1–2.
102. Yakov Kahane, *La Voz Sionista*, Feb. 1950.
103. Shapiro 1971.
104. The best example of this is the emergence of the General Zionists as the centralizing force in the Kehillah, and the exclusion of Jewish communists in Mexico.
105. Avni 1987b:135–136.
106. Austri-Dan (1957:70) suggests that at one point in time, of the fifty-six board members (Rat-mener) of the Kehillah, forty-nine were Zionists or Zionist sympathizers.
107. The Conservative Bet-El Congregation has now established its own cemetery, and calls itself a "community." The separation from the Kehillah only came about after the death of Shimshon Feldman. Now that his son, Israel Feldman, is heading the Kehillah with a more decentralized power group, the Bet-El group has broken away. However, to be defined as a "community" implies that the group contributes to and sustains certain services. Israel Feldman sees that as the major issue with Bet-El, who do not contribute to the local needs of any other organizations, schools, old-aged homes, etc.
108. *Fraindt*, Oct.–Nov. 1962, p. 21. This, of course, is even truer today; there are no political platforms within the few parties that form the directorship of the Kehillah.
109. Kraut 1988:219–220.
110. Ibid., p. 212.
111. Kraut's argument is that the Jewish leaders in the United States have been of all types—protesters, from the periphery, from the center, cultural creators, philanthropists—but those who succeeeded as the power structure grew were mostly those who added national concerns to their idiosyncracies. See also Shapiro 1971; for example, his discussion of Brandeis (61–76, esp. 73): "They were trying [in the United States] to define the term Zionist in such a way as to avoid any potential conflict with their other obligations and loyalties as Americans . . . they became occupied not with Jewish culture, but rather with the structural position of the Jews in American society" (74).
112. Ibid., p. 222.
113. In November 1973, in the first (and up to now the only) national Jewish conference of the community, held in Mexico City, Dr. Horacio Chinich elaborated on the dual loyalties of Jews in Mexico. His emphasis was, though, on legitimizing Jewish attachment to Israel and Judaism, rather than the internal link with Mexico. He made an analogy between the familial love of a child to a mother and father and the love of Jews to their local country as well as to Israel. The 1970s was a terribly insecure period in the relationship between the two countries, as the racism-Zionism formula that Mexico accepted suggests. The implied unity of the analogy seemed nonexistent in the reality of the two countries. The analogy could just as well be used to point out the insecurity and instability in the community, as in the case of divorced parents. In the 1992 vote in the United Nations, President Salinas de Gortari reversed Mexico's position on the issue.
114. Gouldner 1976:35–37, 44.
115. Ibid., p. 246.

116. Ibid., p. 45.

117. Lack of youth in all branches of the Kehillah is widespread. Even at earlier stages, "apathy" and "tiredness" were mentioned in the press. See, for example, *Forois*, March 1940, pp. 26–28; *Undzer Vort*, Jan. 1931, p. 5.

118. *Forois*, Jan. 1944, p. 8.

119. Scattered attempts of youth activity have erupted. The early 1970s had a university group, ODEUJ (Organización de Estudiantes Universitarios Judíos), which searched for a format in which to address its members multiple but nonspecific concerns. They were accepted but also distrusted, and received no special support; the group dwindled when professional life dictated the main concerns of its members. The opportunity to incorporate them into the establishment was avoided. Another short-lived attempt of university-linked activists was the ODRADEC (1982). This was an effort by a handful of left-oriented young professionals who published a few issues of their journal. There is not much one can learn from them, except for their name, which they took from Kafka's story, choosing Odradec, the central character, "the strangest bastard which prehistoric world had begotten with guilt" (as Walter Benjamin describes it). Was Odradec the community they were attacking, or did they feel themselves to be Odradec, the shape that things assume in oblivion? Although linked to the communists, they had no clear agenda or goal, and so soon disappeared. Yet another, less politically threatening example was the journal *Aquí Estamos* (1977–1979), which also did not receive support.

120. Douglas 1979.

121. From my unpublished paper "Youth and Communal Political Elite," presented at the National Jewish Conference in Mexico City, 1973. See also Gouldner 1976:248.

122. Not that the sociological logic of the structure itself was to blame for all the stagnation in the lack of visions for diaspora Jews. The effects of the Holocaust are probably one of the major contributors to this problem.

123. Lewin 1937:204. The Mexican sociologist Rodolfo Stavenhagen (1977) describes nationalism in Mexico for minorities as a forced choice: "The conception of the Mexican nation based on ethnic homogeneity as the national integrating instrument conduced to the rejection of ethnic plurality and cultural diversity as contrary to the national identity. From here we see that ethnic minority groups whether indigenous or by immigration were faced with one alternative: either total assimilation to the majority and to the dominant patterns or existence as a cultural enclave, marginal to the national society, suffering the rejection of the majority."

# CHAPTER 3. PROFILES OF THOUGHT:
# THE PEOPLE BEHIND THE IDEOLOGIES

1. Marx, "The Eighteenth Brumaire of Louis Bonaparte," in Tucker 1972:437.

2. Glantz, in Kahan 1945:169.

3. Eventually, a pattern of continuous thankfulness to the new country takes place. Jews, in their insecurity, go well beyond the thankfulness that other

groups show to their new hosts. In Mexico, moments of crisis often bring out the need to show the thankfulness of the minority. As a random sample, see the autobiography of Shimshon Feldman (1993); "Salomón Cohen funda un Premio similar al Nobel, 'Pro México," *Excélsior*, 10 July 1987; Michelena 1987.

4. Gouldner 1976:79.

5. *Der Veg*, Yubilei Oisgabe, p. 132.

6. Ibid., p. 130. Glantz could not accept Berliner's self-description as an "eternal wanderer." The only "real" problems to think about, Glantz suggested, were the national problems (p. 129). It is ironic that Glantz and Berliner had this difference. While Berliner tried to express his love for Mexico, he empathized with its problems, culture, and history, and made these issues part of his explicit work. He was the poet of pain of that generation. See his *Shtot fun Palatzn* (1936), which includes drawings by Diego Rivera. He coauthored *Drai Vegn* in 1927 with Glantz and Glikovsky. In many of his poems there, one finds the integrationist mood described, but it is clearest, perhaps, in *Shtot fun Palatzn*, when he writes, "I'd like to be in your heaven a star, an eye that sees and shuts up" (202).

7. Broid 1980:9–59.

8. Caso formed, with other young intellectuals 1909, the Ateneo de la Juventud, as a group that wanted to reject positivism and rediscover the classics and humanist thinkers.

9. Of Kahan's eleven books from 1936 to 1964, all but two are about music. (His son, José Kahan, became an accomplished pianist.) In 1945 he wrote *Yidish-Meksikanish* (Judeo-Mexicano) in Yiddish, and in 1961 he wrote *Israel 1960*.

10. Territorialism is a spin-off of Zionism that started in 1905. Though Zionism is a much more comprehensive ideology, the movements divided over the issue of territory. While for Zionism it was imperative that Palestine be the Jewish homeland, Territorialists were ready to settle for any autonomous piece of land. They considered territories in Africa, Australia, and Argentina.

11. President Cárdenas is considered the first modern left-oriented president. Active since before he was eighteen as a revolutionary in the state of Michoacán (1913), he rose to power and as president he helped organize peasants (CNC—Confederación Nacional Campesina) and workers (CTM—Confederación de Trabajadores Mexicanos). He was in search of a "Mexican socialism." In 1938 he nationalized the oil industry while the United States had its attention set on the fascist dangers in Europe.

12. Broid 1980:74.

13. Kahan 1945.

14. The integration ideology in Mexico never developed as it did, for example, in Argentina, where Jews used to justify their life there: e.g., Creolism, the Hispanic-Hebrew tradition, the cult of the Cervantine-Castillian link to the Golden Age of Jews of Spain, etc. See Senkman 1987:255–70.

15. See the article on the Jewish press in Mexico by Glikovsky, in *Der Veg*, Yubilei Oisgabe, p. 30.

16. For the development of thought as helped by freedom, see Beauvoir 1975:20, 24, 27.

17. The Jewish Argentinian writer Albert Gerchunoff (1884–1950) underwent a similar process while building his identity into that of an Argentinian. He attempted to gain, so to speak, "entry to history." See Sosnowski 1987.

18. Some examples of friends: Jorge Cuesta, Torres Bodet, Villaventia, Mariano Azuela, Gonzálo Martínez, Nuñez y Domínguez, Diego Rivera, the brothers Coronel, Lilian Cerrillo, Felguérez, Amor, Areola, Matias Goeritz, Morris Schwartz, Berta Singerman, Sholem Asch, etc.

19. My interview with Glantz. See also Margo Glantz 1981:153.

20. Glantz 1980 (written in Yiddish in 1939).

21. Glantz, Berliner, and Glikovsky 1927:54.

22. Rubinstein, *Meksikaner Temes*, in Broid 1980:86.

23. Yerushalmi 1983.

24. Mannheim, in his *Ideology and Utopia* (1936), refers to this type of thinking as "limited reflexivity"; see Gouldner 1976:281. It must be made clear that Glantz's intention of keeping "older" issues out of his thinking was only programmatic. His writing is full of references to the Jewish God, to older Jewish motives, biblical Hebrew, etc.

25. *Der Veg*, Yubilei Oisgabe.

26. *Der Veg*, Jan. 1929.

27. Sosnowski 1987:297–300: "Belonging always refers to space, to territory. It also refers to identity. . . . Geography is not enough to provide territorial belonging." Sosnowksi, however, sees the hyphen identity as generally a search for meaning and a protection from assimilation-integration—a point, as will be seen below, that Golomb would have disputed strongly. The difference can be accounted for in terms of the different stress that each part of the label attains: from Sosnowski's position, the hyphen is a choice to maintain Jewishness; from Golomb's perspective, the hyphen marks a transitory stage that includes the desire to assimilate while one is still seen as a Jew.

28. *Der Veg*, Yubilei Oisgabe, pp. 130, 132.

29. Glantz himself was faced with the ambiguities of his posture when facing his children's behavior, which probably absorbed at least some of his thought. See Margo Glantz 1981:217. The daughter of Jacobo Glantz and an accomplished writer herself, Margo Glantz describes how she and her sister, when they were children, joined a friend in Popotla while their parents were absent and got baptized, had a first communion, etc. Eventually she married out of the minority. See Margo Glantz 1981:147, 198.

30. See Jan. 1950; May 1950, p. 4.

31. Beauvoir 1975:129.

32. Kahan 1951:81–95.

33. Broid 1980:32.

34. Pocock 1975:35.

35. In Kahan 1951:206–7.

36. He formed the CTM (Confederación de Trabajadores Mexicanos) in the Cárdenas period. His bid for leadership of the peasant organization failed, which eventually limited his political power. See Lerner de Sheinbaum and Ralsky de Cimet 1976:120.

37. The Yiddish concept for this idea is *Doikait*, which means "hereness."

38. Gouldner 1976.

39. For a general study of the Bund, see Johnpoll 1967.

40. We have the story of Shmuel Shapshik recounting that he met Mr. Yeshor, a Bundist, on his second day in the city, and within a week was in the organization.

41. C.Y.S.H.O., the Central Yiddish School Network, formed in 1921 in Poland with 69 schools. In 1925 there were 91 schools attached to it, and in 1929 the number went up to 216 institutions, covering kindergartens, evening schools, secondary schools, and teachers' seminaries.

42. See Tzfas (on Maizel's fiftieth birthday), *Forois*, Nov. 1947, pp. 18–20.

43. He enrolled, for instance, only one of his children in the Yiddish school.

44. Conversely, the Right has thought that the masses are too wrapped up in popular culture, too vulgar to understand the more refined aesthetic culture. Current research suggests a more updated version of what happens in society, specifically in the United States, where people seem to be able to choose from different types of culture without the erasing of class differences. See Lamont and Fournier 1992.

45. As a case study, Maizel fits very well into the theoretical descriptions offered by the French sociologist Bourdieu, who suggests that cultural capital is a general medium of accumulation and recognition for a society. The accumulation and recognition bring up a distinction that is used in many areas of society, certainly in civic symbolic politics. See Hall 1992.

46. Maizel 1948.

47. The Bund in Mexico did not detach itself totally from tradition, religion, and languages, as it did in Argentina. This may have been due to Golomb's influence, as Zadoff suggests, but not totally his doing. From the late 1930s and 1940s on in Mexico, some prominent Bundist teachers in the school system were committed to a more ample view of Jewish elements necessary for continuity. See Zadoff 1988.

48. *Forois*, Jan. 1943, p. 35. On this same ship, in December 1941 in Mexico, Mollie Steimer and Senya Fleshin were met by Jack Abrams, the well-known anarchist, who had been in Mexico since 1926; all were part of the famous anarchist case in the United States in 1918 (see Polenberg 1987).

49. *Undzer Lebn*, 7 Nov. 1929.

50. Bundism is a movement that had absolutely no following in the Sephardic part of the community. Originating in Eastern Europe, Bundism was based on Western values and used Yiddish as a language for consciousness raising. The apathy that was protested in Ashkenazi circles in the 1970s, once the communal life was well defined, was different from the surge of energy that the Sephardic community had in that decade. See Hamui de Halabe et al. 1989.

51. Weber's idea of man as "personality" presents a view of man as attempting to achieve consistency as a cultural being, but in the process makes him rather an ideal type.

52. Interview, 1983.

53. Marx, "On the Jewish Question," in Tucker 1972:24–51.

54. The great exception to this pattern was the case of Mr. Sheinboim. A Jew from Lithuania and a communist already, he arrived in Mexico and managed to

join the official party. Recently deceased, he was the only Jew to join the party, achieving the high rank of general secretary for ten years. He had changed his name to Julio Ramirez; whether this was a pre-joining or post-joining requisite, we do not know. There is almost no information available on him; he made an extraordinary effort to be effaced; his children remember little; and he left no written documents. He seems to have been a practical activist and not a theoretician.

55. The joke that Plekhanov, the father of Russian Marxism, was said to have made about Bundists—as "seasick Zionists"—allows one to question (as others did) the honesty and intention of the Soviet policy towards Jews: they supported Zionists outside the Soviet Union, but persecuted Zionists and Bundists within the country.

56. Some of Bergelson's books were *Arum Vokal, Nokh Alemen, Der Toiber*, and *Peniek*, among others. He joined in the Soviet Realist movement, and the official date of his death is the communal date we know of when most Jewish writers (most of whom were loyal communists) were killed: 13 August 1952. With them, a generation of thinkers was exterminated.

57. Revueltas was a Mexican writer who wrote, among others, *Los Muros de Agua, El Luto Humano, Los Días Terrenales,* and *Los Errores.*

58. See *Leksikon Fun Der Nayer Yidisher Literatur*, 8 vols. (New York: Alveltlekher Yidisher Kultur-Kongres, 1956–1980).

59. Rivke Rosenfeld, another example of a young Polish immigrant who had alliances with the leftist group Shomer Hatzair, became disappointed in the movement's theoretical treatment of Arabs; this contradiction moved her thinking to pro-Soviet leftism, and so she decided to belong to the Communist Party (my interview).

60. *Forois*, Nov. 1947, p. 12. The Bund criticized this position long ago, asking if the Soviet Union would then need to send two ambassadors, one to Palestine and one to Birobidzhan.

61. Though Rosen's description of the school was critical, not all communists felt the same. Shapshik qualified the Yidishe Shule as a nonpartisan effort. However, as will be seen below, neither of the two assessments seems accurate: politics and political objectives were part and parcel of the school's structure.

62. Rivke Rosenfeld was an exception worth mentioning. A teacher and psychologist, she was active in communist circles, too. She published a book on child psychology.

63. Numerical size is one of the strongest variables that accounts for some of the differences in the behavior of this group when compared to the case of Argentina. There the group remained active in an independent structure at the periphery of the central communal organization. See Zadoff 1988.

64. Some remained connected to the communal structure. Julio Torenberg, for instance, became president of the Central Committee in the 1980s with no party affiliation. He gave the Central Committee a more independent field of action from the Kehillah.

65. Rosen contests, among others, that the letters defending the PLO against Israel printed in the national press on this subject using his signature (among

others), in a period when the idea of "peace" was not even remotely used in those circles, were really provocations of the CIA. However, no public disclaimer ever followed.

66. The only Zionist leader who understood this contradiction, according to Rosen, was Nachum Goldman, because he fought for the incorporation of the diaspora in to the mainstream of Judaism.

67. The deproletarianization process of the community—as in other Latin American communities—must also have had something to do with the decrease of sensitivity and patience with this line of thinking.

68. Though *conflict* and *consensus* are concepts well known in the sociological literature, they are mostly used as opposites. Not so here, where they are rather interpreted as manifestations of power exchanges, while consensus is not the absence of power exchanges but rather the submission of a group through conflict. See Bourdieu [1990]:41.

69. Zack de Zuckerman 1994.

70. As an exception, the Dominican Republic agreed to accept 100,000 Jews after the Evian-les-Bains conference, but eventually only 5,000 visas were extended. Mexico also made exceptions for the Spanish refugees.

71. Rosen, *Fraivelt*, March 1944, p. 4

72. *Forois*, Jan. 1943, p. 18.

73. There are many divisive issues within the Central Committee between Ashkenazim and Sephardim that are expressed in cultural differences, language usage, and even style of government. Nevertheless, the two subgroups have remained linked in this peripheral structure, and ambivalence and tension have not destroyed this alliance.

74. See his autobiography (Feldman 1993), as dictated to Sergio Nudelstejer, his collaborator in the Central Committee and friend.

75. Lerner de Sheinbaum and Ralsky de Cimet 1976; Carpizo 1978.

76. See, for instance, Kerr 1994.

77. The Kehillah, for instance, did not send representatives to the Zionist Congress, as it was defined as a nonpartisan organization.

78. The "conservative movement" came fairly late to the Mexican scene (1960s), as an influence of the United States, and was until recently (1990) controlled as a "congregation" rather than considered an independent "community." It acted only as a constituent element of the Kehillah, with the result that the structure and power of the Kehillah remained intact. Attempts to break this status quo have recently been made again as the Bet-El congregation established its own cemetery.

79. Although other Kehillah efforts were launched in the Americas—e.g., Argentina, New York—each was a response to local history. Each effort differed in size; the numbers of Jews involved were by far the greatest in New York, followed by Argentina (which claimed about 100,000 Ashkenazi Jews in the 1930s). The New York case was more a response, as Goren suggests, to the issues of World War I; put in those terms, the case of Mexico was more a response to World War II and Israel.

80. So close was the relationship that Rabbi Avigdor left his *tefilin* (philacteries) to Feldman in his will.

81. The linkage between Kehillah and orthodoxy deserves a study; the number of accommodations the latter has made to keep the relationship going is especially noteworthy.

82. Weber 1964:115.

83. A new center for documentation has been created and sponsored, headed by Alice Gojman de Backal.

84. It should be mentioned that the community produced world-prominent Zionists, too. Leib Dulcin, for instance, became a high-ranking Zionist in the central organization, but left the community, and so is less interesting for our purposes in this study.

85. Esther Aliphas, my interview.

86. This awareness of the importance of traditional Jewish values may have come from the exposure to the traditional family he had married into and the experiences that led to.

87. Gouldner 1976:47. Gouldner explains that if ideology grounds identity, "a person's being becomes contingent on the maintenance of that ideology and thus sets limits on the capacity to change to that ideology rationally."

88. See the general list of publications in his book *Tzum Tokh fun Yidishkait* (1976).

89. Pilovsky 1990.

90. "Integral Judaism" is a term borrowed from Tzvi Schwartz; see *Yidishe Velt*, nos. 3–4. Golomb used it with some qualifications; it meant for him a "people consciousness," as a group of people that possess a common emotional spiritualness emanating from their life-forms, styles, and traditions. See also his *Integrale Yidishkeit* (1962).

91. Golomb, *Yidishe Velt*, nos. 76–78, 1945.

92. See his articles in *Der Veg* and *Di Shtime*: "Briv Tzu Yidishe Tates un Mames." This was a section of the newspaper that he wrote for a time (Letters to Fathers and Mothers).

93. Golomb, (1971), p. 173.

94. Golomb, *Yidishe Velt*, no. 2, 1945.

95. Parsons on Weber's *Sociology of Religion* (1964); see the Introduction.

96. Golomb often became linked to Bundism; though never a Bundist, he received their support and cooperated with them in his educational work in Mexico. However, he was critical of their posture. The "here and now" posture of the Bund was to him empty. He claimed it had no concrete program for Jewish living, even though Bundists continued to speak of "cultural autonomy," which collapsed during World War II. The Territorialists can only be helpful, he thought, if they stop searching for territories. These are not given away. Work must be done in the democratic countries that accept Jews and do not prevent them from building their own economic and cultural environment. *Freeland* should deal with territories where Jews live as "periphery" but not in diaspora. The task, according to Golomb, was not to convince the non-Jew of Jewish merits, but to recognize Jewish life. See *Freeland*, June–Aug. 1952, pp. 5–6.

97. Golomb 1971:170–205.

98. The process Golomb describes is similar to what Dubnov describes as being the problem; see Dubnov, 2nd letter in Bankier 1979. Dubnov was a his-

torian and ideologue for national autonomy who called for affirmation of its heritage for Jewish identity.

99. Golomb 1976:19–20. This point, in its simplicity, is paramount. However, it seems to me that Golomb himself abstracted too much from the specific diasporas in which he found himself. Having changed diasporas, their cultures became fuzzy and abstract to him. I would suggest that part of his inability to connect with the local population during the course of his stay in Mexico was that he himself, being so conscious of the problems of diaspora, as well as so distant from the culture of Mexico as a diaspora, did not manage to allow or define how much was to be "incorporated" of the local culture.

100. Golomb 1971:179.

101. Ibid., p. 19.

102. Ibid., p. 284. See also the Introduction by Zoltán Tar in Lukács 1986:21. Lukács wrote in contrast to Weber's individualism, and expressed a belief in collectivism, suggesting that culture can exist only in conjunction with collectivist values, a point which is very similar to Golomb's.

103. Golomb 1971:72. This is expressed in the Kantian sense.

104. Ibid., p. 131.

105. Ibid., pp. 292–331.

106. See Golomb, *Yidishe Velt*, nos. 3–4.

107. Hirsh Minski, *Fraivelt*, Oct. 1944, pp. 16–17.

108. Dabin, "Dos Yidishe Gezelshaftlekhe lebn in Meksike," *Fraivelt*, Sept. 1946, p. 10.

## CHAPTER 4. CONFRONTATIONS THAT PRODUCED STRUCTURAL CHANGES: FIVE CASE STUDIES

1. The B'nai B'rith reopened in Mexico in 1934.

2. *Forois*, Jan. 1943, p. 18.

3. *Der Veg*, 1936, Aug.–Sept. issues.

4. For our purposes, see Gojman 1988:180

5. Delgado de Cantú 1991:258.

6. *Undzer Vort*, Oct. 1928, p. 10. An answer appeared in the Jewish Press, attempting to rebut these accusations and suggesting that the acrimonious feelings of the host were unjustified. Jews were not parasites, they claimed, and had contributed to Mexico, offering their "life, blood, and wealth," as they did in any country in which they lived. Most arguments of the sort were published in the Jewish press, in Yiddish, thus preaching to the converted.

7. Lerner de Sheinbaum and Ralsky de Cimet 1976:147–48.

8. Gojman 1988:184.

9. For example, in Veracruz, Sonora, Sinaloa, San Luis Potosí, Puebla, Mérida, etc. See *Der Veg*, Yubilate Oisgabe, pp. 111–12, 140–42; *Undzer Vort*, Jan. 1931; *Der Veg*, 25 Sept. 1936.; etc.

10. Gojman 1988:182.

11. *Undzer Vort*, April 1930, p. 4. The article mentions newspapers engaged in publishing anti-Semitic material: *Omega, Tribunal, El Mexicanista*, occasionally

*Excélsior, Gráfico,* and *La Prensa.* Abruch 1971:130 presents a list of anti-Semitic books in print at the time, from Henry Ford's *The International Jews* to other local publications. See also *Der Veg* of the time.

12. See *Der Veg* and Gojman 1988:188.

13. See Abruch 1971.

14. *Forois,* Jan. 1940, p. 18.

15. Leibl Bayon, *Forois,* Jan. 1940, pp. 23–24.

16. Bayon, *Forois,* Jan. 1943, pp. 20–21; see also Korona, *Fraivelt,* Feb. 1944, pp. 10–13.

17. There is an extensive literature pointing to what boils down to similar behavior from Jews in America during World War II in larger, more sohisticated communities that did not necessarily benefit economically. See Dawidowics 1975; Trunk 1979; Penkower 1983.

18. *Fraivelt,* Feb. 1944, pp. 6–8; March 1944, pp. 11–12.

19. *Fraivelt,* April 1944.

20. Toledano 1942, 1951.

21. Penkower 1983:381.

22. Other countries with the same response were Chile, Ecuador, Uruguay, Venezuela, Peru, Argentina, Brazil, Nicaragua, Honduras, and Panama. The only exception was the Dominican Republic, which attempted to help some Jews.

23. Avni 1987a:61, 65.

24. Letter from the Minister of Interior, (Secretario de Gobernación) Lic. Ignacio García Tellez; see Zack de Zuckerman 1994:40.

25. Part of the complaints of the non-Ashkenazim in the Central Committee had been that the most important positions were always in their hands. In the last ten years, from the mid-1980s and onwards, Sephardim have headed the Central Committee, with Ashkenazim only in lesser roles. To some, this was a sign of political democratization. But others among the Ashkenazim explain this situation as evidence for the weakening of the Ashkenazi sector vis-à-vis the Sephardim in general.

26. Weber 1957:194–95. These party-followers shifted alliances often enough, calling into question the parsonian description of groups as rooted into a normative order.

27. Lerner de Sheinbaum and Ralsky de Cimet 1976:100–101.

28. The idea started in 1927, and was launched in 1928; by 1930, the area had been granted the status of "Jewish Autonomous Region." However, in the first few years of the colonization project, the number of Jewish immigrants dropped by half, due to the difficulties of the region, which was located on the border between the Soviet Union and China. The idea aroused wide interest, especially among Jews who believed in Territorialism. Most Zionists were opposed.

29. This regime offered asylum to Trotsky (1879–1940), whose original name was Bronstein and who was eventually killed in Mexico. The Jewish community did not have much to do with him; the painter Diego Rivera and others petitioned for the asylum but were expelled from the Communist Party for it. Jewish communists followed the official line, too (Shmuel Maguidin interview, 1990). At least one interview—in French—took place between Trotsky and Moishe

Rosenberg, Moishe Glikovsky, Abraham Vaisboim, and Kalmen Landoi, in which Trotsky criticized the Birobidzhan experiment. In general, Trotsky did not believe that Jews had any future as a separate people. He was against the Bund, the Zionists, etc. With the reemergence of anti-Semitism in the late 1930s, he admitted that Jews needed a territorial solution.

30. For the parallel of this Russophilia with that of English and American intellectuals during the 1930s, see Coser 1970:144, 234–36.

31. B. T. Goldberg, *Fraindt*, Feb.–March 1963, pp. 15–16. In joining a communist platform, the Bund was trying to bypass old differences between the groups. In their formative years (1890s), all Jewish socialists started out with the sharing of a viewpoint condensed in the statement "Wir Sind keine Juden, Sondern Jiddisch-sprechende Proletarier" (We are not Jews, but Yiddish-speaking proletarians). The more nationalistic among them formed the Bund, while the internationalists joined the communist ranks, linking with the viewpoint that separated them bitterly in later years. World War II brought out the strongest animosities and conflict between the Bund and the communists. For an overview, see Johnpoll 1967.

32. Rosen was then a young activist and editor of the communist *Fraivelt*. Lisker belonged to the young Gesbir and was active in the League, and de Gortari was a well-known Mexican philosopher and sympathizer with communism.

33. The same occurred in the United States, but the path the break took there needs to be researched. See *Der Hamer*, Aug. 1939, p. 15; Sept. 1939; Oct. 1939; especially the articles of M. Katz. It seems that communists rejected the more general socialist publication *Yidishe Kultur* because it did not allow *them* to justify the Pact. The publication defined itself as nonpartisan. Dr. Zitlovsky, Dr. Mokduni, Y. Opatoshu, B. T. Goldberg, Peretz Hirshbein, and H. Leivik all resigned; the journal remained as a Bundist publication for a short time. See Sept.–Oct. 1939, nos. 9 and 10.

34. Bankier 1989:84.

35. *Forois*, May 1940, pp. 13–14, 20.

36. See Johnpoll 1967:239–40.

37. *Fraivelt*, no. 45 (1943), p. 20.

38. *Forois*, Nov. 1949. It has been said that Mikhoels was brutally killed on Stalin's orders in 1948; so was Fefer, who had been a KGB agent for a time. Both were Soviet leaders who engaged in Soviet propaganda in Mexico. Trotsky, the Bulgarian leader Nicola Petkov, Bucharin, Rykov, and others, as well as Moishe Kulbak, Maks Erick, Zalman Reizin, and others, were also killed. See *Forois*, Jan. 1944, p. 15. Eventually, Constantin Umanski, the Soviet ambassador to Mexico, became prisoner of the very "qualities" which had made him so useful at the time. When Jews became suspected of anti-Soviet behavior by Stalin, they were entered on the list of those who would eventually be purged. There is suspicion, though unconfirmed, that Umanski's death in a plane crash in Mexican territory was an assassination. However, another version makes it a pure accident. Mexico had purchased old World War I planes from the United States; two other planes had crashed, and so did the one Umanski used, almost at takeoff, on a trip to Central America.

39. *Fraivelt*, Feb. 1944, pp. 7–8.

40. *Fraivelt*, Jan. 1944, pp. 13–14. (It is said that he understood Yiddish well.)

41. *Fraivelt*, July 1944, p. 45.

42. Bankier 1989:84.

43. Ibid.

44. Katz was in turn attacked by Bundists for sabotaging the memorials for Alter and Erlich; *Forois*, Dec. 1947, p. 17.

45. The coalition was not limited, though, to left-Zionists. There was apparent religious cooperation with communists, since Rabbi Rafalin (an Orthodox Rabbi) published a Shana Tova wish in *Fraivelt*. The Bund protested against such coalitions. *Forois*, Oct. 1948, p. 19.

46. *Forois*, July–Aug. 1944, pp. 8–9.

47. *Forois*, July–Aug. 1944, p. 7. This time the attack went so far as to question the legitimacy of Zionist leadership: "Why are you [Goldman] speaking for all Jews? . . . Zionists feel they represent all!"

48. *KKL Bulletin*, no. 7, Sept. 1930; no. 8, 1930–1931; no. 9, 1931; 1936.

49. Leibl Dulcin, *Farn Folk*, Aug. 1937, p. 12.

50. *Forois*, May 1948, p. 11; July 1949, p. 11.

51. In addition to the conclusion on this point that Johnpoll offers in his *Politics of Futility* (1967), he also suggests that the Bund distinguished itself by offering very poignant and accurate political analysis of the international political scene in the 1930s and early 1940s. They were the first (as early as 1933), Alter specifically, to suggest Hitler's plan with respect to Poland; their criticism of Stalin's totalitarianism as opposed to real socialism was also timely and accurate. See Johnpoll 1967:267–68.

52. Yosef Zaharias, *Forois*, Dec. 1947; Salomon Kahan, *Forois*, June 1949, p. 13. Criticism came from other sectors, too. Jack Abrams, the anarchist in Mexico, distrusted communists, as did they him. He claimed that the Soviet Union could not be considered, as communists suggested, the ideal society versus the Western world, which was in convulsions of strikes and disagreements: "Do not believe in this silence, jail is not a cemetery," he quoted a Russian prison song. Abrams, born in Russia, claimed to have been jailed as a pacifist with Eugene Debs for two-and-a-half years, and was exchanged for a military officer to regain freedom. He was one of the main characters of the U.S. anti-anarchist trial of 1918 (see Polenberg 1987). He finally emigrated to Mexico in 1926. *Forois*, Feb.–March 1947, p. 38; Jan. 1948, p. 13.

53. *Fraivelt*, Aug.–Sept. 1944, p. 5.

54. Hirsh Minski, *Fraivelt*, Aug–Sept., p. 6; *Farn Folk*, 1936, 1937.

55. *Fraivelt*, Nov.–Dec. 1955, p. 6.

56. *Fraivelt*, Nos. 4–5 (1943), p. 23.

57. *Forois*, March 1949, p. 15.

58. *Forois*, Sept. 1949, pp. 13, 15.

59. Canetti 1991:285.

60. Ibid., p. 262; see also p. 269: "Survival . . . carries with it considerable uneasiness for the survivors . . . the dead can never be quite trusted. The more powerful a man was here on earth, the greater and more dangerous is his rancor afterwards."

61. Hirsh Minski, *Fraivelt*, Jan. 1944, pp. 50–53; see also Landoi, *Fraivelt*, March 1944, p. 38; May–June 1944, pp. 33–36. One must point out that the Bund in Europe could not always be criticized as "politically empty," since as a movement they were the first to promote and fight in self-defense against pogroms; their activity to protect Jews from Polish and German gangs started in 1940. In 1941 they started to acquire arms to fight the Nazis, and the idea to organize a nonpartisan "army" against the Nazis in the Warsaw Ghetto was theirs. Finally, Zygielbojm's work in exile was more active than his suicide may point out. See Penkower 1983, chapter 4; and Johnpoll 1967:251.

62. This same criticism was at times also put forward by Zionists. Bundists did on occasion speak of despair and suicide, but essentially agreed and asked to go "back" to life, to "build life." Ideologically, however, they had no vision of how to do it. See *Forois*, June 1944, p. 9; Nov. 1947, pp. 2–3. Indeed, one of their leaders, S. Zygielbojm, in utter despair over the world's indifference to the Jewish plight, committed suicide in London in 1943.

63. *Fraivelt*, April 1944, pp. 33–34. Further explanations of the war became more ideological and abstract. The indications of consolation and hope brought by the Soviet Union to the League people were for the Bund an intolerable absence of mourning before the war was even over. The love for the Soviet Union superseded all Jewish specificity, as when communists claimed that "the Jewish revolt in the Warsaw Ghetto . . . [belongs to the] general fight of all enslaved people" (*Fraivelt*, May–June 1944, p. 53). Although the Bund also universalized its political goals, it did not take well to the universalizing of specifically Jewish events.

64. I use Lucy Dawidowics's title and allude to the fact she pointed out, that this "war" against Jews was absolutely unparalleled, since it was not even a war between equals in political standing. Jews had nothing to wage a war with: no state, no army, no training, no immediate precedent.

65. Bankier 1989; *Forois*, Sept. 1949, p. 15. Leo Katz went to Israel for a time, but moved for health reasons.

66. Committees of "Pro-Palestina Hebrea" were opened since 1943 in Cuba, Uruguay, and Mexico, headed by distinguished personalities in an attempt to gain support of the gentile world. Further, visits to the community were made by international Zionist leaders as mentioned above, but also fund-raising leaders of the Keren Hayesod, such as A. S. Yuris and Manuel Gravier. See Avni 1987b:146–47.

67. *Forois*, Feb. 1948, p. 13.

68. I am indebted to Emil Fackenheim for the concept of the "moral necessity" of a Jewish state in Israel. See Fackenheim 1978:197.

69. For some details on the unsuccessful attempts of Zionists to influence the Mexican position, see Bokser 1991, especially chapter 4. Their accomplishment was perhaps the achieved shift from a "no" vote to an abstention.

70. It is important to note that what won was the ideology as used by a widely spread-out organization rather than a Zionist organization per se. In 1948, two days after the proclamation of the new Jewish state, a pro-Palestine committee was formed—filling the vacuum—to help organize the festivities for the event (*KKL, 50 años*, Mexico: 1980, p. 53).

71. Barry 1980. He refers to the case of busing children in the United States. This policy was used, according to him, as a substitute for experimenting with wider integration issues in real life.

72. Yosef Zacharias, *Undzer Lebn*, 7 Nov. 1929; Leibl Bayon, *Der Veg*, Yubilei Oisgabe, pp. 52–62; Avner Aliphas, "Geshikhte fun Yugunt Dertziung in Meksike," Aliphas Archives; Levitz 1954; Portnoy 1977.

73. The article also stipulates that no religious corporation can have access to educational bodies, especially when these are meant for workers and peasants. It accepts the existence of private schools, but when directed to workers and peasants these must be authorized by the government.

74. Levy 1987:164. Zadoff 1988:19.

75. Aliphas 1942:3.

76. As an expression, "Talmud Tora" means "to study Tora." However, the term became used to designate small schools like the Kheder, supported by the communities and offering Jewish education to children, usually for free.

77. In 1936, Binyomin Kovalsky, Miriam Tchornitzky, and M. Mondlak; in 1937, Fruma Tartak, Leibl Bayon, etc. The visits of Jacobo Pat, Dr. Y. Shatzki, and Av Goldberg gave the school recognition from New York, Argentina, Warsaw, Vilna, Bialystok, and Grodno.

78. Aliphas 1943:10; "Shul un Dertziung," *Undzer Tribune*, no. 3 (1942), pp. 10–15. Other schools that were subsequently set up included Monte Sinai School (1943, Sephardi), Tarbut Sephardi (1944), Teacher's Seminary (1946), Tzedaka Umarpe (1949), etc. (this is just to show the growth of the network in these years; it is not a comprehensive list of educational organizations). The estimated growth of students in the years of 1940 to 1950 and 1953 is from 611 to 2,670 and 3,790 respectively (Zadoff 1988: 11–14).

79. *Forois*, Dec. 1943, pp. 5–7.

80. *Forois*, Dec. 1947, pp. 14, 18.

81. *Forois*, Feb. 1948, p. 21; March 1948, pp. 17–18; April, p. 25.

82. *Forois*, July 1949, pp. 9–11; August 1949, pp. 14–15.

83. *Tog* (New York), 5 Sept. 1949.

84. *Forois*, Nov., 1949, p. 2.

85. Ibid., p. 50.

86. Political party formed in Israel in 1906 by immigrants from Russia, and which had left and right sections within.

87. Kalmen Landoi, "Fertzig Yor, Naye Yidishe Shul Y. L. Peretz," *Der Veg*, 18 May 1990.

88. *Forois*, Nov. 1949, p. 8. Zionists had also at one point suggested bringing Chaim Grinberg (writer and ideological leader of the Labor Zionism, and activist for Tarbut schools) to Mexico to elaborate a school program for Golomb. Golomb responded, agreeing to work jointly on a school program, but categorically rejecting working on a program given to him by Grinberg. The idea never went further.

89. *Forois*, Nov. 1949, pp. 8–10; Dec. 1949, p. 3.

90. *Naye Yidishe Shul, Yor Bukh*, 1 Sept. 1950.

91. When he attempted to publish on two occasions, on specific issues, he was confronted with arguments about lack of space and outright questions on the

"wisdom" of publishing in the local press. *Forois*—from the Bund that defended him—would gladly have given him space. However, he may not have wanted to be identified too strongly with the Bundists and make them his only source of support, since he was not one of them. Bundists allied with Golomb for at least two reasons: the teachers who followed him probably had a working relationship and possibly collaboration on many pedagogical issues; and the movement had in Golomb a prominent (albeit for them partial) spokesman who articulated their defense of the immediate Shtetl-world past—its culture, language, and meaning.

92. Arendt 1980.

93. Ibid., p. 259.

94. Canetti 1991:286.

95. *La Voz Sionista*, 25 Nov. 1949, p. 2.

96. The challenge is equally important for Israel and has been magnified with the peace negotiations of the 1990s. Distinct groups of citizens—Arabs, Christians, etc.—will probably have to be integrated as such in innovative political ways. For parts of this current debate, see Margalit and Halbertal 1994, and the response of Oksenberg Rorty (1995).

97. For a historical comparative analysis of these issues for Jews in other parts of the world, see Birenbaum and Katznelson 1995.

98. Fackenheim 1978:198. "Moral discrimination" is Fackenheim's term for the refusal to allow the Jewish people to have a Jewish state.

99. Wise 1991:39.

100. Diamond 1983.

101. Max Weinreich did for the Yiddish language what Merleau Ponty did for language in general. Looking at language policy as politics is a novel approach, too, since much of language confrontation and change has been explained away as a generational change, normative in its modifications—especially in the case of the United States, the country of minorities. See Weinreich 1975:279–88. The analysis here, then, will be informed by the premises inferred from the above, where (a) language and speech are seen as part of a structural process that defines and is defined by its agents, and (b) the political side to which language has been put to use, which has so often still been missed, is acknowledged.

102. The Tarbut schools belonged to a general movement on behalf of promotion of the Hebrew language and culture.

103. *Forois*, Jan. 1944, p. 31; July–Aug. 1944, p. 9. Profs. Austrijak (a Zionist) and Tsfas (a Bundist) exchanged arguments on languages.

104. These cultural and political views were often mixed by their proponents and used unsystematically to further political goals, but at stake was the maintaining or rejecting of language as a discourse, as a synonym of power. See Sheridan 1980:127–30.

105. *Forois*, Jan. 1948, p. 45. Only after Maizel's death on 16 June 1985 did the Kehillah allow Spanish to be used in its publication. *La Voz de Kehillah* started to appear in 1987.

106. Kahan 1951:94.

107. *Forois*, Dec. 1947, p. 18. In their protocol, it was also added that Spanish would be allowed in their meetings to help those who did not speak Yiddish!

108. The Bund responded for him. They were out to show that the Tarbut school had started to allow Spanish a large place—outside of the secular department, they claimed. It was not only that Hebrew was not about to take the place of Yiddish, but rather that the battle was being lost to Spanish.

109. *La Voz Sionista*, 9 Dec. 1949, p. 3. See *Fraindt*, Sept. 1962, p. 9, on the Danzig Conference of 1932 and Ben Gurion's position and resolutions for Zionism; this case was consistent with the local position on how to act in diaspora towards Yiddish.

110. See Gold 1977. Gold recounts the politicization of the respelling issue in Yiddish between the pro-etyological spelling group (orthodox, Hebraists, and the YIVO) and the pro(morpho)phonemical group (Birenbaum in Tshernovitz, Soviet Yiddish linguists). In the Soviet Union, the Hebrew-Aramic spelling got rejected in 1920 as a rejection of "religion, tradition, and bourgeoise elements" in language. As an anticommunist reaction, these spelling rules were never accepted by the Bund, orthodox groups, or YIVO, though these groups did not fully unify on a standardization of spelling either. (The Bund youth of Warsaw did use the Soviet orthography, in 1932.) This was another facet of political conflict that Yiddish faced parallel to the one described above. The issue of conflict did not, however, surface in Mexico.

111. There are references to the issue in an old Midrash that suggest that Jews were redeemed from Egypt for four reasons, one of them being that they did not change their names and their language (Vayikra Raba 32:5). Other periods—during the Second Temple and after—also recall the issue of languages whose status was not clear (Aramic, later Yiddish) since they were considered ethnic languages, but not holy. Later this turned into a conflict of functions between the languages. (See Weinreich 1973.) The modern stage of the language issue occurred after the Enlightenment. Orthodoxy and the Reform movement debated over the question of prayer—"In which languages can one say it?"—and even on the question of preaching. See Guttman 1977 and Bleich 1986, for the Halachic (legal) and political arguments for usage of Hebrew and Yiddish against the vernacular (German) in the second decade of the nineteenth century.

112. Weinreich 1973:287.

113. De Voss and Ross-Romanucci 1982.

114. The Hebrew renewal has been explained as the sublimation of a desire to "exit" from one's identity. However, similar ambivalent feelings were found in the Yiddish-speaking sector, in their ideological positions and all their modernizing efforts. The question remains as to how much change an identity can go through for it still to be recognized; the conflict between the two is the answer each group gives to this question.

115. Harshav 1986:20. However, Weinreich (1973:283) suggests that Yiddish flourished as belles-lettres because it did not protest its denigrated status.

116. Weinreich, in "Di Geshikhte Fun Der Yidishe Shprakh" (1973), suggests the development of Ashkenaz and Yiddish—group and language–have been parallel. He offers historical examples of when he thinks Ashkenaz initiated its independent cultural development with Gershom ben Judah (960–1040) (Rabeinu Gershom) and the parallel development of an independent language (Yiddish), and

he explains how linguistic structure and social structure mutually affected each other.

117. Fishman 1987, chapter 4.

118. Harshav 1986:7–8. Even in modern Yiddish poetry, one finds confirmation of feelings of ambivalence: "Yiddish poetry certainly harkened back to a remembered collective past, but much more powerful was the original urge it expressed of young men and women to liberate themselves, however briefly and incompletely, from the collective identity of Jews, and worker, and family member."

119. See Rivkin 1939 for a view of the problems the language was thought to solve, and a critique of the thought of Golomb, Zitlovsky, and Olgin. See also Golomb 1939a, 1939b.

120. Harshav 1993, especially part 2. One can read the book using part of Harshav's own subtitle of a chapter as two different sides—one tragic and one happy—of one revolution. Yet there is no need to attach the word "endings" as though this language history is all but finished now.

121. With branches in Russia, the Austrian Empire, England, the United States, Argentina, and Rumania, the Poalei Tzion established a branch in Palestine in 1906 and consolidated in 1907 under the leadership of Ben-Zvi. It advocated class struggle, unions, and strikes. Its first newspaper, *Onfang*, was published in Yiddish; the second one, *Ahdut*, was founded in 1910 and was published in Hebrew. The Poalei Tzion movement was a combination of socialism and Zionism, and started in Russia in 1890s. It had left and right factions that split in the 1920s.

122. The group's full name was "Histadrut Hapoalim ha zeirim be Eretz Israel," and it was founded in 1905 with membership of the Second Aliyah. Though this immigration wave fed both political parties, the Hapoel Hatzair and Poalei Tzion, their fundamental difference was over the latter's acceptance of international socialism. They also differed on their acceptance of Yiddish. The Poalei Tzion started with Yiddish and accepted it abroad, while the Hatzair group rejected it from the start.

123. Pilovsky 1990:360, 20–21. Both groups were engaged in self-definition and in claiming centrality. While the Poalei Tzion was detaching from the Bund, from Bolshevist ideology, the left–Poalei Tzion remained linked to Yiddish.

124. Fishman 1987.

125. Weinreich 1931:65.

126. Ibid. Fishman (1987) shows that the town chosen for the conference skewed the attending population in favor of plain folk, more Zionists than Bundists, and more tradition-oriented Jews than proletarians, which may have had much to do with the predominant view and ultimate perception of the "change of the power" of the Yiddishists.

127. Pilovsky 1990, chapter 1; for example, *Onfang* was eliminated in 1907. Other languages were also discarded and attacked in Eretz Israel, such as German and French, since cultural elites of each tried to reproduce European life there. However, this did not represent an attack on a core Jewish identity, as Yiddish did; neither did these languages and cultures depend on this population to survive.

128. Pilovsky 1990:66.

129. Political factions in Eretz Israel fought, at first, over the issue of Yiddish. Not all agreed immediately. However, since the premise of a need for a test of loyalty was not disputed, Yiddish became the "easy" vehicle. A similar process is described by Diamond in his discussion of the struggle over bilingualism in America (1983:48).

130. Cafferty 1980:4.

131. Diamond 1983:52. See also p. 26 for his description of how, in the case of the United States, variations have occurred over time in the designation of the groups whose languages have been discouraged in an effort to affirm a political reality.

132. Harshav 1993:52. In Wise 1982, the description writer Dan Davin gives of Itsik Manger, a Yiddish poet, contains another reason for the need to escape that some Jews felt–through alcohol–not from a "despising" culture but from a heightened consciousness of the culture and its abiding weight: "And he may have needed it for escape from his often acute consciousness of a past and a people utterly destroyed, a youth which had gone forever, not as the youth of most people passes, to be recalled, sentimentalized, . . . but lost forever with the generation which had no survivors" (2).

133. Wuthnow 1984:75–77.

134. Pilovsky 1990:42.

135. Ibid., p. 33–34.

136. The two general groups most affected by the move described were the orthodox and the very active Poalei Tzion (when they did not meet the requirement); see Pilovsky 1990:33–34.

137. See again Diamond 1983:32, 17.

138. The fight of the Reform Movement in Germany was not for or against Yiddish, but for German.

139. The kind of tendency mentioned above could be suggested as a response to a long, persistently repetitive history of rejection of this minority. See Joshua Fishman, *Oifn Shvel*, July–Sept., p. 5. Fishman describes the fact that Jews from the cities in Europe with statistically more rather than less cultural and linguistic heterogeneity were the ones who joined more readily in the Hebrew project. From this, Fishman suggests that Hebrew as a modern language did not come about from a desire to communicate but rather from a desire to change Jews.

140. A. Chinich, *Der Veg*, 18 June 1949.

141. *Forois*, July 1949, p. 7; also Yosef Rotenberg, *Forois*, Nov. 1949, p. 16.

142. In their introduction to *Voices of the Yiddish* (1975), Howe and Greenberg find Yiddish intellectuals and essayists at a disadvantage from general Western intellectuals, lacking universities and masses of readers to help them polish and experience themselves, but "against these handicaps, the Yiddish writers were blessed with historical passion and ethnical security. They wrote out of a deep conviction as to the centrality of their material; they sensed behind them the vitality of folk energy and martyrdom" (12).

143. *Forois*, 15 Dec. 1948, p. 2. Of the two, the Folk Universitet did not take off.

144. E.g., October 1949, p. 4.

145. Notice that the languages are referred to differently in the newspaper; *Hebrew* is capitalized and *Yiddish* on occasion is not. See, e.g., 13 Jan. 1950.

146. *Forois*, Oct. 1949, p. 10. The metaphor was from the Jewish writer Niger in America, but others also referred to the issue as "two nostrils to breath" (in Sholem Aleichem) and "two feet of one culture" (in Dubnov).

147. *Forois*, Oct. 1949, p. 7.

148. Another thinker who also separates thought and structure is Thomas Kuhn. In his *The Structure of Scientific Revolutions* (1970), he separates social communication from the political network in his methodology on language.

149. "Astonishment" is defined by Ernst Bloch as the awareness of the future that is latent in ourselves and in things, a definition that fits our explanation pattern; see Jameson 1974:133.

150. One of the strongest statements that expresses the same thought of Golomb's is found in Beauvoir 1975: "To abandon the past to the night of facticity is a way of depopulating the world. I would distrust a humanism which was too indifferent to the efforts of the men of former times" (92).

151. Tocqueville reached a similar conclusion on the limitations imposed on people if the past is not forgotten: "Since the past has ceased to throw its light upon the future, the mind of man wanders in obscurity." However, there is another dominant understanding of what thought can do. Coming from a line of thought of Marx, Engels, and Freud, the idea is that thought can be used not to understand but to modify reality, by detaching from old thought. (See Marx's "Theses on Feuerbach.") Foucault (1972b), in his preface to *A History of Sexuality*, volume 2, uses this line of thinking, as well, since thought is a "detacher." The process of thought, if it is to help reach a liberated form of thinking, is different, says Foucault: "The object [is]," he suggests with a Freudian echo, "to learn to what extent the effort to think one's own history can free thought from what it silently thinks, and so enable it to think differently." Foucault, to use him as a paradigmatic example, has a total dissatisfaction with most thought about the past, a position with which Golomb would disagree.

152. It was only in 1995 that the Israeli parliament (Knesset) issued an official recognition to Yiddish and Ladino as Jewish national languages that the state has the obligation to protect.

153. Both languages are taught in the community and remain active; Yiddish is maintained by a subminority.

154. Held 1989:190.

155. Shotter 1993:130–31. The challenge, according to Shotter, is to recognize differences rather than similarities in society, to "demand . . . a unique individuality rather than an atomistic individualism afforded by liberal individualism or state socialism."

156. It was only in 1994 that the Mexican Constitution was amended to legitimize the existence of indigenous and other religious minorities.

157. As an idea, the World Jewish Congress started in 1919, but the first Congress convened in Geneva in 1936, with Stephen Wise and Nahum Goldman as its central figures.

158. See the letters of Kate Knopfmacher, the WJC representative in Mexico, in the World Jewish Congress Archives, Box 231, Folder 23.

159. For the case of Argentina, see Klich 1993.

160. Bokser 1991, chapter 4.

161. "Declaración de Abstención en torno al problema de Palestina," Archivo Histórico Diplomático Mexicano, México, Secretaría de Relaciones Exteriores, 1981, no. 10, p. 192.

162. *Forois*, Dec. 1947, p. 17.

163. The complete list of protesters: A. King, Jacob Abrams, Mary Abrams, Martin Temple, Isaac Leventhal, Walter Gruen, Clara Gruen, Ira Lerner, Virginia Mishnun, Roman Waisfeld, and Dr. H. Jacob. See copy letter sent to the World Jewish Congress in the World Jewish Congress Archives, Box H229, Folder 49a.

164. The sanctions varied in intensity, from rejections to bans to ostracizing.

165. Bourdieu 1990:143.

166. In an attempt to dispel the tension between the community and the government, in 1976 President López Portillo signed decrees granting citizenship to a group of Jewish residents. Since before World War II, citizenship was hardly ever granted to Jews, some of whom were allowed to stay in the country with no papers but with the status of "stateless" (Apatrida).

167. Bourdieu 1990:183.

168. See Berlin 1992:235. He strongly argues that many of the social monsters that men have constructed are the result of the fallacious attachment to an aesthetic model of politics which suggests that society can be made into a perfect work of art.

169. See the quest for pluralism and multiculturalism in Tilly 1992:717. Tilly proclaims that diversity must be "benign pluralism" and not "malign segmentation."

170. Steinberg 1981:44–46.

171. Beauvoir 1975:60–70.

# BIBLIOGRAPHY

## ARCHIVES

Aliphas, Avner. Personal Archive. Mexico.
Brenner, Anita. Personal Archive. Amigos de la Universidad Hebrea de Jerusalem. Mexico.
Maguidin, Shmuel. *Fraivelt Collection*. Mexico.
Rosen, Boris. *Fraivelt*. (The material has now been given to Hemeroteca Nacional de México.) Mexico.
Rotenberg, Yosef. *Forois Collection*. Mexico.
World Jewish Congress. Archive. Mexico section. Cincinnati.

## PERIODICALS

*Der Hamer.* 1939. New York.
*Der Veg.* Mexico.
*Di Shtime.* Mexico.
*Farn Folk.* Mexico.
*Forois.* Mexico.
*Fraivelt.* Mexico.
*Fraindt.* Mexico.
*Freeland.* 1945–1957. Mexico.
*Hilf.* Mexico.
*K. K. L. Bulletin.* Mexico.
*La Voz de la Kehila.* Mexico.
*La Voz Sionista.* Mexico.
*The Nation.* Nos. 199 and 133. New York.
*Naye Yidishe Shul.* Yor Bukh no. 1. Mexico.
*Oifn Shvel.* New York.
*Tarbut Reports.* Mexico.
*Tribuna Israelita.* Mexico.
*Undzer Lebn.* Mexico.
*Undzer Vort.* Mexico.
*Bulletin YMHA.* Mexico.
*Yavne Zhurnal.* Mexico.
*Yidishe Kultur.* New York.
*Yidishe Velt.* New York.

215

## BOOKS AND ARTICLES

Abercrombie, N. 1980. *Class Structure and Knowledge.* Oxford: Blackwell.

Abercrombie, N., et al. 1980. *The Dominant Ideology Thesis.* Boston: G. Allen & Unwin.

Abruch, Miguel. 1971. *Algunos Aspectos del Anti-Semitismo en México.* B. A. thesis. UNAM, Mexico.

Alexander, Jeffrey. 1984. "The Centrality of the Classics." In Giddens and Turner, 11–67.

Aliphas, Avner. 1942a. "A Yor Hebreishe un Natzionale Dertziung." *Tarbut Report* 1.1.

———. 1942b. "Shul un Dertziung." *Undzer Tribune,* no. 3.

———. 1943. "Din Vekheshbon fun a yor arbet in Tarbut."

———. n. d. "Geshikhte fun Yugunt Dertziung in Meksike." Aliphas Archives. Mexico.

Almog, Shmuel. 1988. *Anti-Semitism through the Ages.* New York: Pergamon Press.

Altmann, Alexander. 1981. *Essays in Jewish Intellectual History.* New Hampshire: University Press of New England.

Arendt, Hannah. 1980. "Truth and Politics." In *Between Past and Future.* New York, England: Viking Press.

Ashkenazi, Isaac D. 1982. *Esperanza y Realidad.* Mexico: Beneficencia Sedaká y Marpe.

Austri-Dan, Yeshayahu. 1957. *Di Tzionistishe Bavegung in Meksike, 1953–1957.* Mexico: Federación Sionista en México.

———. 1963. "The Jewish Community of Mexico." *Dispersion and Unity,* Feb., pp. 51–73.

Avni, Haim. 1985. "Territorialismo, Colonialismo y Sionismo." *Rumbos,* no. 13.

———. 1987a. "Latin America and the Jewish Refugees: Two Encounters, 1935 and 1938." In Elkin and Merkx.

———. 1987b. "The Origins of Zionism in Latin America." In Elkin and Merkx.

Bankier, David, ed. 1979. *The Modern Epoch Document,* vol. 2. Jerusalem: Hebrew University of Jerusalem.

———. 1988. "Los Exiliados Alemanes en México y sus Vínculos con la Comunidad Judía, 1942–45." *Judaica Latinoamericana* Jerusalem.

Barker, Nancy. 1980. *The French Experience in Mexico, 1821–1861: A History of Constant Misunderstanding.* Chapel Hill: University of North Carolina Press.

Barry, Bryan. 1980. "Ethnicity and the State." In Bruckner et al.

Bartra, Roger. 1987. *La Jaula de la Melancolía: Identidad y Metamorfosis del Mexicano.* Mexico: Grijalbo Press.

Bazant, Jan. 1977. *A Concise History of Mexico.* New York: Cambridge University Press.

Beauvoir, Simone de. 1975. *The Ethics of Ambiguity.* New Jersey: The Citadel Press.

Bejarano, Margalit. 1988. "Deproletarization of Cuban Jews." *Judaica Latinoamericana* Jerusalem.

Berger, David. 1986. *History and Hate: The Dimensions of Anti-Semitism.* Philadelphia: The Jewish Publication Society.

Berlin, Isaiah. 1992. *The Crooked Timber of Humanity.* New York: Vintage Books.

Berliner, Itzjok. 1936. *Shtot Fun Palatzn: Songs and Poems.* Mexico: El Camino.

Bernstein, Basil. 1971. *Class, Codes, and Control.* London: Routledge & Kegan Paul.

Birenbaum, Pierre, and Ira Katznelson, eds. 1995. *Paths of Emancipation: Jews, States, and Citizenship.* Princeton: Princeton University Press.

Blau, Joseph. 1966. *Modern Varieties of Judaism.* New York: Columbia University Press.

Bleich, Judy. 1986. "Rabbi Akiva Eger and the Nascent Reform Movement." *9th World Congress of Jewish Studies*, div. 3, vol. 3.

Bokser, Judith. 1991. "El Movimiento Nacional Judío: El Sionismo en México." Ph.D. thesis. UNAM, Mexico.

———. 1992. *Imágenes de un Encuentro.* Mexico.

Bonfil, Batalla. 1990. *México Profundo: Una Civilización Negada.* Mexico: Grijalbo Press.

Bourdieu, Pierre. 1990. *In Other Words: Essays Towards a Reflexive Sociology.* Stanford: Stanford University Press.

———. 1991. *Language and Symbolic Power.* Great Britain: Polity Press.

———. 1993. *The Field of Cultural Production.* New York: Columbia University Press.

Branding, D. 1985. *Los Origines del Nacionalismo Mexicano.* Mexico: Ediciones Era.

Brenner, Anita. 1924. "The Jews in Mexico." *The Nation*, 27 August 1924, 211.

———. 1928. "Mexico: Another Promised Land." *Menorah Journal* 14.4.

Breytenbach, Breyten. 1991. "The Long March from Hearth to Heart." *Social Research* 58.1.

Broid, Elizabeth. 1980. "La Diáspora Mexicana: Seis immigrantes Judíos del Siglo XX." B. A. thesis. UNAM, Mexico.

Bruckner, D. J. R., et al., eds. 1980. Conference on Politics and Language; *Politics and Language: Spanish and English in the U.S.* Chicago: University of Chicago Press.

Cabrera González, Ignacio. 1990. "Ni integracionismo ni tesis culturalistas servirán al indígena." *Excelsior*, 22 April, sec. A.

Cafferty, Pastora San Juan. 1987. "Bilingualism in America." In Bruckner et al.

Canclini García, Nestor. 1989. *Culturas Híbridas.* Mexico: Grijalbo Press.

Canetti, Elias. 1991. *Crowds and Power.* New York, Canada: The Noonday Press.

Carpizo, Jorge. 1978. *El presidencialismo mexicano.* Mexico: Siglo XXI.

Carreño, Gloria. 1994. "Pasaporte a la Esperanza." In Gojman et al. 1994.

Chalmers, Douglas. 1977. "The Politicized State in Latin America." In *Authoritarianism and Corporation in Latin America*, ed. J. Maloy. Pittsburgh: University of Pittsburgh Press.

Coriat, Ubando. 1979. "Los Judeomexicanos en México." *Aquí Estamos* 2.8.

Cohen, Ira. 1984. "Structuration Theory and Social Praxis." In Giddens and Turner, 273–309.

Collins, Randall. 1986. *Weberian Sociological Theory*. New York: Cambridge University Press.

———. 1988. *Theoretical Sociology*. San Diego, Calif.: Harcourt Brace Javanovich.

Coser, Lewis. 1964. *The Functions of Social Conflict*. New York: The Free Press.

———. 1970. *Men of Ideas: A Sociologist View*. New York: The Free Press.

Cosío Villegas, Daniel. 1974. "Pasan Atropelladamente periódicos, gobierno e intelectuales." *Plural* 31.

———, ed. 1988. *Historia General de México*. 2 vols. Mexico: El Colegio de México.

Cuddihy, John Murray. 1974. *The Ordeal of Civility: Freud, Marx, Levi-Strauss, and the Jewish Struggle with Modernity*. New York: Dell Publishing Co.

Dash-Moore, Deborah. 1975. *The Emergence of Ethnicity: New York Jews 1920–1940*. Ph. D. thesis. Columbia University, New York.

Dawidowics, Lucy. 1975. *The War Against the Jews*. New York: Bantam Books.

———. 1984. *On Equal Terms: Jews in America 1881–1981*. New York: Holt, Rinehart & Winston.

De Romano, Graciela. 1978. *Orígines del Judaismo Contemporáneo en México*. Mexico: Monte Sinai.

De Voss, George, and Lola Ross-Romanucci. 1982. *Ethnic Identity*. Chicago: University of Chicago Press.

Delgado de Cantú, G. 1991. *Historia de México*. Mexico: Alhambra Mexicana.

Della Pergola, S. 1985. "Demography of Latin American Jewry." *American Jewish Yearbook* 85:51–104.

———. 1987. "Demographic Trends of Latin American Jewry." In Elkin and Merkx.

Della Pergola, S., and S. Lerner. 1993. *Perfil Demográfico, Social y Cultural de la Población Judía en México*. Mexico and Jerusalem: Xerox.

Della Pergola, S., and Uziel O. Schmeltz. 1986. "La Demografía de los Judíos de Latinoamerica." *Rumbos*, no.15, pp. 17–35.

Diamond, Sigmund. 1969. "Language and Politics: An Afterword." *Political Science Quarterly* 84.2.

———. 1987. "Discussion of Barry and Breton Presentation." In Bruckner et al.

———. 1983. *Historical Aspects of Bilingualism in the United States*. New York: Columbia University Center for the Social Sciences.

———. 1992. *Compromising Campus*. New York: Oxford University Press.

Douglas, Mary. 1978. "Judgments on James Frazer." *Daedalus* 107.4.

———. 1991. "The Idea of Home: A Kind of Space." *Social Research* 58.1.

Dreyfus, H. L., and P. Rabinow. 1982. *Michel Foucault: Beyond Structuralism and Hermeneutics*. Chicago: University of Chicago Press.

Elazar, David. 1976. *Community and Polity: The Organizational Dynamics of American Jewry*. Philadelphia: The Jewish Publication Society of America.

———. 1977. "The Kehila." Working Paper 6. Center for Jewish Community Study.

Elkin, Judith. 1980. *Jews of the Latin American Republics*. North Carolina: University of North Carolina Press.

————. 1985. "Latin American Jewry Today." *American Jewish Year Book.*

————. 1989. "Recent Scholarship on Latin American Jews." *JWB Jewish Book Council* 46:108-17.

Elkin, Judith, and Gilbert W. Merkx, eds. 1987. *The Jewish Presence in Latin America.* Boston: Allen & Unwin.

*Encyclopedia Judaica.* 1972. Jerusalem.

Endelman, Todd. 1983. "Native Jews and Foreign Jews in London, 1870–1914." In *The Legacy of Jewish Migration*, ed. David Berger. New York: Columbia University Press.

Erikson, Erik. 1975. *Life History and the Historical Moment.* New York: Norton.

Fackenheim, Emil. 1978. *The Jewish Return into History: Reflections in the Age of Auschwitz and New Jerusalem.* New York: Schocken Books.

Feingold, Henry. 1981. "Jewish Life in the U. S.: Perspectives from History." In *Jewish Life in the U.S.: Perspectives from Social Sciences.* New York: Johns Hopkins.

Feldman, Shimshon. 1993. *Un Hombre Una Vida.* Preface by Sergio Nudelstejer. Mexico: Lito Offset Artístico.

Fishman, Joshua. 1987. *Ideology, Society, and Language.* Ann Arbor: Karoma Publishers.

————. 1990. "Hundert Yor Ivrit Meduberet." *Oifn Shvel*, March, pp. 7-10.

————. 1991. "Ume Ve Loshn." *Oifn Shvel*, July-Sept., pp. 7–10.

————. n. d. "Yidish un Shtimrekht in Nu York, 1915–1921." For *Oifn Shvel* (unpublished).

Foucault, Michel. 1972a. *The Archaeology of Knowledge.* New York: Pantheon Books.

————. 1978. *The History of Sexuality.* New York: Pantheon Books.

————. 1982. "Afterword: The Subject of Power." In Dreyfus and Rabinow, 212.

Friedlander, Judith. 1990. *Vilna on the Seine: Jewish Intellectuals in France since 1968.* New Haven: Yale University.

Gartner, Lloyd. 1987. "Jewish Migrants en Route from Europe to North America." In Rischin.

————. 1988. "The Greatest American Jewish Leaders." *American Jewish History* 78.2:320.

Geertz, Clifford. 1973. *The Interpretation of Culture.* New York: Basic Books.

Gerth, H. H., and C. Wright Mills, eds. 1957. *From Max Weber: Essays in Sociology.* New York: Oxford University Press.

Giddens, Anthony. 1976. *New Rules of Sociological Method.* London: The Anchor Press.

————. 1981. *A Contemporary Critique of Historical Materialism.* Berkeley, Calif.: University of California Press.

————. 1987. "Structuralism, Post-Structuralism, and the Production of Culture." In Giddens and Turner.

————. 1990. *Central Problems in Social Theory.* Berkeley, Calif.: University of California Press.

Giddens, Anthony, and Jonathan Turner, eds. 1984. *Social Theory Today.* Stanford, Calif.: Stanford University Press.

Glantz, Jacobo, Itzjok Berliner, and Moishe Glikovsky. 1927. *Drai Vegn*. Mexico: Grupo Literario Juventud.

———. 1962. "Notas sobre la formación de la comunidad Judía de México." *Israel y La Diáspora* (Mexico), 5721.

———. 1980. *Cristobal Colon*. Israel: I. L. Peretz Press.

———. 1950. *A Kezaies Erd*. Mexico: Tzvi Kessel Fund.

Glantz, Margo. 1981. *Genealogías*. Mexico: Martín Casillas Press.

Gojman, Alicia. 1984, July-Sept. "On Jews." *Wizo* (Mexico), no. 241.

———. 1987. "La Xenofobia en la prensa de Derecha en México, 1930–1945." *Revista de la Universidad*, No. 434, UNAM.

———. 1991. "La formación de la Sociedad cripto Judía en la Nueva España." 6th Conference of the LAJSA. Unpublished ms.

———. n. d. "Migración Oriental Judía de Alepo y Damasco a México." Xerox.

———. 1988. "Minorías, Estado y Moviemientos de la Clase Media en México: Liga Anti-China y Antijudía." *Judaica Latinoamericana*. Jerusalem.

———. 1984. *Los Conversos en la Nueva España*. Mexico: University Acatlán.

Gojman, Alicia, et al. 1987. *La Presencia Judía en México*. Mexico: UNAM, Tribuna Israelika, Multibanco Mercantil.

———. 1994. Trujillas-Indias, una ruta de conversos, vol. 2. Mexico: Kehila Ashkenazi.

———, et al. 1994. *Generaciones Judías en México: La Kehila Ashkenazi, 1922–1992*. 7 vols. Mexico: Comunidad Ashkenazi.

Gold, David. 1977. "Success and Failure in the Standardization and Implementation of Yiddish Spelling and the Romanization." *Advances in the Creation and Revision of Writing Systems*, ed. J. Fishman. The Hague: Mouton.

Golomb, Abraham. 1939a. "Yidish Lebn un Yidisher Kultur." *Yidishe Kultur*, Jan., 20–24.

———. 1939b. "Vegn Maksimum Yidishkait." *Yidishe Kultur*, March, 68–73.

———. 1946. "Jewish Self-Hatred." *YIVO Annual of Jewish Social Studies* 1:250-259.

———. 1962. *Integrale Yidishkait*. Mexico: Imprenta Moderna.

———. 1971. *Tzu di Heikhn fun Yidishn Gaist*. Paris: Imprimerie Abexpress.

———. 1974. *Tzu di Tifn fun Yidishn Gedank*. Israel: I. L. Peretz Press.

———. 1976. *Tzum Tokh fun Yidishkait*. New York: Shulsinger Bros.

González, Luis. 1988. "El Liberalismo triunfante." In Cosío Villegas, 2:909–12.

González Casanova, Pablo, and Enrique Florescano, eds. 1979. *México Hoy*. Mexico: Siglo XXI.

González Navarro, Moises. 1960. *La Colonización en México, 1877–1910*. Mexico: El Colegio de México.

———. 1988. "Las Ideas Raciales de los Científicos, 1890–1910." *Historia Mexicana*, no. 148.

———. 1994. *Los Extranjeros en México y los Mexicanos en el Extranjero, 1821–1970*. 2 vol. Mexico: El Colegio de México.

Goren, Arthur. 1970. *New York and the Quest for Community: The Kehillah Experiment, 1908–1922*. New York: Columbia University Press.

Gouldner, Alvin. 1976. *The Dialectic of Ideology and Technology*. Oxford: Oxford University Press.

———. 1950. *Studies in Leadership*. New York: Harper.

Guttman, Alexander. 1977. *The Struggle over Reform in Rabbinic Literature*. Cincinnati: Hebrew Union College.

Habermas, J. 1972. "Ernst Bloch: A Marxist Romantic." In *The Legacy of the German Refugee Intellectuals*, ed. Robert Boyers. New York: Schocken Books.

Hall, John. 1992. "The Capital(s) of Cultures: A Nonholistic Approach to Status Situations, Class, Gender, and Ethnicity." In Lamont and Fournier.

Hamui de Halabe, Liz, et al. 1989. *Los Judíos de Alepo en México*. Mexico: Maguen David A.C.

Hansen, Roger. 1971. *La Política del Desarollo Mexicano*. Mexico: Siglo XXI.

Harshav, Benjamin. 1986. *American Yiddish Poetry*. Berkeley, Calif.: University of California Press.

——. 1990. *The Meaning of Yiddish*. Berkeley, Calif.: University of California Press.

——. 1993. *Language in the Time of Revolution*. Berkeley, Calif.: University of California Press.

Held, David. 1989. *Political Theory and the Modern State*. Calif.: Stanford University Press.

Hodges, D., and R. Gandy. 1983. *Mexico 1910–1982: Reform and Revolution*. London: Zed Press.

Holander, John. 1991. "It All Depends." *Social Research* 58.1.

Howe, Irving, and E. Greenberg, eds. 1975. *Voices of the Yiddish*. New York: Schocken Press.

Hyman, Paula. 1974. *From Dreyfus to Vichy*. New York: Columbia University Press.

Jameson, Fredric. 1974. *Marxism and Form*. Princeton, N.J.: Princeton University Press.

Johnpoll, Bernard. 1967. *Politics of Futility: The General Jewish Workers Bund of Poland, 1917–1943*. Ithaca: Cornell University Press.

Kahan, Salomon. 1940. "The Jewish Community in Mexico." *Contemporary Jewish Record* 1.

——. 1945. *Yidish-Meksikanish*. Mexico: Zelbs Hilf Press.

——. 1946. *Meksikaner Shriftn*. Mexico: Zelbs Hilf Press.

——. 1951. *Meksikaner Viderklangen*. Mexico: Zelbs Hilf Press.

——. 1954. *Meksikanishe Reflexn*. Mexico: Zelbs Hilf Press.

Kerr, Sarah. 1994. "The Mystery of Mexican Politics." *New York Review of Books*, 17 Nov., 29–34.

Kirshenblat-Gimblet, B. 1987. "Folk-Culture of Jewish Immigrant Communities." In Rischin.

Klich, Ignacio. 1993. "Failure in Argentina: The Jewish Agency's Search for Congressional Backing for Zionist Aims in Palestine (1946)." Jerusalem: Magnes University Press.

——. 1996. "The Chimera of Palestinian Resettlement in Argentina in the Early Aftermath of the First Arab-Israeli War and Other Similarly Fantastic Notions." *The Americos*, July 1996, vol. 53–1, p. 15–43. Washington: The Catholic University of America.

Krause, Corine. 1970. "The Jews in Mexico: A History with Special Emphasis on the Period from 1857 to 1930." Ph.D. thesis. Pittsburgh.

————. 1972. "Mexico Another Promised Land? A Review of Projects for Jewish Colonization in Mexico: 1881–1925." *American Jewish Historical Quarterly* 61 (June): 220–23.

Kraut, B. 1988. "American Jewish Leaders; The Great, Greater, and Greatest." *American Jewish History* 78.2.

Krauze, Enrique. 1976. *Caudillos Culturales en la Revolución Mexicana.* Mexico: Siglo XXI.

Kuhn, Thomas. 1970. *The Structure of Scientific Revolutions.* Chicago: University of Chicago Press.

Lafaye, J. 1977. *Quetzalcoatl y Guadalupe: La Formación de la Conciencia Nacional en México.* Mexico: Fondo de Cultura Económica.

Lamont, Michèle, and Marcel Fournier, eds. 1982. *Cultivating Differences: Symbolic Differences and the Making of Inequality.* Chicago: University of Chicago Press.

Leff, Enrique. 1979. "Dependencia científico-tecnológica y desarrollo económico." In González Casanova and Florescano.

*Leksikon Fun Der Nayer Yidisher Literatur.* 1959–1980. New York: Alveltlecher Kultur Kongress.

Lerner de Sheinbaum, Bertha, and Susana Ralsky de Cimet. 1976. *El Poder de los Presidentes, 1910–1973.* Mexico: IMEP.

Lesser, Harriet. 1972. "A History of the Jewish Community in Mexico City, 1912–1970." Ph.D. thesis. Jewish Teachers Seminary and Columbia University, New York.

Lesser, Jeff. 1994. "Neither Slave nor Free, Neither Black nor White: The Early Chinese in Early Nineteenth-Century Brazil." *EIAL* 5.2:23–34.

Levine, Robert. 1987. "Adaptive Strategies of Jews in Latin America." In Elkin and Merkx.

Levitz, J. 1954. *The Jewish Community in Mexico: Its Life and Education.* Ph.D. diss. Dropsie College.

Levy, Daniel. 1987. "Jewish Education in Latin America." In Elkin and Merkx.

Lewin, Kurt. 1937. In Stonequist.

Liebman, Seymour. 1981. *Los Judíos en México y America Central.* Mexico: Siglo XXI.

Lukács, Georg. 1986. *Selected Correspondence, 1902–1920.* Introduction by Zoltán Tar. New York: Columbia University Press.

Maizel, Tuvie. 1948. "The Jews of Mexico," *YIVO Annual of Jewish Social Science* 2–3:295312. (Published earlier in *Yivo Bleter* 27 [1946].)

Mannheim, Karl. 1936. *Ideology and Utopia.* New York: Harvest Books.

Margalit, Avishai, and Moshe Halberstal. 1994. "Liberalism and the Right to Culture." *Social Research* 61.3.

Martínez Montiel, Luz María. 1988. *La Gota de Oro.* Veracruz: Instituto Veracruzano de Cultura.

Marx, Karl. 1972. "On the Jewish Question." In Tucker.

McPherson, C. B. 1962. *Possessive Individualism.* Oxford: Oxford University Press.

Medin, Tzvi. 1983. *El Minimato Presidencial: Historia Política del Maximato 1928–1935.* Mexico: Editorial Era.

Merton, Robert. 1976. *Sociological Ambivalence and Other Essays.* New York: Free Press.

Meyer, Jean. 1973. *La Cristiada.* 3 vols. Mexico: Siglo XXI.

Meyer, Lorenzo. 1978. *El Conflicto Social y los gobiernos del Maximato.* Mexico: El Colegio de México.

Meyer, Michael. 1979. *The Origins of the Modern Jew.* Detroit: Wayne State University Press.

————. 1989. "Anti-Semitism and Jewish Identity." *Commentary* 88.5 (Nov.).

Michelena, Margarita. 1987. "Hedor y Perfume." *Excelsior,* 18 May.

Miller, James. 1974. *History and Human Existence, from Marx to Merleau-Ponty.* Berkeley, Calif.: University of California Press.

Mishima, Ota. 1985. *Siete Migraciones Japonesas en México: 1890–1978.* Mexico: El Colegio de México.

Moshinsky, Marcos. 1977. "Ser Judío en México." *Aquí Estamos,* no. 1.

Neuser, Jacob. 1989. "Can Judaism Survive the 20th Century?" *Tikkun* 4.4.

Novisky, Anita. 1987. "Jewish Roots in Brazil." In Elkin and Merkx.

Oksenberg Rorty, Amelie. 1995. Response to Margalit and Halbertal. *Social Research* 62.1.

Ortoll, Servando, and Annette Ramirez de Arellano. 1985. "American Catholics and the Mexican Church-State Conflict, 1926–1929." Unpublished ms.

Patai, Raphael. 1950. "The Indios Israelites of Mexico." *Menorah Journal* 38:54–67.

Penkower, Monty N. 1983. *The Jews Were Expendable.* Chicago: University of Illinois Press.

Pilovsky, Arieh. 1990. *Tzvishn Yo un Nein.* Israel: World Council for Yiddish & Jewish Culture.

Pocock, J. C. A. 1971. *Politics, Language, and Time: Essays on Political Thought and History.* Boston: Atheneum.

————. 1975. *The Machiavellian Moment.* Princeton, N.J.: Princeton.

Polenberg, Richard. 1987. *Fighting Faiths: The Abrams Case, the Supreme Court, and Free Speech.* New York: Penguin Books.

Porter, David. 1966. *A Conspiracy of Complacency and Complicity.* New York: Vintage Books.

Portnoy, Ana. 1977. "Cultura e Intelectuales Judíos en México." B.A. thesis. Iberoamericana, Mexico.

Ralsky de Cimet, Susana. 1972. "La Identidad Etnica Minoritaria: Un Estudio de Caso." B.A. thesis. UNAM, Mexico.

Rischin, M., ed. 1987. *The Jews of North America.* Detroit: Wayne State University Press.

Rivkin, B. 1939. "Der Iker vos darf tzukumen der Yidisher Kultur-Ideie." *Yidishe Kultur,* Sept.-Oct., 4-11.

Roth, G., and W. Schluchter. 1984. *Max Weber's Vision of History, Ethics, and Methods.* Berkeley, Calif.: University of California Press.

Rubinstein, Moisés. 1941. *Temas Mexicanos.* Mexico: Nuestra Vida.

Sartre, Jean-Paul. 1965. *Anti-Semite and Jew.* New York: Schocken Books.

————. 1968. *Search for a Method.* New York: Vintage Books.

Sawatzky, H. L. 1971. *They Sought a Country: Mennonite Colonization in Mexico.* Berkeley, Calif.: University of California Press.

Schenkolewski, Silvia. 1988. "Cambios en la relación de la Organización Sionista Mundial hacia la comunidad Judía y el Movimiento Sionista en la Argentina, hasta 1948." *Judaica Latinoamericana.* Jerusalem.

———. 1991. "Los partidos políticos Sionistas en Argentina, 1943–1948." LAJSA. Unpublished ms.

Senkman, Leonardo. 1981. "Latin American Jewry between Revolution and Reaction." *Jewish Frontier,* March 1981:10–13.

———. 1987. "Argentine Culture and Jewish Identity." In Elkin and Merkx, 255–70.

Sennett, Richard. 1976. *The Fall of Public Man: On the Social Psychology of Capitalism.* New York: Vintage Books.

Shabot, Esther. 1990. "El Pensamiento Antisemita de José Vasconcelos." *Estudios Judaicos* (Mexico), no. 8, 37–51.

Shapiro, Yonathan. 1971. *Leadership of the American Zionist Organization, 1897–1930.* Urbana: University of Illinois Press.

Sheridan, Alan. 1980. *Michel Foucault: The Will for Truth.* New York: Tavistock Publications.

Shotter, John. 1993. "Psychology and Citizenship: Identity and Belonging." In Turner, B.

Shulgasser, Berl. 1953. "Colegio Israelita de México." *Jewish Education* 24.

Simmel, George. 1964. *Conflict and the Web of Group Affiliations.* New York: The Free Press.

Smart, Barry. 1983. *Foucault, Marxism, and Critique.* London: Routledge & Kegan Paul.

Sorin, Gerald. 1989. "Tradition and Changes: American Jewish Socialists as Agents of Acculturation." *American Jewish History* 79.1 (Autumn): 37–54.

Sosnowski, Saúl. 1986. "Sobre el Inquietante y Definitorio Guión del Escritor Judeo-Latinoamericana." In *Pluralismo e Identidad: Lo Judío en la Literatura Latinoamericano,* ed. Barylko, Jaime, et al. Argentina: Milá Press.

———. 1987. "Latin American–Jewish Writers: Protecting the Hyphen." In Elkin and Merkx, 297–307.

Souratzky, León. 1965. *Geshikhte fun Yidishn Yishuv in Meksike.* Mexico: Moderna Pintel, S.A.

Soyer, D. 1986. "Between Two Worlds: The Jewish Landmanschaftn and Questions of Immigrant Identity." *American Jewish History* 76.1 (Sept.).

Stavenhagen, Rodolfo. 1978. "El Nacionalismo Mexicano ante las Minorías Etnicas." *Aquí Estamos* (Mexico) 2.4:4.

Steinberg, Stephen. 1981. *The Ethnic Myth.* Boston: Beacon Press.

Stember, Charles, et al. 1966. *Jews in the Mind of America.* New York: Basic Books.

Stonequist, Everett, ed. 1961. *The Marginal Man: A Study in Personality and Culture Conflict.* New York: Russell & Russell.

Swidler, Ann. 1986. "Culture in Action: Symbols and Strategies." *American Sociological Review* 51:273–86.

Takaki, Ronald. 1993. *A Different Mirror: A History of Multicultural America.* Boston: Little, Brown & Co.

Tilly, Charles. 1992. "Future of European States." *Social Research* 59.4.

Toledano, Vicente Lombardo. 1942. "Judíos Mexicanos: Razas Inferiores?" Edit. Universidad Obrera de México.

———. 1951. "Dos Conferencias sobre Israel." Edit. Universidad Obrera de México.

Trillin, Calvin. 1994, 12 Dec. "Drawing the Line." *The New Yorker*.

Trunk, Isaiah. 1979. *Jewish Responses to Nazi Persecution*. New York: Stein and Day.

Tucker, Robert C., ed. 1972. *The Marx-Engels Reader*. New York: Norton.

Turner, Bryan, ed. 1993. *Citizenship and Social Theory*. London: Sage Publications.

Turner, Bryan. 1981. *For Weber: Essays on the Sociology of Fate*. Boston: Routledge & Kegan Paul.

———. 1983. *Religion and Social Theory*. Newbury Park, Calif.: Sage Publications.

Turner, Frederick. 1971. *La Dinámica del Nacionalismo Mexicano*. Mexico: Siglo XXI.

Waxman, Chaim. 1968. *The End of Ideology Debate*. New York: Funk & Wagnalls.

Weber, Max. 1957. "Politics as a Vocation." In Gerth and Mills.

———. 1964. *The Sociology of Religion*. Boston: Beacon Press.

Weinreich, Max. 1931. *Di Ershte Shprakh Konferentz: Barikhtn, Documentn un Opklangen fun der Tzernovitzer Konferentz 1908*. Vilna: YIVO.

———. 1975. "Internal Bilingualism in Ashkenaz." In Howe and Greenberg.

———. 1973. *Geshikhte fun der Yidisher Shprakh*. New York: YIVO.

Williams, Robin. 1977. *Marxism and Literature*. Oxford: Oxford University Press.

Wise, Ruth. 1991. "A Monument to Messianism." *Commentary*, March.

Wolff, K. 1971. *From Karl Mannheim*. New York: Oxford University Press.

Wuthnow, Robert. 1984. *Meaning and Moral Order*. Berkeley, Calif.: University of California Press.

Yerushalmi, Yosef Hayim. 1983. *Zakhor: Jewish History and Jewish Memory*. Seattle: University of Washington Press.

*Yoivl Bukh: Tzvantzig Yor Yidishe Shul in Meksike*. 1944. Mexico: Colegio Israelita de México.

Zack de Zuckerman, Celia. 1994. "Colectividad y Kehila." In Gojman et al., vol. 6.

Zadoff, Ephraim. 1988. "Un análisis comparativo de las redes educativas judías de México y Argentina, 1935–1955." *Judaica Latinoamericana*. Jerusalem.

Zárate Miguel, Guadalupe. 1986. *México y la Diáspora Judía*. Mexico: Instituto Nacional de Antropolgín e Historia.

Zoriada Vázquez, Josefina. 1988. "Los Primeros Tropiezos." In Cosío Villegas, 2:735–818.

# INDEX

Abrams, Jack, 206 n.52, *see also* anarchist
Agudas Akhim congregation, 43,103
Aliphas, Avner, 111–116, 125, 144, 153, 155, 165, *see also* identity, ideologies; ideologue, schools, Zionism
Alliance Israelite of Paris, 15–16
Alter, Victor, 140, *see also* Bund, Bundism
anarchist, 138
anti-Semitism, 3, 11, 14, 19, 23, 46, 78, 118, 101, 128, 131–135, 188 n.36, 190 n.15

Belongingness, 21–22, 29, 30, 35, 75, 180; reciprocal process, 26; ethnic hyphen, 195 n.113. *See also* identity, loyalty, nationalism
Berger, Meyer, 35, 48, 153, 171
Berliner, Itzkhok, 35–36, 77, 80–81; *see also* immigrants, roles (meaningful agents, writers)
B'nai Brith, 14–15, 22, 33–34, 129, 143, 152; *see also* ideologies, schools
Boundaries, x, 11; acceptable behavior, 35, 47, 48–51, 65, 82, 97, 115, 147, 177; ethnic, 94; experiments in, 136–137; ideological, 27–28,33, 93, 122, 147, 152; institutionalization of, 44, 66, 69, 100, 107, 147–148, 172; linguistic, 121, 155–156, 168, 170; political, 47–49, 54, 63, 76, 106, 165, 179, 182–183; *see also* political violence
Brenner, Anita, 22, 23, 50; *see also* boundaries; identity; immigrants

Bund, (Bundism, Bundists), 37, 39, 40, 44–48, 51–52, 54, 58, 64, 67, 77, 84–87, 89–90, 92, 97–99, 102, 105–106, 123–125, 199 n.47, n.50, 200 n.55, 205 n.31, 207 n.61, 166–167, 173; *see also* identity, ideologies; interaction of, 141–144; *see also* structuring

Calles, Plutarco Elías, 10, 31
Camisas Doradas, 32
Cárdenas, Lázaro, 78, 98, 135, 139, 197 n.11, 198 n.36
Carranza, Venustiano, 14
Caso, Antonio, 77, 197 n.8
Catholic church, 4–5, 14, 16, 28, 31
Central Committee (Tzentral Komitet), 32, 57, 58–59, 63, 89–90, 100, 104–105,130, 132, 134–137, 147, 160, 194 n.86, 200 n.64, 204 n.25; *see also* ideologies; Kehillah; structuring
Chinese, 9, 131
citizenship, 20; *see also* minority/majority; nationalism
colonizer, 13; colonization law, 8, 11; territories, 204 n.28, 188 n.30
communists, 37, 39–40, 44–45, 48–49, 54, 64, 93, 95–97, 99–102, 105, 118, 120, 123–124, 138, 140, 142–147, 157–158, 199–200 n.54; anti-Communist, 131; party, 95; youth, 196 n.119; *see also* boundaries, identity, ideologies, structuring; Gesbir, 40, 49; socialist ideas, 77, Marxists, 78, 84–85, 102; organization, 139, 146

227